"Groves and Brown use their years-long study of change in news organizations to lay out ways for managers to thoughtfully consider the roles of institutional culture and mission, professional values, and audience engagement to be more effective innovators in the industry."

Amber Hinsley, PhD, Professor of Journalism at
Texas State University

Transforming Newsrooms

Transforming Newsrooms offers a practical guide to navigating structural and culture change for news organizations facing economic disruption in today's rapidly changing media landscape.

Even when the need for change is obvious, the best ideas and intentions are often not followed by successful execution. This book offers a road map for understanding the obstacles to change in news organizations and how to overcome them. Providing a detailed overview of the ways in which news processes and routines are being fundamentally altered to meet new demands for multimedia, interactivity, and immediacy, the book offers tips to help news organizations better serve communities by understanding what information people need and how they want to engage and collaborate. The book also features a variety of case studies and examples from news organizations of all kinds, including a 10-year in-depth investigation of the *Christian Science Monitor*, the first national news organization to stop its daily presses for a digital report.

Transforming Newsrooms is an invaluable resource for students and media professionals alike, demonstrating how to make research on organizational change actionable and help build a more equitable journalism model that will survive and thrive when we need it most.

Carrie Brown is the founding director of the social journalism master's program at the Newmark Graduate School of Journalism at City University of New York. This program prepares students for careers in engaged journalism, with an emphasis on learning how to listen, understand community information needs, build relationships, and produce tangible impact. Her research centers on how news organizations can adapt to the changing media landscape.

Jonathan Groves is an associate professor and chair of the Communication Department at Drury University in Springfield, MO. He spent 14 years as a reporter and editor at newspapers in Arkansas and Missouri before becoming the first doctoral fellow at the University of Missouri-Columbia's Reynolds Journalism Institute. He has consulted with several organizations undergoing change efforts, and his research focuses on newsroom change and engagement.

CARRIE BROWN AND
JONATHAN GROVES

Transforming
Newsrooms

Connecting Organizational
Culture, Strategy, and
Innovation

Focal Press
Taylor & Francis Group

NEW YORK AND LONDON

First published 2021
by Routledge
52 Vanderbilt Avenue, New York, NY 10017

and by Routledge
2 Park Square, Milton Park, Abingdon, Oxon, OX14 4RN

Routledge is an imprint of the Taylor & Francis Group, an informa business

Library of Congress Cataloging-in-Publication Data
Names: Brown, Carrie, author. | Groves, Jonathan, author.
Title: Transforming newsrooms : connecting organizational culture, strategy,
and innovation / Carrie Brown, Jonathan Groves.
Description: London ; New York : Routledge, 2020. | Includes
bibliographical references and index.
Identifiers: LCCN 2020022736 | ISBN 9781138841260 (hardback) |
ISBN 9781138841277 (paperback) | ISBN 9781315732336 (ebook)
Subjects: LCSH: Journalism–United States–History–21st century. |
Newspaper publishing–Economic aspects–United States–History–21st
century. | Journalism–Technological innovations–United States. |
Christian Science monitor.
Classification: LCC PN4867.2 .B85 2020 | DDC 071/.3–dc23
LC record available at https://lccn.loc.gov/2020022736

ISBN: 978-1-138-84126-0 (hbk)
ISBN: 978-1-138-84127-7 (pbk)
ISBN: 978-1-315-73233-6 (ebk)

Typeset in Joanna
by River Editorial Ltd, Devon, UK

Contents

Acknowledgments   ix

Introduction   1

Uncovering Your Values   **One**   18

Deciphering Your Culture   **Two**   37

The *Christian Science Monitor*: A Decade of Change.
Part One – Making a Radical Shift for Survival   51

Developing Your Strategy   **Three**   75

Developing an Entrepreneurial Mindset   **Four**   91

The *Christian Science Monitor*: A Decade of Change.
Part Two – Page Views Are Not Enough   111

Engagement – Applying the Model   **Five**   131

Leading through Change and Resistance   **Six**   153

The *Christian Science Monitor*: A Decade of Change.
Part Three – Retrenchment   173

Conclusion – Developing Your Road Map   206

Index   233

Acknowledgments

We have too many fellow researchers and journalists to thank from over the years for their contributions and conversations, but we would be remiss not to highlight at least a few of the key players who helped shape our thinking over the years, especially our mentors and colleagues at the University of Missouri-Columbia, where the two of us met more than a decade ago. Dr. Michael Diamond, the founder of the University of Missouri's Center for the Study of Organizational Change, forever shaped our thinking, first in his classes and later as a member of our respective dissertation committees. Thanks also to our anonymous reviewers on our drafts, whose comments helped shape this book into its final form.

Thank you to the generous journalists at the *Christian Science Monitor*, the *Milwaukee Journal Sentinel*, and all the other news outlets who gave their time and insight to helping us understand organizational culture and change, and especially to the leaders who took the chance on letting us into their newsrooms.

We would also like to thank the team at Focal Press for their endless patience as we struggled to balance the demands of our families, our teaching, our administrative responsibilities, and our writing. Thanks especially to Margaret Farrelly and Priscille Biehlmann for guiding us across the finish line.

From Brown:

First and foremost, this one is for my husband, Grant, who puts up with me. Without his support, care, and cooking, this book would have been impossible.

I would also like to thank Bill Kovach and Tom Rosenstiel, who taught me that journalism was more of a calling than a career when I had the good fortune of working for them in the early 2000s.

Elements of Journalism was a guiding light for this book and all the work I do. Kovach once told me that journalism would only die if we let it; this book is among my best efforts to live up to his example.

Finally, I am tremendously grateful to my colleague and friend Jeff Jarvis at the Newmark Graduate School of Journalism at CUNY for his unflagging support in good times and bad. His insight into how we can better listen to and serve audiences helped inform many aspects of this book as well as my teaching.

From Groves:

I would like to thank Dr. Esther Thorson, Dr. Margaret Duffy, and Dr. Earnest Perry for their guidance as I started down this scholarly road, as well as the many journalists I've worked with over the years who helped nurture and inspire my love and passion for the craft.

Thanks also to Drury University and the Association for Education in Journalism and Mass Communication for providing funds to support our Christian Science Monitor research, as well as Ann San Paolo, who devoted countless hours to transcribing our research interviews.

Most of all, I want to thank my family—Cindy, Samantha, Jenna, and Nathan—for their unwavering love and support through this long process.

In early 2020, just as we were wrapping up this book, a seismic event rocked the news industry and the world. The spread of coronavirus and COVID-19 disrupted media more rapidly and forcefully than even the Great Recession of 2008 or the transition to digital. The crisis revealed two truths: Information needs have never been more vital, and organizations that hope to survive have no choice but to rethink their business strategies and how they do their work. We hope our model for change will help.

Despite the surge in interest in news and record traffic as the pandemic gathered steam, many news organizations still struggled.[1] Gannett furloughed and laid off employees.[2] The *Cleveland Plain Dealer* cut more than half its workforce, leaving 14 in the newsroom to produce a newspaper for a metropolitan area with more than 2 million people.[3] Poynter began a rolling tally of layoffs from around the United States at news organizations large and small.[4]

The moment demands bold ideas. Even before the virus hit, digital advertising was being swallowed up by Facebook and Google, and local news in many places was barely hanging on, beset by crippling cutbacks and decisions from corporate owners[5] guided less by public service than the desire to squeeze out every last dollar of profit.[6]

This model can also help new outlets born of this crisis rethink how to express core values to build a journalism of greater service to communities that is more equitable and diverse.

Newsrooms that had been moving slowly in the direction of listening to and engaging their audiences must accelerate their pace. The funding models of the future involve direct support in the form of subscriptions, memberships, or public funding, all of which demand deeper relationships and trust. This shift is not easy for journalists used to standing above the fray, but this book will offer a variety of examples and specific steps you can take to transform your culture and strategy, and keep learning.

Drawing on our background as former journalists, our research is inspired by the belief that democracy requires an inclusive news ecosystem that can sustain itself. Over the years, our academic work has revealed that journalism must not only innovate; the field must learn to match good intentions with solid strategy and the ability to maneuver entrenched newsroom cultures.

Using knowledge from scholars on organizational change and leadership, we've studied a variety of news organizations as they tried to make sense of the uncertain future and adapt to new technologies and processes while attempting to adhere to their deeply held core values. One of those projects involved a decade of visits to a single organization, the *Christian Science Monitor*, where we observed the long-term evolution of one of the nation's first newspapers to eliminate its daily print edition in favor of digital. Over the years, we witnessed resistance to change in a variety of forms; we also observed a willingness to experiment as journalists increasingly understood that their jobs and the organization's survival were on the line.

In this book, we will track the successes and failures of the *Monitor* and other news organizations over the past decade and extract lessons that can help newsrooms avoid some of the mistakes caused by cultures resistant to change. We pull insights from academic theories of management that apply to the news industry, and examples from other industries that have weathered disruption. Our framework is a multilevel model of change to help journalists think through who they are and how they might evolve in today's ever-shifting media landscape. This model can apply to well-established older media companies but also to digital upstarts and nonprofit news organizations.

THE ESSENCE OF STRATEGY: HOVERING ABOVE THE NOISE

One key element of our model is strategy. Organizations have historically relied on strategic thinking to guide their competitive course over the longer term. Good leaders rise above the daily demands to see beyond the temporary trends and the immediate tugs of unexpected threats and crises. With this broader view from above, leaders avoid being consumed by the everyday and can remain focused on their

Transforming Newsrooms:
A Model for Change

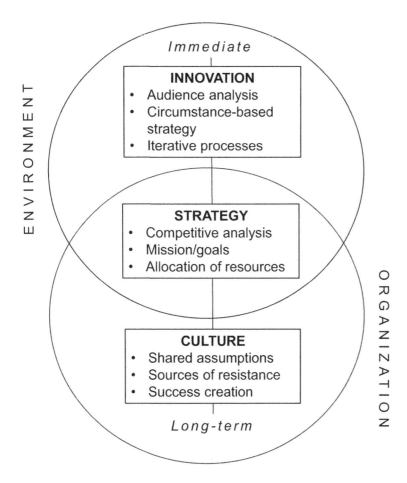

Figure 0.1 Our model of change integrates ideas from multiple disciplines. Leaders must work across the levels for meaningful change to take hold.

overarching mission. To succeed, they must offer steady guidance that isn't easily jarred by the erratic shifts of financial markets and the lure of untested technologies.

Harvard Business School professor Michael Porter developed one of the primary frameworks for analyzing the competitive forces in any industry.[7] Leaders must scan the environment to determine their organization's place in the competitive landscape. How will their products and services compete effectively? Porter notes the importance of delineating between *strategic positioning* (identifying your distinctive product/service for the customer that is different from your competitors) and *operational effectiveness* (providing the lowest-cost product/service by being more efficient than your competitors), especially in the age of the Internet.[8] Strategic positioning, he argues, creates long-term competitive advantage; the efficiencies created by operational effectiveness can eventually be mimicked and on their own will not sustain an organization over the long term.

The long view is important for leading an organization. But it can engender a cautious decision-making bureaucracy that prevents risky but creative ideas from rising to the surface. It can create unintended incentives that lead employees to avoid risk. In such a safe environment, projects often take months or years to develop until they're fully tested, researched, and vetted.

In today's digital news environment, new ideas must not gestate for months. Organizations must develop new structures that allow suggestions and recommendations to bubble up quickly and get into the marketplace for testing and evaluation.

MAKING INNOVATION MORE THAN JUST A BUZZWORD

With the big success of some tech startups, many organizations have embraced tactics rooted in the work of innovation researchers such as Harvard Business School professor Clayton Christensen, which he first articulated in his seminal 1997 book *The Innovator's Dilemma* and expanded on with co-author Michael Raynor with *The Innovator's Solution*. These books provide a structure for understanding how successful firms are disrupted by new, market-expanding products or services, and help leaders craft strategies to fend off such threats. In this book, we also draw upon models for rapid iteration aimed at entrepreneurs, such as *The Lean Startup* by Eric Ries, which offer insight for newsrooms into how to develop and test new ideas and products.

In our model, we think of innovation on a shorter time horizon than strategy. It is more outwardly focused, on the user and the audience, and offers immediate, testable suggestions that will give you either tangible, visible results or failures that you can learn from. At the heart of this thinking: Break out of the "build it, and they will come" mindset, and develop products and services that respond effectively to specific citizen needs and desires, their "jobs to be done," in Christensen's parlance.[9] Instead of a product-first mentality, news organizations must start by thinking of their audiences at the initial development stage of any new product or service. This shift from the gatekeeper mindset, in which the journalist always knows what news is most important, helps shake stagnant organizations out of complacency and can inspire quick-moving experimentation and change.

Shifting to an audience-first frame is difficult for many news organizations that have become accustomed over the decades to dictating the topics and direction of the public conversation. For decades, editors and journalists decided what was "news," what stories and packages would appear in the evening edition or newscast. But the Internet changed that power dynamic. No longer beholden to news decisions of press barons and network executives, anyone with a computer and an Internet connection could become his or her own broadcast station, printing press, or wire service. By the dawn of the new century, the fragmented attention of audiences, split among hundreds of media choices, had cut into the circulations and viewer numbers of legacy media.

Recognizing the shift in media habits, the American Press Institute looked at ways to apply Christensen's ideas to help newspapers adapt.[10] Back in 2005, it developed the Newspaper Next project and the N2 Innovation Method for helping organizations identify new ways to meet community needs. It provided templates and worksheets. It offered workshops and case studies. The *Dallas Morning News*, the *Boston Globe*, and Gannett were among the major industry players that participated in the initial experiments, and the project was later expanded to other sites that developed new publications and websites to satisfy customer needs.

Today, many of those projects have faded as failed experiments, lost as the leaders who drove the innovations moved on to other ideas and organizations; in many cases, they weren't given much time to prove their effectiveness.

Often, the problem with such efforts is they come across as top-down reflexive responses to threats in the competitive landscape. Especially in larger conglomerates with upwardly mobile leaders, rank-and-file employees can be (rightly) suspicious—or even blatantly rebellious—when managers propose radical new efforts that seem at odds with traditional routines and values.

So how do reflective leaders balance strategic thinking with the dynamism and risk of innovation? By understanding their organizational cultures.

THE FOUNDATION OF CHANGE: ORGANIZATIONAL CULTURE

To strike the right balance for your organization between strategy and innovation, it's vital to understand who you are and the values that bind the people together in your organization into a cohesive whole to do the journalistic work. The oft-used adage "Culture eats strategy for breakfast," attributed to management consultant and professor Peter Drucker, is profoundly applicable to newsrooms.

Culture is the foundation of our model. Unless leaders understand the deeply embedded values of their organization's members, even the most carefully plotted strategies and new initiatives will fail.

Indeed, it isn't for lack of ideas or will that news organizations have struggled to cope with digital transformation. Over and over, we have seen good intentions and smart ideas fail to make a dent in a news organization's long-established ways of doing things. As frustrating as resistance to change can be, the challenge makes sense when understood as more than just laziness or a few recalcitrant individuals stubbornly refusing to change.

Journalistic organizations often develop myths and narratives around their coverage triumphs: the award-winning breaking-news stories, the paradigm-shifting investigations, the long-form narratives and documentaries. And the historical demand for deadline-driven content for newscasts and news columns has led to deeply embedded journalistic routines and cultural norms that are difficult to alter or break. People often resist change because the old ways of doing things worked so well for them in the past.

Edgar Schein, a professor emeritus at the MIT Sloan School of Management who developed a foundational model of organizational culture, calls these deep-seated norms "underlying assumptions," the often-unconscious ideas that organization members agree upon to accomplish their shared work.[11] Newer organizations often have an easier time innovating than older ones that have assumptions more deeply embedded by past successes. Even in startups, however, cultures established by founders can develop and solidify quickly, making ongoing evolution difficult.

Understanding culture means not just hearing what people *say* about their work, but comparing that with what they actually *do*. Think about how many newspapers spent years broadcasting their need to be "digital first" but found their efforts blocked by a powerful underlying assumption about the lingering prestige of breaking a story on the front page. For example, the Milwaukee Journal Sentinel stated its goal of prioritizing digital beginning in the mid-2000s. However, in 2007, the morning and afternoon news meetings one of us observed for several months almost never included a single mention of the web, as editors debated what stories should get prominent positions on the front page. In 2014, the New York Times innovation report pointed out that it too continued to struggle with the same issue despite years of effort.[12] In late 2017, a survey by the International Center for Journalists found that newsrooms around the world were still lagging when it came to adopting a digital-first mindset and developing necessary new skills such as social media verification or knowledge of how to use analytics strategically.[13]

The strategy and innovation levels of our model offer guidance for altering organizational processes and adapting to the environment; they are not as helpful, however, for understanding the psychological processes at work during change efforts. Schein refers to the presence of "disconfirming data" that induces psychological distress, such as anxiety or guilt.[14] Applying Schein's model, managers and leaders must use stress to motivate change—without threatening the identity or integrity of the journalists. Offering support such as training or other resources to mitigate anxieties about learning new skills helps as well.

Leaders cannot simply mandate a new culture. Organizations must develop new routines that fit in the context of the existing culture and use concrete expectations and rewards to encourage members to embrace risk and experimentation. New successes will inspire and embed new habits and assumptions.

This book will explain how leaders can coax their cultures toward greater experimentation. We suggest they need to examine carefully what is rewarded and punished, and recognize the critical role they play as leaders, not only in what they say but in every action they take, no matter how subtle.[15] Staffers are quick to notice not only the more obvious internal awards or raises, but also how attention and praise are distributed.

To instill a spirit of continual innovation, organizations not only need to be prepared to test their assumptions consistently with the people who will use their product and consume their content. They must also be ready to adjust course quickly when tests show that something isn't working. Failure is difficult for individuals and organizations to absorb and may trigger a variety of defensive responses; however, it must be welcomed for a culture of learning to grow and thrive.[16] We will explore some of the ways in which entrepreneurs and experts on organizational learning overcome these types of obstacles.

DEVELOPING THE MODEL

Our interest in newsrooms and how they can adapt to the digital, mobile world grew from our own experiences as former journalists. After four years as a reporter, Groves moved into the management ranks, with stints as a section editor, a page-one editor, an online editor, and finally, an assistant managing editor at a Gannett newspaper before becoming a management researcher and professor. He witnessed firsthand the tension faced by newspaper journalists trying to weave in the increasing demands of web updates and multimedia content on top of their print responsibilities—in an environment of shrinking resources and declining circulation.

After stints as a reporter and editor, Brown spent four years managing the traveling curriculum program for the Committee of Concerned Journalists. That experience sparked her lifelong passion for finding ways to keep the enduring values of journalism strong in new media forms. Brown visited nearly 30 newsrooms around the United States, including major dailies as the New York Times, Chicago Tribune, and San Francisco Chronicle, working with leading journalists to host workshops in which staffers and managers came together to discuss how to better align their practices with their goals. Informed by the book *The Elements of Journalism* by Committee of Concerned Journalists' co-chairs Bill Kovach and Tom Rosenstiel, these traveling workshops revealed journalists' ongoing commitment to core values such as watchdog reporting, verification, and independence. But they also showed that even the best of intentions and most creative ideas are not enough when faced with a managerial mandate to change.

We met at the University of Missouri, where we had both come to pursue doctoral degrees with the hope we could help current and future journalists navigate the changing media landscape. Under the tutelage of Dr. Michael Diamond, then-director of the Center for the Study of Organizational Change at the University of Missouri, we recognized that a method rooted in cultural analysis could help newsrooms. He highlighted myriad examples across industries of cultural obstacles that prevent organizations from effectively adapting to environmental changes.

Since that time, we have analyzed newsrooms through a cultural lens. Often, when we explain our approach to newsroom leaders, the spark of recognition is immediate: *This*, they tell us, is what we need.

For this book, we have drawn from years of research into newsrooms, both others' as well as our own. In that time, we have shadowed journalists on the job, talked with people working in various organizations, and seen the struggles evolve over time with the advent of social media and the rise of mobile.

Our collaboration began when we participated in the New Media, Enduring Values project led by Geneva Overholser, Esther Thorson, and Margaret Duffy at the University of Missouri. Three news organizations—the *Milwaukee Journal Sentinel*, WHO-TV in Des Moines, and American Public Media in Minnesota—participated in a yearlong initiative beginning in 2006 to bring journalism's core values to life on the web. Each news organization developed an online project exemplifying one of three key values drawn from *The Elements of Journalism* by Bill Kovach and Tom Rosenstiel: verifying the accuracy of information, finding ways to make important news more relevant, and creating a public forum for discussion.

We contributed to the project by providing research on media use, helping to monitor impact, and studying the effectiveness of efforts to change the newsrooms' processes. We interviewed 25 key players, asking about their roles in the project, their perceptions of the effectiveness of its implementation within their organization, and the impact of explicitly introducing core values into the process.

In 2008, Brown spent 10 weeks at her hometown newspaper, the *Milwaukee Journal Sentinel*, sitting at a desk in the newsroom, attending morning and afternoon news meetings, and interviewing 53 staffers from all departments and levels of the newsroom hierarchy. At the time of the study, the paper's two top editors had recently called for nothing short of a "culture change" and the adoption of a "web first" mentality in the newsroom, and her questions sought to understand how the paper was making this transition and what challenges it faced. Since then, the *Journal Sentinel* has changed ownership twice, and as a Gannett paper, as recently as January 2019 was still experiencing buyouts and layoffs in its substantially smaller newsroom.

In 2009, Groves conducted a similar study at a family-owned daily newspaper with a circulation of less than 50,000, located in a mid-sized U.S. city. He returned to the paper regularly over a five-month period, observing its process to develop content for multiple platforms and conducting interviews with 35 newsroom employees.

In late 2009, we embarked on what would become a 10-year longitudinal study of the *Christian Science Monitor*, encompassing 10 visits to the Boston newsroom. That year, the *Monitor* became the first nationally circulated newspaper to replace its daily print edition with its website and a weekly print magazine. In addition to wide-ranging interviews with staff from all departments and job titles, we attended meetings, shadowed staffers, and observed the shifting news-production process at work over time.

By observing the *Monitor*'s transformation, we were able to document shifts in its news-gathering efforts and coverage. For example, in the early years, immediacy and page views rose as critical measures of success, and later, engagement and other measures of reader loyalty evolved to become important. By studying the same organization over such a long period, we were able to see its many successes and failures and how, time and again, its culture influenced its response to change.

In 2013, Brown spent a week in the newsroom at WMC-TV in Memphis, interviewing 13 staffers. While the main thrust of her work there was examining the kinds of skills broadcast journalists of today need, she also learned about the station's efforts at engaging readers and some of the ways local television stations are responding to new dynamics in the field.

In addition to our formal research and professional work, we've spent the past 15-plus years as close observers of changes in the journalism industry, carefully monitoring new developments in the industry reported in the trade press and leveraging our many contacts in academia and in newsrooms globally. We have attended many academic and industry conferences over the years. And both of us are highly active on social media, with access to the latest accounts from the many journalists we follow and have come to know well.

As the founding director of the social journalism program at the Newmark Graduate School of Journalism at City University of New York (CUNY), Brown has had the opportunity to closely follow the latest digital shifts in New York media and work with organizations like ProPublica, MIT, and First Draft in educational partnerships. As department chair of the Communication Department at Drury University in Missouri, Groves has closely tracked changes in his local media ecosystem, regularly visiting with news organizations and journalists in his community. In 2018, he spent his sabbatical studying the rise of podcasting and its effect on journalism and storytelling with visits to news organizations around the country.

As former journalists passionate about the importance of news for democracy, we were not, in a sense, "outsiders" in the newsrooms we studied. Our backgrounds allowed us to acclimate quickly to newsroom settings and routines. As researchers, we realized the potential hazards and limitations of that connection as well. Throughout our research process, we remain sensitive to our possible biases and sympathies, and document our own psychological reactions to organizational immersion.

But our unique blend of experiences—professional and academic—allowed us to develop our model as a usable framework for helping journalists think about their work at multiple levels while on the job.

OUR MODEL: THINKING ACROSS LEVELS

In our newsroom experiences, we have connected with many types of leaders: charismatic, authoritarian, collaborative. Some embrace traditional strategic thinking with a reasoned analysis of the competitive environment, a method that has deep roots in management thinking. It provides a base to ensure newsrooms have a strong vision and mission.

But clinging to the tried and true can inhibit change and creative problem-solving. If we remain too attached to an insulated view of ourselves, we hunker down with what we are good at—even if those skills are not what our audiences want or desire. Bureaucracies can stiffen as longtime managers begin to protect their turfs and their profit margins. Often, it takes a raucous, disruptive leader, willing to challenge the status quo, to uproot a staid organization and inspire innovation and change. We saw this to some degree at the Monitor when Jimmy Orr, who came to the paper with a background in politics, not journalism, pushed hard to up the paper's metabolism to match the demands of the web.

However, focusing too heavily on risk and iteration can mean never committing to a guiding vision. Both the strategy and innovation levels we have outlined in the model of change offer tactical prescriptions for products and services. They can result in new procedures, processes, and routines that often can lead to improvement in audience numbers and financial gains. But such successes will not last if they are not considered in the context of the foundational level of the model: the cultural level.

Leaders and managers—especially those wanting to move up in larger corporations—often focus efforts at the strategy and innovation levels to spark quick change and produce immediate results. The issue is such changes don't often last because deeply embedded cultures often default back to what they know and are comfortable with. Experienced front-line employees have learned to wait out the change effort of the moment, knowing that it, too, shall pass, only to be replaced by the next big idea.

Professionals at every level tend to think of organizations as "things," structures that exist apart from those who work within them. We disagree. We embrace the approach of psychodynamic theorists who focus on the living, breathing nature of organizations: *People* make up organizations, and as a result, we must understand the emotions, behavior, and psychology of those within in order to move the organization in the direction guided by the organization's strategic vision and mission.

Astute leaders exhibit emotional intelligence, an ability to connect with their employees on a psychological level that inspires commitment and dedication. They understand the cultures of the organizations they lead, and are aware of their role in creating and maintaining those cultures. The older an organization is, the more entrenched its culture becomes. To manage such organizations, leaders must engage in a process of understanding who they are as an organization. By respecting the culture and nurturing the organization's psyche, strong leaders can coax change while allowing employees and managers to maintain their identities and senses of self.

In our view, these three levels move in tandem; one relies on the other in an interlocking but flexible structure. Innovation done without regard to the organization's strategic vision will fail over the long term. Understanding the organization's culture helps articulate a strategic vision that jibes with the values of those committed to the organization, and what innovative structures may fit within the organization. Simply cutting and pasting the best practices from innovative organizations such as ProPublica or Google is destined to fail without a complete understanding of who you and your organization are.

APPLYING THE MODEL: A PATHWAY TO CHANGE

Our model is meant to help leaders visualize how to think at all levels when considering change. We have created steps that will walk leaders and managers through each level to develop meaningful change and move the organization gradually toward a vibrant workplace that consistently challenges its long-held assumptions and pushes itself to improve.

Change should not be viewed as a one-time process; it needs constant tending and nurturing. As organizational researcher and consultant Chris Argyris noted, the ideal of an organization that consistently challenges the status quo is rarely attained.[17] We recommend continually engaging in a process of self-evaluation and self-reflection to ensure new initiatives are considered at every level of the model.

Most organizations know they need to change to adapt to new technologies and market conditions, and they impose news structures and new routines on the staff without a proper understanding of who their employees are—and more importantly, what their organization is as a whole.

We recommend turning the process upside down. Start at the foundation by understanding your culture. By uncovering the underlying assumptions everyone uses to accomplish work, you can understand your role in the competitive landscape and create your vision for the future. Only then can you decide how to spark innovation and move the structures and routines of your organization forward.

We see the model applied in a three-step process:

Discovery: Understanding Your Values and Organizational Culture
In chapters 1 and 2, we show you how to use interviews, focus groups, and observation techniques to determine the underlying assumptions at work in your organization. Organizational researchers frequently see a disconnect between what people *say* their values are and how they *act* when they perform their work, and we have found such inconsistencies at organizations we have studied.

Culture is best understood through a complex interplay of processes, reward systems, and work routines. Historical successes and achievements embed strongly held assumptions about how work should be accomplished. This stage concentrates on uncovering those connections.

Surveillance: Understanding Your Space in the Competitive Landscape and Developing Your Strategy
In Chapter 3, we provide you with tools for analyzing your competitive landscape and finding your place within it.

Many organizations have participated in long-term visioning exercises over the years to develop mission statements and multiple-year plans for the future. But often, those carefully crafted ideas remain framed on a wall or bound on a shelf, rarely to be consulted in the frenetic day-to-day obligations of meeting budget requirements and responding to ever-changing consumer needs.

A coherent strategy, developed in concert with an understanding of the organization's culture, can provide a stable guide for day-to-day initiatives. It helps determine how much risk an organization may be willing to bear. It also offers comfort and security in times of upheaval.

Top leaders must continually scan the competitive environment for threats and opportunities, and determine how best to apply and adjust the long-term strategic goals and mission. But the adjustments must be made with deference to the cultural assumptions at work in the organization.

Transformation: Developing New Routines and Processes to Foster
Innovation and Ongoing Learning in the Ever-Changing Landscape
Only after gaining a clear perspective of your organization and its values can you look to developing and implementing new structures to foster change and develop new ways of work. In Chapter 4, we draw upon design thinking, among other methodologies and theories, to offer techniques for inspiring change in your workplaces and mechanisms to continually test and tweak these efforts.

With this foundation, in Chapter 5 we help you think through bringing true engagement efforts into a newsroom. In Chapter 6, we discuss how to overcome resistance that is likely to arise during such transformation efforts.

For news organizations, the biggest challenge comes from the need to embrace an audience-first perspective. Journalists adhere strongly to a sense of social responsibility and the notion of serving as a check on government in society, especially in countries with representative democracies such as the United States and the United Kingdom. But often, journalists also write for their peers and sources, and fear pandering to the lowest common denominator in ways that don't serve the public good. By using frameworks rooted in the work of Christensen and Ries, we help you identify the audience's "jobs to be done," and figure out ways to fulfill those jobs that are in line with your strategy and, most importantly, with your cultural values.

NOTES

1 Hanaa' Tameez, "At Least Coronavirus has Been Good for Online News Traffic (We're Trying to be Optimistic)," *Nieman Lab*, March 18, 2020, www.niemanlab. org/2020/03/at-least-coronavirus-has-been-good-for-online-news-traffic-were-trying-to-be-optimistic/.

2 Jason Bogage, "Gannett Will Furlough Workers at More than 100 Newspapers over the Next Three Months," *Washington Post*, March 30, 2020, www.washington post.com/business/2020/03/30/gannett-newspapers-furloughs/.

3 Sam Allard, "22 Plain Dealer Newsroom Staff Laid Off in Advance Union Purge," *Cleveland Scene*, April 3, 2020, www.clevescene.com/scene-and-heard/archives/2020/04/03/22-plain-dealer-newsroom-staffers-laid-off-in-advance-union-purge/.

4 Kristin Hare, "Here Are the Newsroom Layoffs, Furloughs and Closures Caused by the Coronavirus," Poynter, June 19, 2020, www.poynter.org/business-work/2020/here-are-the-newsroom-layoffs-furloughs-and-closures-caused-by-the-coronavirus/.

5 Penelope Muse Abernathy, "The Rise of a New Media Baron and the Emerging Threat of News Deserts," UNC School of Media and Journalism's Center for Innovation and Sustainability in Local Media, October 16, 2016, http://news paperownership.com/changed-landscape/.

6 Elizabeth Greico, "Newsroom Employment Dropped Nearly a Quarter in Less Than 10 Years, with Greatest Decline at Newspapers," Pew Research Center, July 30, 2018, www.pewresearch.org/fact-tank/2018/07/30/newsroom-employment-dropped-nearly-a-quarter-in-less-than-10-years-with-greatest-decline-at-newspapers/.

7 Michael Porter, *Competitive Advantage* (New York, NY: Free Press, 1985), 4–11.

8 Michael Porter, "Strategy and the Internet," *Harvard Business Review*, 2001, 63–78.

9 Clayton Christensen and Michael Raynor, *The Innovator's Solution* (Boston, MA: Harvard Business Review Press, 2003), 74–75.

10 American Press Institute, "Newspaper Next: The Blueprint for Transformation," 2006, www.americanpressinstitute.org/wp-content/uploads/2013/09/N2_Blueprint-for-Transformation.pdf.

11 Edgar Schein, *Organizational Culture and Leadership*, 4th ed. (San Francisco, CA: Jossey-Bass: 2010), 28.

12 Joshua Benton, "The Leaked New York Times Innovation Report Is One of the Key Documents of This Media Age," *Nieman Lab*, May 15, 2014, www.niemanlab. org/2014/05/the-leaked-new-york-times-innovation-report-is-one-of-the-key-documents-of-this-media-age/.

13 Shan Wang, "Many Newsrooms Around the World Are a Little Lagging with It Comes to New Tech and a Digital First Mindset," *Nieman Lab*, October 6, 2017, www.niemanlab.org/2017/10/most-newsrooms-around-the-world-are-a-little-lagging-when-it-comes-to-new-tech-and-a-digital-first-mindset/.

14 Schein, 301.

15 Schein, 237.

16 Chris Argyris, *Reasons and Rationalizations* (New York, NY: Oxford University Press: 2004), 2.

17 Argyris, 10–11.

One

In September 2017, protests erupted in St. Louis when a white former police officer was acquitted in the killing of a black man, Anthony Lamar Smith.[1] With dogged effort on the streets and social media, Black Lives Matter activists had succeeded in raising the issue of police conduct in black communities to greater prominence in mainstream news sources that had previously largely ignored it. Faced with this latest development in St. Louis, the social newsgathering team at NowThis jumped into action to cover the verdict and protests with real-time reporting based entirely on a @newsroom account on Twitter.[2] Two pioneers in social newsgathering, P. Kim Bui and Andy Carvin, led the team, combining speed with verification and transparency.

Bui told *Columbia Journalism Review*:

> We've learned that eyewitness accounts are paramount to good
> reporting. We've learned that building community really makes
> a difference if you spend time talking to people, asking questions,
> answering questions, and being incredibly transparent. We're both
> very big about tweeting as we learn things, being open about what
> we know and what we don't know, and that's something news
> organizations are starting to do more of.[3]

It wasn't long ago that reporting and distributing a story using Twitter as the primary tool, as NowThis did after the verdict came down, would have been considered blasphemy.[4] Even today, resistance to using social media for reporting and feedback remains among some established journalists, despite the possibilities for connecting with previously untapped corners of their communities. But many have embraced these tools as part of their newsgathering routines, as social media use has become commonplace among journalists and citizens alike.[5]

Why are there still such disparate levels of adoption? The answer lies in understanding how any new tool or practice is evaluated by journalists: through the lens of core journalistic values instilled by schools, institutions, and organizations.

This chapter will explain how these deeply held values of the craft shape, enable, or inhibit change in critical ways. Many journalists enter the field as idealists, hoping to make a difference in their communities and bring problems to light, and journalistic values are rooted in their identities as professionals and as people. Multiple studies over the years have shown that journalists will resist any change they perceive—correctly or incorrectly—will affect the quality of their work or threaten to undermine these core principles.[6] Thus, a critical aspect of successful change in newsrooms is recognizing that embracing technologies and/or practices does not have to mean abandoning these values; indeed, tapping into them is necessary and important.

The practical application of values can be a subjective process. Reasonable people may not always agree on which activities are or are not in line with core principles; each organization is going to have to do the work to identify how its own people think and feel about specific cases. We cannot overstate the danger of using the language of values inauthentically; there is no faster way to breed contempt. But the bottom line is those in the newsroom will usually resist—openly or covertly—any change that they perceive will undermine their core principles.

JOURNALISTIC VALUES ENDURE

Unlike other aspects of newsroom culture that can be unconscious, uncovering the guiding journalistic values is easier because so many are widely held. They are a common part of the industry's socialization process in journalism schools and early career development.

As part of their work with the Committee of Concerned Journalists, Bill Kovach, Tom Rosenstiel, and their staff conducted interviews, focus groups, and surveys with hundreds of journalists around the country about the values they felt defined their work.[7] In the book *The Elements of Journalism*, they summarized their findings as 10 widely shared principles, and the book, which has been revised and updated three times since its original publication in 2001, is frequently taught in journalism schools around the United States (see Box 1.1).

BOX 1.1 THE ELEMENTS OF JOURNALISM

Bill Kovach and Tom Rosenstiel

These essential principles that underlie good journalism were identified through extensive surveys of reporters and editors, academics, and the public.

- Journalism's first obligation is to the truth.
- Its first loyalty is to citizens.
- Its essence is a discipline of verification.
- Its practitioners must maintain an independence from those they cover.
- It must serve as an independent monitor of power.
- It must provide a forum for public criticism and compromise.
- It must strive to keep the significant interesting and relevant.
- It must keep the news comprehensive and proportional.
- Its practitioners must be allowed to exercise their personal conscience.
- Citizens, too, have rights and responsibilities when it comes to the news.

In the 2014 edition, the authors noted how dramatic changes in technology had disrupted but not killed journalism principles:

Journalism and the elements of journalism should concern all citizens today even more than they once did precisely because the distinctions between citizen and journalist, reporter and editor, audience and producer are not vanishing but blurring. Journalism isn't dying. It is becoming more of a collaboration. And journalists are not being replaced or becoming irrelevant. Their role has become more complex and more critical.[8]

Newsrooms may prioritize the individual principles differently, but they are an excellent starting point for understanding what shared values should guide digital change efforts.

The core principles identified in *Elements* reflect the profession's highest aspirations of serving the public in a democratic system, and many people are attracted to the field because of them. Historically, these core values arose as journalism evolved into a bona fide profession requiring specific skills and training, and served as a defense against critics who disparaged journalists' work as biased or slipshod.[9] Given that journalists' work is inherently public and that they depend on the trust of the public for viability, the ability to defend the profession was important and helped embed these values further.

"I honestly believe a well-informed public is a major characteristic of a flourishing democracy," one journalist said in response to a Committee of Concerned Journalists survey created and administered by Brown about why they got into the field, echoing many other respondents. "Wide-ranging and high-quality journalism is a central component of making a well-informed public a possibility." Another said: "I was intensely interested in participating in a free press as a vital element of our society."

Study after study by ourselves and other academics has confirmed that any change effort that does or is perceived as undermining those values will be met with active or passive resistance, even in newsrooms that increasingly recognize that change is vital.[10] Looking back to the early 2000s, for example, the industry buzzword was "convergence," as news organizations sought to cope with digital change by establishing print and broadcast partnerships. One study of four "converged" newsrooms at the time found strong staff resistance because of a widespread perception that the changes were made purely for economic and not journalistic reasons.[11] Leaders had not been clear or convincing about how to execute change in ways congruent with core values, and ultimately the staff members from different media backgrounds were not working together in productive or consistent ways, the study found.

In her extensive study of how the *Capital Times* in Madison, Wisconsin, handled its transition from print to a web-only news product in 2008, University of Wisconsin professor Sue Robinson found that "the key to making these transitions 'successful' lay in getting people to think about technology not as another tool (i.e. labor device) but as a journalistic concept itself, one that could enhance the calling of the profession."[12] She talked to journalists who said their digital work seemed more ephemeral, making it feel like it had less journalistic heft and meaning. In our own work, we, too, have seen journalists view newer forms of storytelling and engagement, such as blogs and comments, as less valuable forms of the craft.[13]

A more recent case study of a news company that was undergoing three interdependent yet distinct changes found that technological change is easier than change that requires journalists to build stronger relationships with their audiences.[14] While journalists understood the merits and necessity of adapting to new technologies and platforms like mobile alerts and social media, "they resist changes they see as disruptive of journalistic autonomy, damaging to the news product, and communicated poorly by company leadership."[15] And as in previous studies, this one concluded that "acceptance is unlikely unless newsworkers come to understand this set of innovations as compatible with deeply held convictions about the role of journalism in society or come to believe this change will result in better journalism."[16]

Research suggests that organizations of all kinds, not just newsrooms, that adapt to their changing environment by building on existing strengths and values often have the most success.[17] It is easier and more realistic to change behaviors than to ask people to rethink their fundamental purpose. As we'll discuss further, there are a number of ways staff can undermine directives they don't agree with.

THE TENSION BETWEEN IMMEDIACY AND ACCURACY

By the time Bui and Carvin were launching @newsroom to cover the protests in St. Louis in real time, the relentless 24/7 news cycle, fueled first by cable television and then by the Internet, wasn't a new phenomenon. But the speed of social media can produce many tensions with one of the defining principles for journalists: the importance of verification, or the imperative to check facts and get it right.[18]

Journalists worry about errors slipping into their work and believe that mistakes are costly in the eyes of the public. They are concerned about having less time to report, potentially leading to an increased reliance on press releases.[19] But on the other hand, hitting pause on the Publish button is not always the option that serves readers best in an environment in which rumors may be exploding across social media platforms. Audiences have come to expect quick, easy access to the latest news on their phones. And most importantly, social media can surface diverse perspectives that rarely found their way into mainstream news in years past.[20] Before activists created the #BlackLivesMatter hashtag and vaulted the movement onto the national news agenda, police shootings of African-Americans weren't reported on regularly.

In workshops conducted at newspapers around the country in the early 2000s, Kovach, Rosenstiel, and other leading journalists who worked as facilitators for the Committee of Concerned Journalists offered a potent visual example of how the media landscape for dealing with rumors had changed. Journalists were like cowboys standing guard at a gate, but the fence around it had disappeared. The cattle were roaming all over the field. Some of the "people formerly known as the audience"[21] or less scrupulous media organizations could easily use new communication tools to bypass the former gatekeepers and spread rumors widely.

The response to this dilemma was not, of course, to give up on verifying facts and throw values out the window. But continuing to stand at the gate silently watching rumors run rampant was not a good solution either. Instead, the answer of news organizations was for journalists to serve as more of a "sensemaker" or a "referee," letting the audience know which facts had been verified and which journalists were still in the process of checking out.

In today's environment, journalism is becoming less about the story, or the package, or the post. It is about the process, the unfolding narrative as it is being verified.

Ultimately, the core of this approach to verification is transparency—being open with audiences about what you do and don't know, as well as giving them a peek at the processes you use to check facts.[22] In the past, when it was possible to keep rumors out of public view, not publishing anything was a viable option. Today, silence is often not the best way to serve the public. And in many ways, the digital world offers a host of strategies that make "sensemaking," transparency, and verification easier, including links to source documents, the ability to quickly reach out to large numbers of people for confirmation, and a greater focus on data journalism.

Kovach and Rosenstiel were writing, researching, and leading workshops at a time during which cable news outlets and some of the earliest blogs were among the most likely to be publishing information that hadn't been vetted in accordance with traditional journalistic standards. With the rise of social media in the mid-to-late 2000s, the gatekeeping model went from life-support to dead.

Journalists like Bui and Carvin developed new ways of thinking about verification in a digital world that pointed a way forward for organizations seeking to navigate change with values in the fore-front, producing not only better journalism but more staff buy-in. In his book *Distant Witness*,[23] Carvin describes how he covered the Arab Spring using social media, developing intimate connections with on-the-ground sources there who helped him to sift rumor from fact in an open dialogue. If an unconfirmed rumor was making the rounds on Twitter, Carvin would flag this piece of information, ask for input in assessing its veracity, and keep audiences informed of the results as they developed. In a speech at the International Symposium on Online Journalism in May 2013,[24] Carvin argued that we need to use social media to slow down the news cycle rather than speed it up, challenging the public to question what they are hearing and explaining what it will take to verify it. As he put it:

> To inform the public is to tell them what we think they should know. To create a more informed public is to help them become better consumers and producers of information—and hopefully achieve their full potential as active participants in civil society.

Carvin and Bui's approach combines core values with the tools, needs, and sensibilities of a digital world. Instead of just asking journalists to "do more"—master more tools, use more platforms, etc.—this more thoughtful change in practice provides a better fit with culture. Both of them applied this technique first at Reported.ly, a venture of First Look Media, and then later at NowThis. Using social media as their platform, the teams at both organizations built relationships with people around the world that helped them surface important breaking news and sift rumor from fact in an open, transparent way.[25]

Another example of how such teams operate was during the shooting at the French satirical newspaper *Charlie Hebdo*.[26] Reported.ly staffers based in Europe caught early tweets mentioning the shooting and jumped into action, using more than 200 Twitter lists with valuable sources around the world. The team worked to verify names of potential suspects that were circulating online, helping to "organize the chaos" on social media.[27]

Carvin wrote:

A handful of individual Twitter users were quoting three specific names of suspects, but nothing had been confirmed yet. A few news outlets decided to run with the names early, but once again I thought back to the Boston (Marathon) bombing (of 2013) and how several people had their reputations tarnished because they were erroneously connected to the attack. It was clear that the three names were circulating more and more widely, so we concluded it was important to acknowledge that names were floating around, but that it was still important to be extra cautious in situations such as this.[28]

Unfortunately, however, far too few newsrooms have adopted practices like these that place a premium on transparency and reporting using social media, a study by Jane Elizabeth, then at the American Press Institute, found.[29] Indeed, both First Look Media and NowThis ultimately dropped their support for this kind of work, laying off Carvin, Bui, and others on their team. Journalists are more comfortable using social media in ways that don't require them to change their relationship with their audience or their practices, Elizabeth found. In other words, most usage tends to be promotional—broadcasting links to content in ways that do not deviate much from older models of journalism.[30] Elizabeth argued that this misstep is a huge missed opportunity for newsrooms seeking to do more original reporting, even with smaller staffs. Instead of treating social media teams as simply there to grow audience, these staffers could work more closely with other reporters to find and verify information and engage audience members in the process. By integrating social media editors in ways that honor journalism values, their work is also likely to be more widely accepted and welcomed in newsrooms.

Journalists looking for resources on how to use social media for reporting and collaboration with citizens while setting high standards for vetting the information that gets circulated can turn to resources from First Draft, which focuses on combating information disorder. The organization offers online courses that teach a variety of techniques and tools for checking the veracity of photos, videos, and other kinds of content.

In 2019, resistance continued to build among journalists against platforms such as Facebook and Twitter because those sites had failed to curb harassment, while hoovering up advertising dollars and failing to prevent manipulation by bad actors.[31] But while the companies behind the platforms may have to change, the need for journalists to use social media to be part of the conversation endures, and can be bolstered if we plan consciously to use them in ways congruent with core values.[32]

NEW MEDIA, ENDURING VALUES

Another example of aligning a change effort with core journalistic values in a deliberate way is a project we participated in beginning in mid-2006. The New Media, Enduring Values project brought together three news organizations and the University of Missouri, the Committee of Concerned Journalists, and the Donald W. Reynolds Journalism Institute in an attempt to experiment with and evaluate a values-driven approach to change.

Each participating news organization developed an online project focusing one of the core values outlined in The Elements of Journalism. For example, the Milwaukee Journal Sentinel chose verification and developed an education coverage initiative that encouraged readers and stakeholders to improve accuracy by reporting errors and contributing their expertise and perspectives.

As part of the team at the University of Missouri tasked with evaluating the results of this effort, we found that this approach was perceived as successful in creating staff buy-in and enthusiasm. Not surprisingly, each project still ran into obstacles related to newsroom culture that we will discuss later in the book; commitment to core values is necessary but not sufficient in and of itself to produce significant organization-wide change. But considering the typical level of resistance to change documented in newsrooms, it was striking that many participating staffers said in interviews that they were willing to let go of typical daily routines in order to focus on developing more multimedia and interactivity for these projects. Many also told us they were willing to take on extra work to develop the new skills necessary to enhance their work in the project.

At the outset of the project, *Journal Sentinel* staffers said the task seemed vague. Sure, as journalists it was natural and easy to talk internally about verification, but what practical, concrete steps could they take to enhance this principle in the digital world that would be meaningful to readers? However, as they began to build greater interactivity and participation into their education coverage, they began to see that tools designed to make it easier for readers to question a fact or add a different perspective to the story enhanced accuracy.

COMMITTING TO INVESTIGATIVE JOURNALISM IN A DIGITAL WORLD

In today's troubled times for news organizations, it has been difficult to sustain the kinds of time-consuming investigative work that represents journalism's highest aspirations. One of the newspapers we studied, however, identified watchdog reporting as one of its core values and found a way to sustain its commitment to this kind of work by making it a top priority.[33]

At the Investigative Reporters and Editors conference in San Francisco in June 2014, the *Milwaukee Journal Sentinel* lit up the ballroom at the awards ceremony as the only organization that took home two prestigious national awards, and was named a finalist for another.[34] One of these stories, "Deadly Delays," which the judges said "exposed a shocking practice at many of the nation's hospitals" of lax screening of newborns for rare diseases, also won an award from the Online News Association.

The wins were not an anomaly. Since 2008, the paper has won three Pulitzer Prizes and has been a finalist four times, during what has been an unquestionably difficult financial period in the newspaper industry's history. "I think that is the stuff we got into the business to do, to do great journalism, and that is good for morale," an editor we interviewed said. "As long as people feel like they can do their work well and do meaningful work, they will be happy."[35]

Reporters we interviewed told us how much they valued having top managers who prioritized and supported investigative work in ways that were no longer widespread among metro dailies, particularly after the Great Recession, and how this sustained commitment amid threats to the industry helped them continue to do their best work even during change. Ultimately, however, even the *Journal Sentinel* has struggled to maintain its investigative priorities, especially under its current ownership by a publicly traded company. In 2017, it lost one of its top investigative reporters to the *New York Times*, and by January 2019, the paper had undergone more layoffs.[36]

While not a tale of unmitigated success, the relatively high internal morale and quality of work the paper has been able to sustain offers lessons for the investigative nonprofits that continue to pop up around the country, as well as any organization under less ownership pressure to cut costs.

THE ROOTS OF MODERN JOURNALISTIC VALUES

The advent of the Internet is far from the first time the journalism industry has faced a crisis of identity.

At the turn of the twentieth century, frustrations with yellow journalism—with its emphasis on sensationalism and celebrity—led to a rethinking of the craft: Could the empirical approach of science be brought to bear to make the methodology of journalism more uniform and reliable? The *New York Times*, the *Christian Science Monitor*, and other news organizations embraced the ethic of the modern era and worked to bring a standard method to gathering facts accurately and completely, with an eye toward context and completeness. Soon, journalism schools began dotting the U.S. landscape to improve the professionalism of practitioners.[37]

In the 1920s, influential writer and thinker Walter Lippmann outlined the idea explicitly in *Liberty and the News*, calling for journalists to adopt a scientific mindset, which calls for "unity of method, rather than aim."[38] Bringing a vigorous focus on verification of facts would help minimize the effect of inherent biases in reporters. As Bill Kovach and Tom Rosenstiel put it: "In the original concept, ... the journalist was not objective, but the journalist's method could be."[39] Journalists began to see the objective pursuit of truth embedded in their work. News organizations worked to separate their advertising executives and opinion writers from their reporters to keep this notion of objectivity sacrosanct.

Other changes to the business of news also favored an objectivity of method and a less partisan style of news than was popular in America in the nineteenth century. New technologies of distribution meant greater reach, and with it the need to avoid offending potential readers with a wide variety of views.[40] But sensationalism did not disappear. During World War II, a group known as the Commission on Freedom of the Press—better known as the Hutchins Commission—came together to produce a report on the state of journalism, a forebear of the work by the Committee of Concerned Journalists. After four years of interviews and public hearings, the Hutchins Commission articulated a vision of a socially responsible press, one concentrated on contributing to a democratic society more than to the bottom line. Like Lippmann, the report noted the journalistic imperative to help the public understand the complex issues of modern life:

> The account of an isolated fact, however accurate in itself, may be misleading and, in effect, untrue. ... The press now bears a responsibility in all countries, and particularly in democratic countries, where foreign policies are responsive to popular majorities, to report international events in such a way that they can be understood. It is no longer enough to report *the fact* truthfully. It is now necessary to report the *truth about the fact*.[41]

Journalists were not always successful at moving beyond stenography. In the 1950s, Sen. Joseph McCarthy held public hearings that became witch hunts in search of communists, and reporters dutifully chronicled the hearings without questioning the truth behind that chronicle, until noted broadcaster Edward R. Murrow confronted McCarthy directly on the CBS airwaves.[42]

A few years after this journalistic triumph, Murrow raised another issue—with his own industry. In a keynote speech at the 1958 convention of the Radio-Television News Directors Association (now the Radio Television Digital News Association, or RTDNA), he questioned the television networks' focus on profits over conscience, entertainment over news, and put forth a challenge: What if the networks dedicated part of their programming to the important topics of the day?

> This instrument can teach, it can illuminate; yes, and even it can inspire. But it can do so only to the extent that humans are determined to use it to those ends. Otherwise, it's nothing but wires and lights in a box.[43]

Such historical touchpoints resonate with journalists today, especially when documented and popularized in books and movies. When the New York Times fought to publish the Pentagon Papers, and Washington Post reporters Bob Woodward and Carl Bernstein dug tenaciously into the Watergate burglary to connect the threads to the White House, legions of journalists were inspired to take on the mantle of watchdog; even today, these events have broad cultural resonance, as evidenced by the 2017 Hollywood film The Post. A decennial national survey of journalists showed that more than three-quarters believe that "investigating government claims" remains a key role for the profession—the highest since the survey has been conducted.[44]

Prior to the Internet age, news organizations also set the civic agenda for what the public thought about and discussed. As the gatekeepers of information, journalists decided what stories were published and aired, what facts the public got to see, as news organizations created the "first rough draft of history."[45]

Today, that work is no longer done solely by news organizations. In 1997, blogger Matt Drudge became the first to reveal details about President Bill Clinton's affair with intern Monica Lewinsky.[46] In 2004, an online campaign of non-journalists questioned the veracity of CBS anchor Dan Rather's reporting about President George W. Bush's National Guard service.[47] And now, in the age of social media, citizens with mobile phones are just as likely to capture news as it happens as professional journalists. The new paradigm requires journalists to become more collaborative in their thinking, to open up the process to the public and amateurs.

But journalism schools have been slow to adapt to this evolving reality. Most programs embed the history of modern journalism into their curricula and ultimately their graduates. With more than 92% of journalists having a college degree today (compared with 58% in 1971), many graduate with these ideals and perspectives top of mind.[48] One study across eight countries found that journalism students interested in hard news viewed their professional role as watchdog or citizen-oriented (what the public "should know") instead of consumer-oriented (what the public "wants to know").[49]

LETTING THE PUBLIC IN

Journalism's fundamental mission is grounded in public service. "To provide citizens with the information they need to be free and self-governing" is the purpose of journalism, according to Kovach and Rosenstiel.[50] It seems obvious that two of the core principles—loyalty to citizens and providing a forum for public criticism and compromise—can be enhanced by deepening relationships and participation among the people we serve. And the two-way nature of digital and social media has built audience expectations that interactivity and engagement are the norm.

So why can efforts to embrace a more participatory audience be controversial and resisted in newsrooms? Because it depends on how efforts to change journalism practice are framed with regard to these values.

Putting the audience at the center of everything you do can sound like marketing-speak to journalists hardened by long experience dealing with PR officials seeking to spin for profit. And even though journalists understand that change is required at a time of economic precarity, pushing for a more active role for the audience can seem like pandering for clicks. In both conscious and unconscious ways, an audience-centric approach can feel like a threat to journalists' authority as arbiters of what is important and what sources of information can be trusted. It strikes at the core of their identity.

Thus, an organization seeking to promote more engagement has to be clear about the ways in which it can enhance, and not detract, from reporting and truth-telling. For example, many of the investigations by the Pulitzer Prize-winning news site ProPublica are powered by its readers, thanks to a dedicated team that uses a variety of crowdsourcing techniques to gather information from a wide range of sources and build community.[51] Showing the newsroom that engaged journalists could enhance award-winning investigations brings the team credibility.

Before you explore the culture of your own organization, it's important to keep the centrality of these journalistic values in mind. They have formed over the past century and have become ingrained in the industry and the university programs that train journalists. These embedded ideals can inspire journalists' best work, but they can also threaten the introduction of new ideas that challenge journalists' autonomy and authority in story creation and reporting— ideas that are necessary to survive in today's interactive, participatory news environment (see Box 1.2).

BOX 1.2 KEEPING CHANGE ROOTED IN JOURNALISTIC VALUES

It's helpful to keep key questions in mind as you initiate change efforts in your own newsroom. Encourage conversations about how new initiatives help deepen reporting and improve connections with the communities your organization covers.

- How do these tools and processes help us improve our ability to capture the key rumors to verify in our communities?
- How can we be more transparent about our work to engender community trust? Look for opportunities to share original reports, raw audio and video, and spreadsheets and databases to allow audiences to see what formed the basis of the stories.
- How do the interactive platforms allow us to improve our ability to serve as a public forum for the communities we serve?
- How can we inspire and moderate fruitful discussions in our communities in online social spaces?
- How can we use these tools to connect with previously hard-to-reach segments of our communities?
- In what ways do these tools allow journalists to do their jobs more efficiently and effectively? How can we streamline and automate previously arduous tasks with new tools?

NOTES

1 Joel Currier and Christine Byers, "Heated Protests Follow Stockley Acquittal," www.stltoday.com/news/local/crime-and-courts/heated-protests-follow-stockley-acquittal/article_c7ee91ad-e65b-5da6-84cb-0b478078c8cb.html.

2 Meg Dalton, "Q&A: A Social-focused Journalist on Reinventing Newsgathering," *Columbia Journalism Review*, September 27, 2017, www.cjr.org/united_states_project/now-this-news-newsroom st louis.php.

3 Dalton.

4 Alecia Swasy, "I Studied How Journalists Used Twitter for Two Years. Here's What I Learned," Poynter, March 22, 2017, www.poynter.org/tech-tools/2017/i-studied-how-journalists-used-twitter-for-two-years-heres-what-i-learned/.

5 Pew Research Center, "Social Media Fact Sheet," June 12, 2019, www.pewinternet.org/fact-sheet/social-media/.

6 See Jonathan Groves, "The Roots of Journalistic Resistance: Blogs, Comments, and the Challenge to Verification in a Newspaper Newsroom," conference paper, International Communication Association Annual Meeting (2011); Peter Gade, "Newspapers and Organizational Development: Management and Journalism Perceptions of Newsroom Cultural Change," *Journalism & Communication Monographs* 6, no. 1 (2004), 3–55; Peter Gade and E. L. Perry, "Changing the Newsroom Culture: A Four-Year Case Study of Organizational Development at the St. Louis Post-Dispatch," *Journalism & Mass Communication Quarterly* 80, no. 2 (2003), 327–347; Kathleen Hansen, Mark Neuzil, and Jean Ward, "Newsroom Topic Teams: Journalists' Assessments of Effects on News Routines and Newspaper Quality," *Journalism & Mass Communication Quarterly* 75, no. 4 (1998), 803–821.

7 Bill Kovach and Tom Rosenstiel, *The Elements of Journalism, Revised and Updated 3rd Edition: What Newspeople Should Know and the Public Should Expect* (New York, NY: Three Rivers Press, 2014).

8 Kovach and Rosenstiel, 2.

9 Michael Schudson, *The Sociology of News*, 2nd ed., Contemporary Societies Series (New York, NY: W. W. Norton & Co., 2002); Barbie Zelizer, *Taking Journalism Seriously: News and the Academy* (Thousand Oaks, CA: Sage, 2004).

10 See, for example, George L. Daniels and C. Ann Hollifield, "Times of Turmoil: Short- and Long-Term Effects of Organizational Change on Newsroom Employees," *Journalism & Mass Communication Quarterly* 79, no. 3 (September 2002): 661–680, doi:10.1177/107769900207900308; Gade, "Newspapers and Organizational Development"; Mark Neuzil, Kathleen Hansen, and Jean Ward, "Twin Cities Journalists' Assessment of Topic Teams," *Newspaper Research Journal* 20, no. 1 (January 1999): 2–16, doi:10.1177/073953299902000101; Sue Robinson, "Convergence Crises: News Work and News Space in the Digitally Transforming Newsroom," *Journal of Communication* 61, no. 6 (2011), 1122–1141, doi:10.1111/j.1460–2466.2011.01603.

11 Jane Singer, "Strange Bedfellows? The Diffusion of Convergence in Four News Organizations," *Journalism Studies* 5, no. 1 (2004), 3–18. doi:10.1080/1461670032000174701.

12 Robinson, 25.

13 Groves.

14 Brian Ekdale, Jane B. Singer, Melissa Tully, and Shawn Harmsen, "Making Change: Diffusion of Technological, Relational, and Cultural Innovation in the Newsroom," *Journalism & Mass Communication Quarterly* 92, no. 4 (December 2015): 938–958. doi:10.1177/1077699015596337.

15 Ekdale, Singer, Tully, and Harmisen, 940

16 Ekdale, Singer, Tully, and Harmisen, 958.

17 Edgar Schein, *Organizational Culture and Leadership*, 4th ed. (Edison, NJ: Jossey-Bass, 2010).

18 Kovach and Rosenstiel.

19 Robinson.

20 Deen Freelon, Lori Lopez, Meredith D. Clark, and Sarah J. Jackson, "How Black Twitter and Other Social Media Communities Interact with Mainstream News," Knight Foundation, February 27, 2018, https://kf-site-production.s3.amazonaws.com/media_elements/files/000/000/136/original/TwitterMedia-final.pdf.

21 Jay Rosen, "The People Formerly Known as the Audience," PressThink (blog), June 27, 2006, http://archive.pressthink.org/2006/06/27/ppl_frmr.html.

22 Kovach and Rosenstiel.

23 Andy Carvin, *Distant Witness* (New York, NY: CUNY Journalism Press, 2013).

24 Andy Carvin, "#ISOJ Keynote: Can Social Media Help Us Create a More Informed Public?" *MediaShift*, April 21, 2013, http://mediashift.org/2013/04/isoj-keynote-can-social-media-help-us-create-a-more-informed-public111/.

25 Andy Carvin, "Welcome to Reported.Ly!" *Medium*, December 8, 2014, https://medium.com/reportedly/welcome-to-reported-ly-3363a5fb7ea5.

26 Justin Ellis, "Reported.Ly Puts Its Social-First Journalism Model to Work Covering the Charlie Hebdo Attacks," *Nieman Lab*, January 13, 2015, www.niemanlab.org/2015/01/reported-ly-puts-its-social-first-journalism-model-to-work-covering-the-charlie-hebdo-attacks/.

27 Ellis.

28 Andy Carvin, "Baptism by Fire: What We Learned Covering #CharlieHebdo on our 3rd Day," *Medium*, January 8, 2015, https://medium.com/reportedly/baptism-by-fire-what-we-learned-covering-charliehebdo-on-our-3rd-day-fc6f479c6235.

29 Jane Elizabeth, "After a Decade, It's Time to Reinvent Social Media in Newsrooms," American Press Institute, November 17, 2017, www.americanpressinstitute.org/publications/reports/strategy-studies/reinventing-social-media/.

30 Elizabeth; Sue Robinson, *Networked News, Racial Divides* (Cambridge: Cambridge University Press, 2017).

31 Farhad Manjoo, "Never Tweet," *New York Times*, January 23, 2019, www.nytimes.com/2019/01/23/opinion/covington-twitter.html.

32 Jeff Jarvis, "Journalism Is the Conversation. The Conversation Is Journalism," *Medium*, January 27, 2019, https://medium.com/whither-news/journalism-is-the-conversation-the-conversation-is-journalism-22a8c631e952.

33 Adrienne LaFrance, "What Does the Milwaukee Journal Sentinel Know that Your Newsroom Doesn't?" *Nieman Lab*, September 27, 2013, www.niemanlab.org/2013/09/what-does-the-milwaukee-journal-sentinel-know-that-your-newsroom-doesnt/.

34 Investigative Reporters & Editors, "2013 IRE Award Winners," www.ire.org/awards/ire-awards/winners/2013-irc-award-winners/#.VGVgavnF90x2014.

35 Confidential interview, personal communication, March 10, 2008.

36 Bruce Murphy, "Journal Sentinel Loses Six More Staff," *Urban Milwaukee*, January 3, 2019, https://urbanmilwaukee.com/2019/01/03/back-in-the-news-journal-sentinel-loses-six-more-staff/.

37 The University of Missouri created the first university-level school of journalism in 1908 (http://missouri.edu/about/history/journalism.php), and Columbia University launched its program—a decade in the making—in 1912 (www.journalism.columbia.edu/page/5-history-of-the-journalism-school/5).

38 Walter Lippmann, *Liberty and the News* (New Brunswick, NJ: Transaction Publishers, 1995), 58.

39 Kovach and Rosenstiel, 102.

40 Schudson, 89.

41 Commission on Freedom of the Press, *A Free and Responsible Press* (Chicago, IL: University of Chicago Press, 1947), https://archive.org/details/freeandresponsib029216mbp. Emphasis in original.

42 PBS, "Edward R. Murrow—This Reporter," www.pbs.org/wnet/americanmasters/episodes/edward-r-murrow/this-reporter/513/.

43 Edward R. Murrow, "Edward R. Murrow's 1958 'Wires & Lights in a Box' Speech," www.rtdna.org/content/edward_r_murrow_s_1958_wires_lights_in_a_box_speech#.VOKX5XZLRNF2015.

44 Lars Willnat and David H. Weaver, *The American Journalist in the Digital Age, Key Findings* (Bloomington, IN: Indiana University, 2014), http://news.indiana.edu/releases/iu/2014/05/2013-american-journalist-key-findings.pdf.

45 Jack Shafer, "Who Said It First: Journalism Is 'The First Rough Draft of History'," *Slate*, August 30, 2010, www.slate.com/articles/news_and_politics/press_box/2010/08/who_said_it_first.html.

46 Michael B. Salwen, Bruce Garrison, and Paul D. Driscoll (eds), *Online News and the Public* (Mahwah, NJ: Lawrence Erlbaum, 2005).

47 Salwen, Garrison, and Driscoll.

48 Derek Thompson, "Report: Journalists Are Miserable, Liberal, Over-Educated, Under-Paid, Middle-Aged Men," *The Atlantic*, May 14, 2020, www.theatlantic.com/business/archive/2014/05/report-journalists-are-miserable-over-educated-under-paid-middle-aged-men-mostly/361891/.

49 Folker Hanusch and Claudia Mellado, "Journalism Students' Professional Views in Eight Countries: The Role of Motivations, Education, and Gender,"

International Journal of Communication 8 (January, 2014): 1156–1173, https://ijoc.org/index.php/ijoc/article/view/2416.

50 Kovach and Rosenstiel, 17.

51 Terry Parris, Jr., "How the Public Fueled Our Investigations in 2017," ProPublica, January 11, 2018, www.propublica.org/article/how-the-public-fueled-our-investigations-in-2017.

Two

"Digital first!" was a constantly heard mantra among newsrooms during the early twenty-first century. Top editors made speeches. Banners got hung in newsrooms. Memos were written and updated on email listservs. The journalism trade press was full of advice and exhortations. And most people we interviewed during our research told us they recognized that embracing the web was critical to survival, even if they would have preferred to remain "ink-stained wretches."

"Digital first," we found, means more than just publishing articles online immediately rather than holding them for print; it means the organization prioritizes all aspects of its digital product. And increasingly, *digital* meant *mobile*, the space where news was more likely to be consumed with the rise of smartphones.[1]

But often, reality did not match intent. The first place one could see the mismatch was in news meetings, where leaders plan coverage and debate which stories deserve prominent placement in the newspaper or on the newscast. Steeped in tradition and prestige, these meetings remained stubbornly focused on the legacy platform.

The *New York Times* was one prominent example. A five-month immersive study by researcher Nikki Usher in 2010 confirmed that rewards and evaluations for reporters at the paper remained centered on A1 productivity and that the paper struggled to adapt to new practices that required constant updates and new multimedia skills that few long-tenured staffers had.[2] It was not until mid-2014 that the *Times* finally changed its "Page One" afternoon news meetings to have more of a digital focus.[3] As the paper's leaked "innovation report" noted:

> The newsroom is unanimous. We are focusing too much time and energy on Page One. This concern—which we heard in virtually

every interview we conducted, including reporters, desk heads, and masthead editors—has long been a concern for the leadership. And yet it persists. Page One sets the daily rhythms, consumes our focus, and provides the newsroom's defining metric of success.[4]

It was not until 2015 that executive editor Dean Baquet announced that the paper would officially retire its system of pitching stories for the front page of the print edition.[5]

Today, we are finally seeing digital prioritization become reality in newsrooms we have studied. But each new evolution of technology or practice since, from social media to mobile, has also often gotten more lip service than actual embrace in daily routines.

What causes this gap between intention and execution? Culture.

CULTURE: THE FOUNDATION OF CHANGE

Culture is fundamental to understanding why people in organizations resist change. It explains why a newsroom could remain in the thrall of Page One or the top of the 5 p.m. newscast for so long, even though a growing share of the audience comes to news via social media or mobile based on when it is most convenient to them.

Management scholar Edgar Schein defines organizational culture as a set of shared assumptions that have been learned by a group to solve its problems.[6] These "problems" may involve both how the organization adapts to the external environment as well as how it functions smoothly internally. Organizations, therefore, are often victims of their own successes. It is common sense that people are reluctant to give up activities that proved successful in the past and even brought them accolades. For newspapers, delivering "the daily miracle" on doorsteps each morning—and now, feeding the online beast 24/7—is a tricky problem, and the routines that make it all possible are particularly hard to adjust.

To understand an organization's culture, you have to examine three things, according to Schein. The first are what he calls *artifacts*, or processes and physical structures. These can offer a variety of clues about what the organization values. The others are *espoused values* and *underlying assumptions*. Espoused values are the group's conscious, articulated goals, beliefs, and values. Underlying assumptions are the taken-for-granted, sometimes unconscious, generally non-discussed assumptions about what is important and the "right" way to do things. These assumptions are what really govern actions in an organization. The key is uncovering them.

It's not that news leaders didn't mean it when they said "digital first!" It's not as if a print focus in news meetings was an act of deliberate sabotage. It is that underlying assumptions about the prestige of print as a career-maker blocked news organizations' ability to focus on digital. As one interviewee in Milwaukee told one of us:

> I think a lot of people rose to prominence based on their knowledge of [print-based] practices, and if these practices are no longer relevant, the basis for their prominence is questioned. It is a scary time for people, even if they don't show it.[7]

The higher up you are in a newsroom hierarchy, the more you had to lose in power and status as the paper made its transition to the digital era. Some of the skills and daily tasks of top leaders increasingly became irrelevant; deciding which stories will get top billing on the paper's front page was long the most prestigious task in a newsroom, and as this decision fades in importance, so does some of the power associated with it. Keeping print primary at these meetings maintained the authority of those who rose to prominence on print-centric skills.

The lingering importance of "Page One" was of course not the only underlying assumption that contradicted a news organization's stated goals; it was just one of the longest-running and more obvious. Some underlying assumptions are more idiosyncratic and depend on an organization's history. For example, the Milwaukee Journal Sentinel developed an underlying assumption that conflict should be avoided at all costs after a bruising merger in 1995 between what was then the morning paper, the Sentinel, and the afternoon paper, the Journal. While the merger was more than a decade past at the time of our research and there had been considerable staff turnover since, many interviewees said that it still shaped the paper's norms in subtle but powerful ways, often blocking the ability to embrace change. One editor said:

> I think that people here just feel like they don't have the stomach for [another change like the merger]. Even top people that were here through it remember it as ugly and terrible.
>
> I think they think that they already went through that and don't want to again. I think that is partly why the pace of change has been slow ... There is still a lot of talk about the merger. It took eight or nine years for wounds to heal.[8]

As a result, in this conflict-averse culture, managers worked around people who refused to go along with digital efforts, rather than confronting them, at least in the earlier stages of the transition.

Other underlying assumptions we've uncovered include a belief that change is an individual-level issue, rather than a systemic one. Schein observes that assumptions about the nature of human relationships affect the ways in which organizations resolve conflict and make decisions. An individualistic way of viewing organizational life can cause leaders to focus on "who is with us/against us?" rather than examining how larger systemic factors affect organizational effectiveness.[9]

Newsroom leaders in one organization we studied, for example, generally operated on the underlying assumption that individual resistance was one of the biggest impediments to change: essentially, that some people just don't "get it." In this kind of culture, people who jumped in and tried new things, without necessarily asking permission or talking in advance about what they planned to do, were generally the most likely to be praised by top managers. However, in interviews, some of those perceived as most resistant to change rattled off a series of ideas for how to make their job more digitally-focused, but they were either encountering obstacles or had the kind of personality in which they were less likely to take action without specific direction and feedback.

DETERMINING YOUR OWN CULTURE

News organizations share similar cultures, and some of the underlying assumptions listed above may look familiar. But it is critical that you take steps to identify the elements of your own culture. If possible, we recommend bringing in someone from outside the organization to help you in this process. As noted previously, underlying assumptions are often unconscious and taken for granted, and while you should recognize their validity once they've been identified, they can be hard to spot when you yourself are a member of the culture. An outsider who doesn't share these assumptions can more easily identify them.

The next step is gathering information from people from all departments and levels of the newsroom hierarchy to learn about what is impeding people's effectiveness in their work and ability to change. This information-gathering phase should include interviewing staffers as well as observing meetings and examining group emails, memos, or other documents.

To establish trust, Michael Diamond, founder of the University of Missouri's Center for the Study of Organizational Change, says it's important that whoever is gathering information stresses that he or she is not going to make any personnel recommendations. If people believe that the objective is to figure out who should be fired or laid off, respondents will not be honest in interviews. The larger goal of a cultural review is to develop the ability to recognize problems, deal with conflict constructively, learn from mistakes, and develop and execute necessary changes to solve problems, Diamond recommends.

It's also important to note that it is rare for an organization's problems to be solved by simply hiring a different or "better" employee or manager; underlying factors like employees' expectations, communication processes, and organizational systems are far more important.[10]

You need buy-in and support from leadership to effectively assess culture. This inquiry is likely to turn up some information that is sensitive and uncomfortable, if it is done correctly, and you cannot do that without explicit and ongoing support from those in charge.

When we examine a newsroom, we ask questions about the organization and perspectives from each position, such as:

1 *Questions that get at the quality and style of internal communication.* How do people find out what's going on? Do they primarily use formal or informal channels? What is the relationship like between different departments and between leaders and staff? You want to be able to identify gaps in information-sharing and underlying areas of tension that keep people from communicating important information.

2 *Questions about leadership, which is a critical element of culture and change.* How does newsroom leadership communicate goals and expectations? Do people feel they know what leaders' expectations are and how they will be evaluated? What kinds of feedback do they receive? How are decisions made, and who has input? What kinds of actions are rewarded or punished?

3 *Questions about organizational strengths and competencies.* What are the newsroom's greatest strengths? What are some examples of successful change efforts or initiatives? What about people's jobs do they enjoy the most or feel the most proud of? You want to find out what the organization can build on or expand.

4 *Questions about organizational barriers.* What are the newsroom's greatest challenges? What are some of the greatest obstacles people face in their day-to-day work? What kinds of things block change in this organization, or inhibit personal or overall organizational effectiveness? How can these challenges be overcome? We have often been surprised by how this simple question can yield a number of insights, even some that are unexpected to newsroom leaders.

5 *Questions focused on support and investment.* What kinds of opportunities for learning or training have people had, and what do they wish they had? One of the biggest barriers to change is a feeling of incompetence, so this question can identify areas in which opportunities for education could break down barriers to change.

6 *Questions related to the alignment between values/mission and proposed changes.* As noted in Chapter 1, even the mere perception of misalignment can block change, so you want to dig into this area a bit. Do existing or proposed changes to the day-to-day routine enhance core values? More broadly, do people feel like they are able to uphold their values in their work?

7 *Questions relevant to an interviewee's position and responsibilities.* Perspectives from throughout the hierarchy provide insights about communication flow and connections between leadership and particular newsroom enclaves.

In addition to asking the above questions of individuals and recording the responses, observe how people interact with each other and communicate electronically. Pay special attention to any gaps between what people say and how they act in meetings or in casual conversations with each other. For example, leaders identify a priority in an interview but then emphasize a different area when speaking to staff at a meeting. Sometimes, they may not even be conscious of this disparity.

Work with someone who has experience organizing and analyzing such wide-ranging organizational information, such as an academic researcher or consultant, because if the collection is done correctly, there will be a lot of data to sift through. A thorough analysis should systematically identify key themes, the points that people bring up repeatedly. These repeated themes will lead to the underlying assumptions described above.

CONNECTING CULTURE TO CHANGE

Once the organizational culture is identified, consider the implications. How is it affecting your newsroom's effectiveness and its ability to adapt?[11]

Often, these implications are immediately apparent once you have surfaced the underlying assumptions. You may see areas where communication is breaking down and people are operating based on untested assumptions about what others think and do rather than real information. For example, at the *Journal Sentinel*, an underlying assumption that conflict must be avoided at all costs led to frequent breakdowns in communication because people didn't want to provoke disagreement. As a result, the research uncovered that some people believed that other people and departments were more resistant to change than they actually were, or were resistant for different reasons than was believed.[12]

Frequently in newsrooms we have seen that aspects of organizational culture push people to focus more on internal politics than on the external threats to survival. Without clear, consistent direction on what their goals and priorities should be, lower-level managers often become engaged in struggles over power and resources. People move to prevent their departmental budgets from being cut, or simply fail to take any kind of action at all. Energy and effort are spent fighting colleagues rather than being directed at finding new ways to adapt to changing economic forces.

There's no simple solution to this problem, but it cannot be addressed until you are at least aware of the dynamics and how they are operating in your organization and can find ways to discuss them openly. Given the state of the industry today and throughout the past 15 or more years, most journalists we've interviewed are highly motivated to try to fix these internal problems because they recognize that threats to organizational survival are strong. As a result, identifying the issues in a clear and understandable way often means that the specific solutions present themselves relatively easily.

Another area to explore is how your organization's culture may be sparking defensive reactions, which scholars have found can be triggered by any stressful situation in which an individual's or a group's sense of identity, competence, or self-worth are threatened.[13]

The most common defensive mechanisms or "routines" may include splitting (viewing people or ideas or concepts as all good or all bad), projection (attributing undesirable parts of the self to others), regression (returning to immature behaviors that may have been utilized in long-past conflicts, like name-calling), or repression (unconsciously blocking from memory certain uncomfortable feelings and thoughts).[14]

Kyle Pope of *Columbia Journalism Review* offered one example of how defensive mechanisms were playing out across the industry in early 2019. Beset by massive layoffs and attacks by online trolls and the president of the United States, journalists turn inward, seeking solidarity with each other, Pope wrote.[15] This reaction is a normal response to fear and external attack, essentially an example of the "splitting" described above. It means that journalists increasingly tune out critics, filtering complaints through the lens of partisan politics in a way that positions them as rising above the conflict.[16] But this behavior has consequences when it comes to adapting to new newsroom practices that recognize the growing power of the audience.

As both Pope and Jay Rosen of New York University pointed out, the *New York Times* in 2018 eliminated the public editor position, its designated reader advocate and listener, even as subscriptions became a greater part of the revenue mix.[17] At the same time, the organization launched an advertising campaign called "The Truth" that, as Pope put it, was "something pulled out of the vault from the days when newspapers were the voice of god, watching and ruling from on high."[18] The defensive turn inward thus results in practices that are contrary to what the business environment suggests is critical.

Once simmering issues that trigger these kinds of defenses are identified, it is easier to elicit more constructive and collaborative responses. Also, as we mentioned in Chapter 1, defensive mechanisms are more likely to be activated if journalists feel their core values are threatened—another reason to think carefully about how new efforts mesh with journalistic principles.

Elements of organizational culture can inhibit leaders from pushing people hard enough for change or helping staffers build the skills and feelings of competence they need to change.[19] If there is not enough pressure, people will not be motivated to alter comfortable routines. If there is too much, however, with few opportunities to train and build new competencies, defensive mechanisms are activated and people simply shut down. Striking this delicate balance is difficult, but it is a key function of leadership.

ORGANIZATIONAL STRUCTURE AND PROCESSES

An organization's culture is also expressed through its structure and processes. It's important to see how well these align with goals and how they might be blocking change.

Organizational scholar Michael I. Harrison talks about the importance of seeing organizations as dynamic "open systems" of interdependent parts.[20] A key source of ineffectiveness and inability to change is poor fit between these different parts, he argues, and you can often identify poor fit through outmoded structures or processes.

Harrison says the factors to pay attention to in terms of fit include inputs, or the available resources, such as budgets, staff, and technology; outputs, or what is produced, whether it is a product, a service, or knowledge; the environment, or the overall context in which you are operating, which may be changing rapidly, especially in the case of media. Where do these areas work against one another? Where are problems with the handoff between these areas?

Structure includes the ways in which the newsroom is organized—whether this is defined by hierarchy or a more vertical alignment of authority. In addition to more formal organizational charts and the relationships between different departments, there can also be informal cliques or favorites of the boss who wield influence.[21] A report by American Press Institute called these "tribes" that self-organize along the lines of job title, level of experience, perceived power, and personal relationships.[22] Tribes can be both positive and negative, but they can block change if they become competitive; a key role for leaders is to unite them in a shared mission, the report said.

Processes are daily routines that have been established over time as the way to get work done. In its 2014 Innovation Report, the *New York Times* explained how ingrained processes can be:

> Another suggested that the relentless work of assembling the world's best news report can also be a form of laziness, because it is work that is comfortable and familiar to us, that we know how to do. And it allows us to avoid the truly hard work and bigger questions about our present and our future: What shall we become? How must we change?[23]

Structures that worked well in traditional media environments do not always translate to the digital realm. Most newsrooms were built on hierarchy to meet deadlines predictably and consistently. Content typically moved through the newsroom in a carefully orchestrated progression through a series of baskets, where it was handled step-by-step by each of the appropriate departments and levels of the newsroom hierarchy; formal news meetings brought together decision-makers from each department at key points in the production process.

Organizational culture expert Schein noted that how an organization views time is an important aspect of its culture, and a linear, "monochronic" time orientation was well-suited to an environment in which meeting deadlines is critical and a high level of coordination is required.[24]

But for newsrooms producing news for digital, there is no clear end-point. Publication and deadlines are ongoing. Therefore, digital appears to necessitate what Schein calls a "polychronic" time orientation, suited for when several tasks need to be worked on at once.[25] This circumstance often means that traditional hierarchies are destabilized and flattened, allowing tech-savvy, lower-level employees to be empowered to make more of the digital decisions about publishing without the usual chain of approval. The ability to make changes post-publication also mitigates some of the risk.[26] As Schein writes, a polychronic time orientation arises in complex, relationship-driven work that is often completed in phases.[27]

One editor at the *Journal Sentinel* described digital work as developing more of a "wire service mentality"; the goal is to get a couple of paragraphs up on the site as quickly as possible that can then be updated and added to later on.[28] The conflicting time orientations suitable to each form of publishing go a long way toward explaining why it is difficult for even those willing to change to adapt. The monochronic time orientation persists not because of individual resistance among organizational members, but because it has historically provided the most appropriate solution to the problem of filling a newspaper or newscast each day. Increasing production speed and frequency also left many staffers at places like the *New York Times* exhausted, especially since they were still expected to provide authoritative second-day pieces for print.[29]

The newsroom's daily routines are resistant to change because they serve as a stabilizing force that brings order to the chaotic process of channeling unpredictable happenings into digestible news.

Culture is complicated because it involves human relationships and assumptions that we often don't even realize we have. But understanding culture is ultimately the most important aspect of any organizational change effort. Even at newer digital news outlets, organization members quickly develop and embed underlying assumptions about the right way to do things. Though they do not have to wean themselves from a traditional medium, they do find themselves having to consider new strategies and business models as Facebook and Google change their algorithms or conventional wisdom about the importance of video waxes and wanes. Habits ingrained by previous successes are hard to break, regardless of whether your organization is one year or 100 years old.

Diagnosing the key components of your culture is the first step to moving forward.

NOTES

1 Sophia Fedeli and Katerina Eva Matsa, "Use of Mobile Devices for News Continues to Grow, Outpacing Desktops and Laptops," Pew Research Center, July 17, 2018, www.pewresearch.org/fact-tank/2018/07/17/use-of-mobile-devices-for-news-continues-to-grow-outpacing-desktops-and-laptops/.

2 Nikki Usher, *Making News at the New York Times* (Ann Arbor, MI: University of Michigan Press, 2014).

3 Joshua Benton, "The Leaked New York Times Innovation Report Is One of the Key Documents of this Media Age," *Nieman Lab*, May 15, 2014, www.nieman lab.org/2014/05/the-leaked-new-york-times-innovation-report-is-one-of-the-key-documents-of-this-media-age/.

4 Joshua Benton, "The New York Times Is Restructuring its Page 1 Meetings to be More Digital (as that Big Report Suggested)," *Nieman Lab*, May 29, 2014, www.niemanlab.org/2014/05/the-new-york-times-is-restructuring-its-page-1-meetings-to-be-more-digital-as-that-big-report-suggested/.

5 Benjamin Mullin, "Dean Baquet: NYT Will Retire 'System of Pitching Stories for the Print Page 1'," Poynter, February 19, 2015, www.poynter.org/reporting-editing/2015/dean-baquet-nyt-will-retire-system-of-pitching-stories-for-the-print-page-1/.

6 Edgar Schein, *Organizational Culture and Leadership*, 4th ed. (Edison, NJ: Jossey-Bass, 2010), 73–74.

7 Confidential interview, personal communication, May 12, 2008.

8 Confidential interview, personal communication, May 8, 2008.

9 Schein, *Organizational Culture and Leadership*, 241–245.

10 Michael Harrison, *Diagnosing Organizations: Methods, Models, and Processes*, 3rd ed. (Thousand Oaks, CA: Sage, 2004), 127–128.

11 Schein, 325–327.

12 Carrie Brown, "New Media, Enduring Values: Managing Change at a Digital Newspaper in the Digital Age," PhD Dissertation, University of Missouri, 2008.

13 Lionel Stapley, *Individuals, Groups, and Organizations Beneath the Surface: An Introduction* (London: Karnac, 2006).

14 Manfred Kets de Vries, *The Leadership Mystique: Leading Behavior in the Human Enterprise*, 2nd ed. (Upper Saddle River, NJ: FT Press, 2009).

15 Kyle Pope, "Getting Over Ourselves," *Columbia Journalism Review*, Winter 2019, accessed May 2, 2020, www.cjr.org/special_report/getting-over-ourselves.php/.

16 Pope.

17 Jay Rosen, "Next Time You Wonder Why New York Times People Get so Defensive, Read This," PressThink, October 21, 2019, http://pressthink.org/2018/10/next-time-you-wonder-why-new-york-times-people-get-so-defensive-read-this/.

18 Pope.

19 Schein, 252–253.

20 Harrison, 27–29.

21 Harrison, 98–100.

22 Jeff Sonderman and Tom Rosenstiel, "A Culture-Based Strategy for Creating Innovation in News Organizations," American Press Institute, May 27, 2015, www.americanpressinstitute.org/publications/reports/white-papers/culture-based-innovation/.

23 New York Times, "Innovation Report," March 24, 2014, www.scribd.com/embeds/224608514/content?start_page=1&view_mode=scroll&access_key=key-TiQrYKIlOq2iHdtIubdB&show_recommendations=true.

24 Schein, 127–129.

25 Schein, 128.

26 Sue Robinson, "Convergence Crises: News Work and News Space in the Digitally Transforming Newsroom," Journal of Communication 61, no. 6 (2011), 1122–1141.

27 Schein, 128.

28 Brown, 2008.

29 Usher.

Part One – Making a Radical Shift for Survival

In October 2008, editor John Yemma walked into the Pulitzer-decorated newsroom of the *Christian Science Monitor* and announced that the daily newspaper would stop the presses.

Its work would carry on—on the web and in a weekly print magazine. But the "daily miracle" on dead trees would cease in 2009.

"Digital first!" has been the reluctant mantra of newspapers and other legacy media organizations for the past decade-plus as they grapple with the recognition that news consumption habits have changed in countless ways. But the *Monitor* was the first national newspaper that turned that rhetoric into inescapable reality by killing the print daily entirely.

The imperative for change was clear, even though the *Monitor* retained a strong reputation among academics and journalists for its prize-winning, often internationally focused journalism. It wasn't just that the newspaper business as a whole was suffering mightily from increased competition and falling advertising rates. The *Monitor* was facing a major cut in an operating subsidy that had helped to support its journalism since its founding. Though the *Monitor* was not a religious publication, the First Church of Christ, Scientist, in Boston owned the paper and largely funded its operations. In 2008, the church decided to slash its subsidy from $12 million per year to $4 million by 2013. Although the church didn't cite declines in the number of the faithful as a reason for this cut, the number of branch churches and practitioners had been declining steadily since the 1960s.[1]

Unless the news organization could find a way to build new revenue streams to make up for the church's declining subsidy, it was staring down a future of debilitating cuts to its staff and other resources.

To make matters worse, the paper had fallen into a stagnant period of low readership; at the time Yemma took the helm, its subscriptions numbered just 52,000 (down from a high of 220,000 in 1970), and the website was getting 5 million page views per month.[2] Even without pressure from the church to raise revenue, its journalists were aware that a paper that isn't being read has little influence.

Yemma brought a new vision: boost page views to more than 20 million per month within five years to increase advertising revenue and make the *Monitor* a vibrant part of the national news conversation.

Accomplishing that goal would require a major shift in practices and mindset. The *Monitor*'s journey since that time provides an ideal case for working through our model to understand how leaders and organizations must consider culture, strategy, and innovation simultaneously for meaningful change to happen.

For 10 years, the *Monitor*'s leadership and staff graciously allowed us to continue to return to the newsroom to observe their transformation. Through surveys, more than 100 confidential interviews, and many hours of observation, we have chronicled and analyzed the frustrations, the relief, the successes, and the failures.

BEGIN WITH THE PAST

Origin stories are critical to understanding organizational cultures. In 1908, church founder Mary Baker Eddy, tired of the sensationalistic yellow journalism of her day, sought to improve the media environment by founding a newspaper rooted in rigor. In the *Monitor*'s first edition, Eddy set forth the mission that still resonates with staffers today. "The object of the *Monitor*," she declared, "is to injure no man, but to bless all mankind."[3]

To this day, *Monitor* staff remain strongly aware of and committed to what they call *"Monitor* values" or *"Monitor* journalism." In our interviews over the years, many have continually used those phrases as they referred to the importance they place on offering context and explanation: "We talk about being solution-based journalism. We don't go into the fray; we try to push the discussion in a new way that is productive."[4]

In strong cultures, tangible artifacts embed and reinforce stated beliefs. The *Monitor* stylebook affirms the organization's mission:

> To blaze its own path of clean, constructive journalism, broad in appeal, high in character, powerful in helpfulness, the *Monitor* tries hard to develop stories that are not routine, articles that are original, interesting, and important to human progress. ... Our aim is to bring light rather than heat to a subject. The purpose is to heal. When exposing evil, we don't call names or sling adjectives; we record acts and official charges. Warmth, compassion, even humor, can help the *Monitor* serve as 'a most genial persuader.'[5]

An organization founded in accordance with something as deeply personal and tightly held as a religion is going to have especially powerful underlying assumptions that make up workplace culture and fuel resistance to change. Delving into its history helps uncover the cultural roots of resistance to change. An organization's founder and early years can play a powerful role in establishing values, routines, and underlying assumptions about what kinds of actions and behaviors will be rewarded and punished. Past successes cause the behaviors that produce them to be seen as immutable, especially as people rise through the ranks based on their mastery of certain skills. Similarly, past traumas, both personal and within the organizational context, can cause avoidance or prompt defensive mechanisms.

Another significant past influence on the *Monitor* was its previous troubled attempts to adapt to technology.[6] In the mid-1980s, the *Monitor* bet big on broadcast. It started producing radio and television news programs, bought Channel 68 in Boston, began transmitting shortwave radio broadcasts, and started its own 24-hour cable station.[7]

The cable station, known as Monitor Channel, folded in April of 1992 after less than one year on the air. The channel provoked turmoil in the organization, including the resignation of a number of leaders, especially after the church disclosed it had borrowed $41.5 million from pension funds to cover costs as it was launching these expensive new initiatives.[8] More than $200 million was invested in the channel, and though it was close to its target of reaching 5 million households by May 1992, it would have needed 25 million to be profitable.[9]

Although all of this occurred nearly 20 years before the *Monitor* made its big digital shift, past failures can still frame how influential, long-term members of organizations view change. Several longtime staffers we interviewed brought up these failed forays into broadcasting when we asked how the organization was dealing with change; one called it "the time when the organic material hit the ventilating device" and said it had been an even more difficult time for the organization than the current digital shift.

"You know, there's that memory out there—that if something doesn't work, they'll shut it down," one editor told us in 2009. "Would they actually let the *Monitor* shut down? I don't know."[10]

THE CHANGE BEGINS

Yemma began the early months of his tenure as editor faced with rallying the staff behind the radical change to come. The *Monitor*'s top new goals as a web-primary publication were: (1) immediacy, or publishing news online as quickly as possible and jumping on any trends; and (2) increasing page views. As Yemma put it,

> Mary Baker Eddy launched us in 1908. Each year of the 100 years and four months since then our predecessors have charted their course by the values she instilled. It's up to us now.[11]

Unlike predecessors who supported the traditional "wall" separating the editorial and business sides of the organization, Yemma saw the publishing division as an ally and teamed with then-publisher Jonathan Wells to develop a possible path toward sustainability. Working with consultants, the *Monitor* crafted a unique value proposition to bring Eddy's vision into a twenty-first-century focus: "Explaining world news to thoughtful people who care about solutions."

Restructuring was necessary, and the newsroom reconfigured workflows to accommodate the website and new weekly magazine. The changes also meant trimming unneeded positions, and to ease the pain, management first offered buyouts to volunteers. As Yemma explained in a February 2, 2009, Q&A memo to the staff:

Q: If after Feb. 16 you need to reduce the staff further with layoffs, how will you decide which staffers get laid off?

A: We are first looking at the jobs and tasks necessary to carry out our core publishing mission. That mission, of course, is changing as we move to a web-first strategy with a weekly print edition. We know that we have to do without certain positions and will have to narrow our editorial focus. In general, if the work associated with a particular position is no longer needed, that would be a position we would not continue to staff.

Q: How will I know if I have one of the jobs essential to the new strategy?

A: I realize that the picture is not yet entirely clear. I'm afraid that is unavoidable at this point. Editors are currently working to develop new staff configurations and workflows. We are bringing on board new technology (the new web content-management system) and reconfiguring K-4 [the *Monitor*'s publishing system at the time], both of which have production and staffing implications.[12]

The newsroom ultimately cut its staff by 22% at the time of the transition, from 96 to 75 people, mostly through buyouts and attrition.[13] The new weekly magazine had six employees dedicated to editing and production, and staff writers on the national and international desks—the two largest parts of the operation—would rotate in for various assignments to help fill the weekly.

Most of the journalistic effort, however, would be concentrated on the website. The new focus meant new routines.[14] For most organizations, getting out of well-worn daily grooves is one of the hardest parts of change, as people gravitate back to their comfortable rhythms. But because the *Monitor* had completely eliminated the daily print edition, it didn't have to fight the temptation to keep the focus on the legacy product. As a result:

- Schedules changed. Editors needed to cover the site from 8 a.m. to 8 p.m. each weekday and on weekends. Under the old system, writers would file by 11:30 a.m. or noon, and afternoons were often dedicated to planning.
- The newsroom purchased a new eZ Publish content-management system, which would democratize the ability to update the website, giving more power to people lower in the organizational hierarchy.
- Writers and editors had to juggle between weekly stories, which were more akin to the 800- to 1,200-word stories of the daily print edition, and web stories. For search engine optimization (SEO) purposes, writers were expected to write shorter posts (500 words or less) and update more frequently. This increased metabolism was hard for reporters and editors to get used to, and many told us they felt like they were just churning out content with less time for thought or reporting.

CHANGE AGENT

Yemma got a key assist from then-online editor Jimmy Orr, a former Internet strategist for President George W. Bush and California Gov. Arnold Schwarzenegger whose swashbuckling style and willingness to take risks infuriated some but also pushed the staff along. Successful change efforts require change agents willing and able to challenge the status quo.

In this case, Orr had been empowered to experiment. He set up some WordPress blogs outside the editorial system to test the effect of content choices on traffic. His "The Vote" blog was an early web traffic driver that embraced somewhat controversial but hot story topics. He remained a constant voice for adopting SEO strategies including trend-driven story selection. He was the type of disruptive agent that scholar Everett Rogers describes as necessary for innovations to take hold.[15]

One editor said of Orr:

> He broke a lot of eggs, which you had to clean up ... He had this great energy, was always pushing boundaries. A lot of what he did got people worked up, especially longtime reporters and editors, but we needed that to some extent.[16]

In some ways, the staff was ready for the shakeup:

> The underlying thing about the whole transition is that if you do good work but no one sees it, what is the point? So even if you have to do something that's populist in order to draw readers, but then those readers come and they'll see other things that are good, then that is the premise on which, I think, we now operate.[17]

Orr himself contended that the most important but difficult shift for journalists was realizing that they had to care about what their audience wanted, regardless of their own desires. "Some people really just don't get it," he said.

LEADING THROUGH A MAJOR CHANGE

During our visits, the door to Yemma's corner office was usually open for passers-by, and in the early days of the transition he worked hard to keep the lines of communication open, with email memos and occasional town-hall meetings led by him and Jonathan Wells. As time went on, though, some in the newsroom felt he did not communicate enough, especially as the town halls became less frequent.

One staffer told us: "We are on board, but as passengers," noting that while their leaders would respond to questions and had official open-door policies, they rarely reached out or spent much time talking to people more casually.[18] And even when the town halls were happening more frequently, they were described by many as not particularly illuminating, often covering topics that had already wound their way through the rumor mill.

During moments of change, people tend to need more communication than usual from their leaders, even to the point that it feels repetitive. Yemma and other top managers felt like they were highly accessible to all, but many we interviewed described them as relatively aloof. We have seen this phenomenon in other news organizations during change efforts. Leaders often think of themselves as approachable and assume all is well if there are no audible complaints. But frustration often percolates beneath the surface. At the *Monitor*, one interviewee acknowledged the appeal of a "hands-off" leader, but added there were times when they could have used more reassurance, more discussion of new initiatives because of the magnitude of the changes.[19]

As often happened at legacy news organizations in the early days of the Internet, the *Monitor* set up its web production team as its own unit, physically separate and distinct from reporting desks such as national and international news. Though these "prod-team" members wrote blog posts, they were often viewed as production workers who posted content, not as "real" journalists. As the transition began, editors regularly distinguished between posts written and edited by *Monitor* journalists and blog content, a perception that may have stemmed in part from differences in filing workflow.

To combat skepticism from other editors, Orr had adopted a proving-ground mindset. He experimented with trend-driven tactics on his own blog to generate traffic, and pushed the boundaries of the *Monitor*'s typically staid headlines and topics to lure visitors. On a May 12, 2009, post for The Vote about Florida Gov. Charlie Crist running for the U.S. Senate, Orr used the headline: "Crist to run for Florida's Senate. Anti-Crist says bring it on." After an internal complaint, it was changed to "Florida's Crist to run for U.S. Senate." Orr also wrote about South Carolina Gov. Mark Sanford's admitted affair after the politician had been reported missing on the Appalachian Trail on June 21, which also happened to be Naked Hiking Day. He highlighted that coincidence in the headline, to the chagrin of others in the newsroom. Despite the opposition, the headline remained intact.[20]

By July 2009, Orr's The Vote blog accounted for 20% of the site's page views, and the Innovations blog had increased traffic from 206,886 page views in April to 343,679 in June.[21] The successes weren't limited to Orr's department, however. With more frequent updates, the national news desk had doubled its monthly numbers to 1.1 million page views in June, and overall site traffic had risen 25% over the previous year.[22] Innovation efforts require tangible successes, and good results in an adventurous department can inspire others to experiment, as long as those successes are shared across the organization.

The good news extended to the Monitor's other products, too. The organization had converted over 90% of its newspaper subscribers to the weekly magazine; its circulation was about 50,000 as of July 2009.[23] And the Daily News Briefing, a printable PDF with a selection of web stories from csmonitor.com, a Christian Science editorial, and a 180-word note by Yemma, was emailed each weekday morning to 1,500 subscribers paying $5.75 a month.

RESISTANCE

Despite the successes in terms of page views and subscribers, Yemma still detected angst among the Monitor's journalists, who worried that the organization was becoming more focused on quantity than quality. He tried to address the concerns directly in a July 4, 2009, memo to the staff:

Are our standards being compromised as we publish shorter articles on the Web? There's much discussion of this in the newsroom. I hope the discussion never stops. We must always examine what we are doing to ensure that our journalism lives up to the values of the *Monitor*. Short-form and long-form should both have those values. Blog posts, photo galleries, videos, podcasts should as well. Light-hearted pieces and complex articles dealing with troubling issues, too.[24]

By the fall, the organization had begun other initiatives to build traffic and revenue. It had hired an outside firm that specialized in SEO. The *Monitor* also looked to syndicate its content through databases and other channels, and the publishing arm had teamed with a consultant to improve access to a broader base of advertisers. For August, the website had 7.5 million page views and about 3 million unique visitors.[25]

Tensions remained, however. With the memory of the lay-offs still fresh, staffers worried about what would happen if the newsroom failed to meet page-view targets, and concerns about the quality drain with shorter, more frequent posts had not dissipated by the time of our first research visit in December 2009. Interviewees at the time expressed concerns that the new style was not "*Monitor* journalism"—deeper, distinctive stories that were contextual, explanatory, and solutions-oriented. In the web-first environment, though, there was little time to develop such stories. Speed and frequency were prized, with the hope that a *Monitor* post would appear within a cluster of stories on the front of Google News or atop a Google search.

One editor told us, "When you do much shorter stories … ultimately you were putting out, like, a 400-word piece on something that's fairly newsy, so you have to make it read straight and read well. But there isn't that much craft involved."[26] The changes threatened not only their organizational identity, but also their sense of journalistic credibility. One staffer went so far as to refer to it as "prostituting," while another said, "I'm, like, really embarrassed by what we're doing."[27] It is this kind of perceived challenge to professionalism that can thwart change efforts.

To win page views, writers had to chase fleeting trends, often covering topics that had not been part of the *Monitor* mix previously. If they waited too long, they would miss the window to work their way into Google News. To many, this speedy, aggregated content—often relying on wire reports rather than original reporting—didn't feel like *Monitor* journalism, yet those posts consistently brought the most page views, according to analytics reports. One interviewee referred to it as "derivative journalism."[28] Another editor explained the distinction:

> One's reported, and the other is sometimes just a reframing of the subject, a write-through. Its level of value-added is much lower. So when your reporters as well as your readers are seeing that the lower value-added content gets the most traffic, what does that tell them? Discouraging.[29]

One staffer said:

> I mean, we're up there with all the different newsiest online organizations [in Google]. The downside would be, we're doing a lot more sort of culture war stuff—headlines with [Sarah] Palin in it and like gee-whiz electronic gadgetry stuff—simply to get traffic. Little blogs that might be a good read but don't really have much reporting—if any—are sort of what gets all the traffic; that, and photos of the day. So it's a little disheartening to be traipsing through the jungle, risking your life in the areas that I cover for my readers, if that's not going to get any traffic at all. All management seems to care about is traffic.[30]

One traffic-garnering tactic became standard practice: explaining the "Google Doodle," the occasional graphic replacement for the Google logo at Google.com to honor an anniversary or historic event. On October 7, 2009, the logo had been replaced with a simple barcode, and a 230-word post on the *Monitor*'s Horizons blog explaining what it meant—the barcode homage spelled "Google"—became a top draw at csmonitor.com. "That kind of was a tipping point, a watershed moment, where we saw the potential there'," one writer said. "Because not only was it something people were searching for, but there was this huge—it was like a funnel, going to whatever was at the top of that search result that Google was driving."[31]

When it came to experimentation, the leadership allowed the staff to experiment with different types of content to garner traffic, especially in the online department. Such permission from above is vital for employees trying to navigate uncertainty during change efforts. Others in the newsroom had taken on a test–learn–adopt mentality, although many staffers still had not embraced analytics-driven journalism at this point. But key opinion leaders—a required constituency to help change efforts proliferate—had begun thinking about their work processes differently. Deputy national editor Mark Sappenfield had started tracking successful stories via spreadsheet to learn which topics and writers were garnering the most views, and he used that data to understand what topics and techniques connected with the audience most effectively. Among his lessons: Page views didn't always come on the first day of posting. A late link could sometimes bring thousands of page views later in the cycle.

The csmonitor.com home page had become the de facto front page in newsroom discussions, and much of the planning effort each day focused upon what content would land there. Though most of the traffic came to the site through other means, the hope of becoming a valuable portal, one that people would bookmark in their browser as a place to check regularly, remained.

The daily news meetings began with review of the previous day's page-view reports, a departure from the traditional news meeting that once focused on what top editors thought was the most important news of the day. Results shared during the November 30, 2009, meeting showed continued success at drawing traffic, with 9.4 million page views for the month, 25% above the budgeted plan. But the reports kept affirming an uncomfortable fact: Online audiences were not drawn to the *Monitor*'s international news stories—its key point of distinction in the past—and the page-view reports demoralized some reporters.

"Here's a guy who's traveled to Afghanistan, risking his life to write stories, and he's seeing that he's never in the top 20," an editor told us. "You know, that kind of feedback he's getting is that, 'What you're doing is not helping us.' That's hard, you know."[32]

HITTING THE MAGICAL MILESTONE

As 2010 began, the new content-management system had gone live, allowing all reporters and editors without any coding knowledge to post to csmonitor.com. And numbers kept growing across the board. By the one-year anniversary of the web-first experiment in March, the organization had reached 14.5 million page views per month across departments, and the weekly's circulation had grown to 77,000. Because of the number of page views, ad revenue had also surpassed the original forecast for March 2010, although revenue per page view had come in lower than expected.[33]

June 2010 brought a stunning milestone: The newsroom had reached its target of 25 million monthly page views three years ahead of plan. With success came a growing acceptance of this new form of work at the *Monitor*. Successes are critical for creating new organizational stories that nudge the culture toward a redefined sense of itself. Reporters and editors had learned how to churn content more quickly and had become adept at identifying which topics would generate page views. One editor who had expressed grave concerns during our first visit felt better by our July 2010 visit: "Yemma said we would get more efficient, and we really have."[34] Another said: "We are less meaty, less original. But I'm surprised by how much good has come out of it in terms of responsiveness and efficiency."[35]

Orr, who had been at the *Monitor* since 2007, parlayed the traffic success into another job.[36] In July, he accepted a position as deputy editor, online, at the *Los Angeles Times*, and the *Monitor*'s international editor Dave Scott, a well-respected journalist among the staff, was tapped to fill the web director role.[37] Some said they were heartened that a more traditional journalist was filling the role, but many of the techniques Orr had pioneered remained in use.

With the *Monitor* rising in the eyes of Google and Quantcast among the top 250 most-traveled U.S. sites on the web, several journalists told us it was exciting for the organization to be seen as relevant again. "I've invested enough in my career to want us to succeed," said one long-time *Monitor* journalist. "I don't want to be the one who has to turn the lights out on this place."[38]

The trend-chasing had taken a toll on the staff, though. Keyword-laden headlines were written to please algorithms, not readers, and shifting between the online and print mindsets was sometimes a struggle. In the print era, staffers often had a moment to stop and think once the noon deadline had passed. "Now, we can never breathe," an editor told us in July 2010. "We are on, all the time. I'm on essentially from 5 to 5. There is no sense of, 'It's OK to just read the news for a minute here.' Now there is always something, always something to edit, etc."[39] Another writer echoed that exhausted frustration. "There just isn't time with this schedule to step back and think strategically about coverage. It's just shoveling it out," the writer said. "I can tell you, having been an editor, that's not satisfying."

Some staffers, too, wanted to focus their energy on their web content instead of writing for the weekly because they worried that their jobs depended on page views; some mentioned a sense of accomplishment from completing multiple short stories each day and seeing the concrete results in terms of positive metrics.

Setting quantitative goals can produce unintended consequences, as people use whatever means necessary to satisfy the spreadsheet. Several in the newsroom were openly skeptical of the trend-driven strategies used to reach the 25 million mark, especially since the site's bounce rate—the number of users who view a single page before leaving—had remained above the initial 84%, an indicator that the *Monitor* was not fulfilling its long-term strategic goal of building an online community around the brand. The web revenue also had not affected the staffing situation, and the promise of doing more *Monitor*-style journalism had not come to pass. With Orr's departure, the foot came off the accelerator, and the demand for such frenetic updating slowed. One editor estimated that the 20 original posts a day had dropped to 13 to 16, allowing writers more time to develop angles and deeper stories.

On the publishing side, though, some felt that the phrase "*Monitor* journalism" was being used as a bulwark against change. "The newsroom has to give up the idea that they can just do whatever interests them," one business-side staffer told us. "So if the readers want a weekly column about what is going on at the White House, give that to them, even if that's not what you feel like doing."[40]

Some had also begun thinking about alternative ways to measure success, such as depth of visit or visitor return rate. The problem was, as some interviewees noted, any benchmark of success could ultimately be gamed, as some felt had been done to reach the page-view milestone.

Whatever direction the organization took next, one truth had emerged: The *Monitor* had become very, very good at grabbing page views.

MULTIPLIERS

After topping the 25 million mark, traffic settled into an average of about 19 million page views per month, and by the fall of 2010, it became apparent that two page views per visitor would not be enough to generate hoped-for revenue. Home-page traffic, a proxy for the destination audience that had chosen the *Monitor* as an online news source, remained persistently flat.

Though the *Monitor* had more monthly unique visitors than Slate at the time, the *Monitor*'s depth of visit was far lower, meaning visitors were looking at fewer pages during each visit than Slate's audience. To tackle this issue, the online staff had begun experimenting with a new form of content dubbed "multipliers."[41] This experiment pushed Scott to work more closely with the business department because such changes to the site required the resources of the tech-development team, which had to satisfy advertising and business goals, as well as the needs of the editorial department.[42]

These reusable features were reminiscent of BuzzFeed, which had emerged as a top destination by that time. The multi-page blocks of related content, delivered in stair-step fashion, were tailor-made to increase page views. Galleries would provide photos a page at a time, allowing users to flip back and forth among the images. Quizzes would guide users through with questions on separate pages to test their knowledge. And numbered lists would be delivered item by item, page by page. As one editor explained during our January 2011 visit:

> If we can do that, it means that for the staff overall … you're not constantly having to generate more content to acquire more page views … so you're not taxing your editorial staff as much. It means that when people come in, they stay longer, as opposed to having to fire things at the search engines, at Google News or Yahoo.[43]

During our January 2011 visit, a quiz called "How much do you know about the US Constitution?"[44] had inspired more than 200,000 page views in a single day, and by that time, quizzes and multipliers had become part of the morning meeting conversation. Despite these efforts, the bounce rate had still not dropped. Social media efforts remained inconsistent, partly because Facebook and Twitter did not consistently generate the same referrals of Google News and search engines, and though the newsroom was testing an iPad app, mobile had not become a priority yet.[45] At this point, the strategic direction was less clear. By 2011, town-hall meetings had dropped off, with email memos the more frequent form of communication from Yemma.

"People on the editorial side feel like they've bent over backwards to triple the traffic," one editor said during our January 2011 visit,

> and they were promised from publishing that amazing things would happen if we only did that, and (it) seems like they're moving the goal posts a little bit and saying, 'Oh well, we still need to get to higher levels of traffic before the revenue really kicks in.' So I feel like there's a lot of doubt still on the editorial side as to whether the ad revenue that's projected is actually for real.[46]

The weekly remained an important slice of the revenue pie. Circulation held steady at 70,000 subscribers, but that level put the newsroom at a strategic crossroads. It was too low for the publishing department to win over mass-market advertisers, as the publication was still considered niche. But the printing and marketing cost to reach the 300,000-circulation threshold would make it unprofitable. And the organization couldn't raise the subscription price without board approval.

At this time, the international desk had begun carving out time to affirm the organizational mission. As a group, editors had begun reading and discussing the book *Commitment to Freedom: The Story of the Christian Science Monitor*, the history of the *Monitor*'s early decades written by Erwin D. Canham, who had served as the paper's editor for 50 years. In the opening section, Canham writes:

> the *Monitor* has always been profoundly dedicated to a crusading, reformative approach to human affairs. But it is an affirmative reformation, rather than an alarmist attitude. It springs from the profound purpose of the *Monitor* to contribute to the regeneration of all mankind.[47]

It served as a cultural reinforcer in a still uncertain time.

APPLYING THE MODEL TO THE INITIAL CHANGES
Organizational culture is deeply embedded by past successes and changes slowly. A dramatic, disruptive shock—such as

eliminating the print edition—shakes up routines and processes that have been locked in place by years of success. We repeatedly saw how underlying assumptions about the best way to do journalism remained powerful and interfered with change at the *Monitor*, even as its espoused values touted its all-in digital commitment. But gradually, new successes did slowly push greater acceptance of different ways of working.

Though Pulitzer Prizes and awards can serve as sources of pride and inspiration, they can also create barriers to change. People often relive those past glories as proof of their competence and strength. Past successes cause the behaviors that produce them to be seen as unchangeable, especially as people rise through the ranks based on their mastery of certain skills.

Similarly, past traumas, like the *Monitor*'s failed bets on broadcast, can cause avoidance or prompt defensive mechanisms. As Pablo J. Boczkowski of Northwestern University points out, technological change in many newsrooms has been more evolutionary than revolutionary, in part because early failures to innovate in the 1980s and 1990s—including videotex, once the target for significant investment by some media chains but ultimately not adopted by the public—shaped their ability to adapt for years to come as leaders learned another costly mistake.[48] The *Monitor* was affected by similar fears.

Artifacts help uncover the organization's underlying assumptions. In the newsroom, it's impossible to avoid the physical proximity to the Mother Church and evidence of ties to the Christian Science Publishing Society, which also publishes the denomination's religious publications and texts. Although the *Monitor* is not a religious publication, belief in the organization's mission was closely tied to the religious views of many staffers.

When staffers repeatedly invoked the phrase "*Monitor* journalism" in our interviews as something they felt duty-bound to protect, they revealed how much of an extension of self and identity the mission had become. Changes were thus perceived to be potential threats not only the organization, but also the roles and core identities of individuals.

"The *Monitor* story before was a very particular kind of story," one editor told us in December 2009, just months after the daily presses had stopped. "You always looked for a larger analytical story on any given news point. You just didn't do the news story, you know. You always did something larger than that, and you always looked ... to be more analytical about it."[49]

Another said:

A lot of what people are interested in is not what I signed up to write about when I went to journalism school. ... The *Monitor* was particularly insulated from all that for so long because, you know, we were the serious newspaper, and we did serious topics, which was great, but then nobody read us. And now, you're suddenly thrown into a much more commercial way.[50]

The newsroom had come to value being above the day-to-day fray of the journalistic pack, an ethic forged by the *Monitor*'s unusual distribution system through regular mail in addition to its philosophical orientation. That delay between printing and delivery forced writers to develop stories and angles with longer shelf lives, with analysis akin to a news weekly, rather than a daily newspaper. Over the years, the reflective style had won accolades from academics, peers, world leaders, and the public.

One editor told us:

I'm really embarrassed by the home page. I mean, I think there is still good stuff, but the top 10 list is just so embarrassing. I mean, every other paper filters out their blogs, and we don't. So we've got all sorts of crazy stuff up there every day, and you come to us and it looks like Huffington Post Light, and just way more salacious than we've ever been, and irreverent. And you know, I guess that's another thing I feel about *Monitor* journalism; it doesn't need to be stiff, and I think it has been at times, but it should have a certain poise and elegance and like graciousness to it. I think that's something that set us apart.[51]

The staff recognized the power of naming new routines and new items, such as "multipliers" and "roundups." Such a language gave the staff a vocabulary for understanding of this new way of accomplishing work, and making sense of uncertainty as a collective is key to organizational survival. Successes led to new co-created cultural norms. Such norms provide comfort; it's why a family metaphor arises so often in workplaces and organizations. When outsiders threaten the sanctity of underlying assumptions, conflict and resistance arise. Within the *Monitor* context, this fear and frustration in the early days was focused on Jimmy Orr and the online production team. Only after proven successes did some in the newsroom grudgingly accept this shifting reality.

Communication from leadership is critical at these moments. As a Christian Scientist and a former *Monitor* reporter, Yemma recognized and appreciated the deep commitment to Eddy's original mission, and nods to the church founder would find their way into his staff memos. In an interview with the *Monitor* at the time he was hired as editor, he affirmed the commitment to Eddy's founding principles, saying she launched the paper at a time

> when objectivity, accuracy, and fairness were in short supply. Now,
> at a time when news organizations are struggling to establish
> a sustainable economic base, the *Monitor*'s role is more crucial
> than ever in providing careful reporting, compassionate analysis,
> and a clear-eyed view of the world.[52]

Rewards and punishments are levers that leaders and managers can adjust as well. In his memos, Yemma highlighted the good journalistic work of the previous months, but his focus regularly turned to page views and revenue. By the end of the SEO era, several people in the newsroom had begun concentrating on these benchmarks to define their own success.

Another factor that can spur culture change is anxiety about survival of the organization, and *Monitor* staffers were clear that change wasn't optional. Many interviewees had come to the realization that the publication had lost relevance over time, and the current path was financially unsustainable. As one editor told us early in the process:

> Ultimately, everyone knows this is not a decision that we made based on preference, but on need. And I think ultimately, everyone wants to succeed. And there might be a little bit of dragging of heels, but ... I don't think there's anyone who's actively working to undermine the effort.[53]

By the summer of 2010, buoyed by page-view successes, the culture had begun the change. Those in the newsroom began to believe in their ability to adapt to the new digital landscape, and their confidence grew as the news organization appeared more frequently on Google News and atop Google searches. But pockets of resistance remained, and as we will see, the success would not last.

At the strategy level, leaders and managers must be clear how they are allocating resources to help with change. At the *Monitor*, the staff reductions and restructured organizational chart made clear that the main focus was the web; the web production and magazine production staffs were roughly the same size. The national desk, which did better traffic-wise, was also larger than the international desk.

Potential revenue streams would also dictate how the organization would focus its efforts in the months and years ahead. Despite the energy directed toward the web, the print weekly still generated millions in revenue and would need to remain as part of the mix for the near future. Web revenue had a long way to grow before it would be able to supplant that amount, and editors and reporters had begun to doubt its strength as a strategic goal after the page-view achievement failed to generate the predicted revenue.

On the innovation level, the test-first, get-permission-later approach Orr took often clashed with some of the editors, who sought to take a more reflective, methodical approach to change. Importantly, Yemma backed Orr while regularly reminding the staff of the organization's history and tradition. He tried—not always successfully—to place that innovation in the context of the culture.

But Yemma was willing to alter routines and processes, and allow experimentation to take place. The newsroom experimented with podcasts, comments, videos, and multipliers, some of which were dropped after they failed to generate traffic or revenue.

Over time, newsroom opinion leaders embraced a constant state of experimentation that led the newsroom to try a number of ideas and let those things that failed fall by the wayside. Through this ethic, members made several discoveries, including the power of explaining the Google Doodle, the importance of Google News to traffic referrals, and the ability of frequent blog posts to bring visitors to the website.

By the end of the SEO era, change had come, but not easily or without struggle.

NOTES

1 Caroline Fraser, "Dying the Christian Science Way," *The Guardian*, August 9, 2019, www.theguardian.com/world/2019/aug/06/christian-science-church-medicine-death-horror-of-my-fathers-last-days;
Stoyan Zaimov, "Christian Scientists Looking to Grow Membership Amid Shrinking Numbers," *Christian Post*, June 15, 2012, www.christianpost.com/news/christian-scientists-looking-to-grow-membership-amid-shrinking-numbers.html.

2 Damien Pearse, "US Paper Stops the Presses to Focus Online," *The Guardian*, October 29, 2008, www.theguardian.com/media/2008/oct/29/christian-science-monitor.

3 Mary Baker Eddy, "Something in a Name," *Christian Science Monitor* 1, no. 1, November 25, 1908.

4 Confidential interview, personal communication, July 10, 2010.

5 Christian Science Monitor (1997) "Christian Science Monitor Stylebook," In-House Binder, p. 2.

6 Pablo J. Boczkowski, *Digitizing the News: Innovation in Online Newspapers* (Boston, MA: MIT Press, 2005).

7 Peter Steinfels, "Fiscal and Spiritual Rifts Shake Christian Scientists," *New York* Times, February 29, 1992, www.nytimes.com/1992/02/29/us/fiscal-and-spiritual-rifts-shake-christian-scientists.html?ref=christian_science_monitor&pagewanted=1.

8 Times Staff and Wire Reports, "Media," *Los Angeles Times*, April 16, 1992, http://articles.latimes.com/1992-04-16/business/fi-1064_1_monitor-channel.

9 Seth Faison Jr., "New Deadline for Monitor Channel," *New York Times*, April 6, 1992, www.nytimes.com/1992/04/06/business/the-media-business-new-deadline-for-monitor-channel.html.

10 Confidential interview, personal communication, December 1, 2009.

11 Confidential interview, personal communication, March 25, 2009.

12 Memo, February 2, 2009.

13 Confidential interview, personal communication, November 30, 2009.

14 Memo, March 25, 2009.

15 Everett M. Rogers, *Diffusion of Innovations*, 5th ed. (New York: Free Press, 2003).

16 Confidential interview, personal communication, July 11, 2010.

17 Confidential interview, personal communication, December 1, 2009.

18 Confidential interview, personal communication, July 26, 2010.

19 Confidential interview, personal communication, July 26, 2010.

20 Jimmy Orr, "Sanford Disappears to Hike Appalachian Trail (on Naked Hiking Day)," *Christian Science Monitor*, June 23, 2009, www.csmoni tor.com/USA/Politics/The-Vote/2009/0623/sanford-disappears-to-hike-appalachian-trail-on-naked-hiking-day.

21 Memo, July 4, 2009.

22 Memo, July 4, 2009.

23 Memo, July 4, 2009.

24 Memo, July 4, 2009.

25 Bill Mitchell, "Circulation, Page Views Up at Christian Science Monitor, but Solvency Yet Not in Sight," Poynter, August 5, 2009, www.poynter.org/news/circulation-page-views-christian-science-monitor-solvency-not-yet-sight.

26 Confidential interview, personal communication, December 1, 2009.

27 Confidential interview, personal communication, December 1, 2009.

28 Confidential interview, personal communication, November 30, 2009.

29 Confidential interview, personal communication, December 1, 2009.

30 Confidential interview, personal communication, November 29, 2009.

31 Confidential interview, personal communication, January 7, 2011.

32 Confidential interview, personal communication, December 1, 2009.

33 Memo, April 2010; confidential interview, personal communication, July 28, 2010.

34 Confidential interview, personal communication, July 21, 2010.

35 Confidential interview, personal communication, July 26, 2010.

36 *Los Angeles Times*, "Jimmy Orr, Deputy Editor, Online," July 13, 2010, http://latimesblogs.latimes.com/readers/2010/07/jimmy-orr-deputy-editor-online.html.

37 Confidential interview, personal communication, January 11, 2011.

38 Confidential interview, personal communication, July 24, 2010.

39 Confidential interview, personal communication, July 22, 2010.

40 Confidential interview, personal communication, July 28, 2010.

41 Confidential interview, personal communication, January 6, 2011.

42 Confidential interview, personal communication, January 6, 2011.

43 Confidential interview, personal communication, January 6, 2011.

44 Warren Richey, "How Much Do You Know about the US Constitution? A Quiz," *Christian Science Monitor*, January 6, 2011, www.csmonitor. com/USA/Politics/2011/0106/How-much-do-you-know-about-the-US-Constitution-A-quiz/famous-phrases.

45 Confidential interview, personal communication, January 11, 2011.

46 Confidential interview, personal communication, January 10, 2011.

47 Erwin D. Canham, *Commitment to Freedom: The Story of the Christian Science Monitor* (Boston, MA: Houghton Mifflin, 1958), xvi.

48 Boczkowski.

49 Confidential interview, personal communication, December 1, 2009.

50 Confidential interview, personal communication, January 7, 2011.

51 Confidential interview, personal communication, December 4, 2009.

52 David Cook, "John Yemma Named Monitor Editor," *Christian Science Monitor*, June 9, 2008, www.csmonitor.com/USA/2008/0609/p25s08-usgn.html.

53 Confidential interview, personal communication, November 30, 2009.

Three

Strategy sounds so twentieth century.

It's what MBAs talked about in the 1980s and 1990s, when junk bonds and leveraged buyouts were fashionable. Today, the business press is all about innovation: *Disrupt yourself. Fail fast. Iterate.*

There's something to be said for the currently-in-vogue slogans, especially in such a fast-moving environment as the media industry. New technologies and platforms rise and fall with shifts of consumer fancy, and organizations must experiment to survive and thrive.

Before diving headlong into transformation, however, you must thoroughly understand your long-term strategy and how your organization's mission and core competencies fit into the competitive landscape. Without a consistent strategy at the root of decision-making, an organization risks exhausting its workers with change for change's sake.

For years, many newspapers had few local competitors, could set the rates they wanted for ads, and had little need for sophisticated strategy. But the explosion of media options in the Internet era created a host of competitors for attention and the need for diversified revenue streams.

When we think about change, we start at the level of culture. How does the organization's understanding of itself undergird how you and your employees accomplish work? With that foundation, you can then move to the level of strategy, which fits between the internal focus of culture and the short-term agility required for innovation. It provides a framework to guide day-to-day tactics and operations, and requires you to take a longer perspective on organizational sustainability.

Thinking at the strategic level forces you to sort through what distinctive skills your organization brings to the marketplace. How do you use your resources most effectively to focus on the unique value you offer? What are the risks you may face? And what is your vision for the future, one, three, five years from now?

Articulating a long-range vision with a statement of purpose helps avoid knee-jerk mistakes and nonsensical snap judgments based solely on the persuasive speculations of futurists. We often see a "shiny diamond" syndrome, where leaders and managers constantly shift direction based on the hot idea or technology of the time. For example, long-time industry watcher Ken Doctor has noted how Gannett's "on-again, off-again innovation history" means that "real questions of corporate authenticity and staying power bedevil any grand pronouncements."[1]

Over the past 15 years, the online Voice of San Diego has focused on a set of guiding values articulated on its website under a page titled "What We Stand For." It is not interested in stenographic coverage of the community; it is about understanding community issues and uncovering solutions. "Journalism is best when pursued with purpose," the page declares.

> It is easy to take stances against small problems but we want to tackle San Diego's big problems. When we do that, reporters and editors should be clear about what they're trying to achieve. ... We pressure leaders to solve widely accepted problems and local challenges.[2]

Using that statement of purpose to guide its strategy, the small newsroom eschews sports and instead focuses on topics related to community betterment, such as education, arts, housing, and border issues. It is an approach that has found a strong base of commitment in its community. According to its 2018 financial report submitted to the Internal Revenue Service, the organization pulled in 30% of its $1.7 million annual budget from memberships. At the end of the "What We Stand For" page, it affirms its promise to members: "Our mission and our values help us keep our focus on the issues and challenges that will define San Diego for decades."[3]

Having this clear, transparent mission allows Voice of San Diego to decide what to do, but perhaps more importantly, what not to do in a time of limited resources. It positions itself as a unique player in the local news ecosystem by concentrating its energies on a specific area of differentiation.

The best strategy is pragmatic and usable, one that journalists can and will draw on consistently to make daily decisions about how to operate and solve problems. A solid strategy and the tactics used to execute it help create, shape, and reinforce culture. The challenge—especially for for-profit corporations—is adhering to that strategy in lean times, when it's tempting to cut too deeply to meet short-term financial targets or radically shift strategic imperatives without evidence.

Placed at the center of our model, the strategic level pushes leaders to think about how the organization and the environment intersect and affect one another. This chapter will guide you to developing your own strategy.

COMPETITION AND THE NEWS BUSINESS

In his seminal book *Competitive Advantage*, Harvard Business School's Professor Michael Porter calls for developing strategy by evaluating the five primary forces in the competitive landscape:[4]

- *The threat of new competitors.* How likely is it that new businesses will come into the marketplace? How high are the barriers to entry?
- *The threat of substitutes.* Are there alternative products and services that could be used instead? Are there cheaper or better alternatives?
- *The bargaining power of suppliers.* How much power do suppliers have in terms of pricing and competitiveness?
- *The bargaining power of buyers.* Is it easy for customers to switch products and services?
- *Rivalry among existing competitors.* How many players are vying for the same customers and users? How intense is the competition? Does it lead to price battles that affect profitability?

Each item has a direct impact on pricing or investment costs for products and services, which ultimately affect profitability. Applying Porter's framework to the media landscape reveals an increasingly competitive market, and media companies are trying several strategies to survive and diversify their revenue sources.

Barriers to entry in the newspaper business were once much higher, with high-speed presses providing an expensive wall against new competitors trying to reproduce the economies of scale of the incumbent newspaper.[5] By the 1980s, many towns had become single-newspaper markets, and there was little threat of substitution.[6] Local radio and television did not have as many reporters as their newspaper counterparts, and other local media could not offer as large or as reliable an audience for advertisers as newspapers.[7]

In the digital world, though, barriers to entry are minimal. In the new-media environment, the intensity of rivalry among competitors increases because so many sites, including Facebook, Craigslist, and YouTube, disrupt the profit model by undercutting the advertising and/or content traditionally offered by legacy news organizations.[8] The threat of substitutes increases as well, as readers are no longer beholden to their local newspaper for national and international news, features, and advertising.

Analyzing these forces in the media landscape reveals just how overwhelmingly competitive the environment is. Local organizations might continue to find a competitive foothold in their markets, but there, potential profitability—especially with much lower advertising rates for online media—cuts into the appeal of the traditional advertising model and requires new revenue streams, such as memberships, subscriptions, event sponsorships, or sales of repurposed content. A 2019 Pew Research Center analysis found that while print circulations continued to decline sharply, revenue from digital advertising accounted for 35% of industry revenue in 2018, up from 17% in 2011.[9]

FINDING YOUR NICHE

With this analysis in mind, the question becomes: *How will your organization find the distinctive place in its market to appeal to users?*

Porter's process involves analyzing the value chain, the way an organization combines and uses its resources to create value. For example, how does the organization tap into its human and capital resources effectively? As Porter notes, companies tend to dissect costs according to existing accounting systems, and often the categories used by the financial department can misrepresent the true nature of costs and their potential returns for the organization.[10]

Instead, a value-chain analysis connects costs and assets with the ultimate value they create for the organization.

In a news organization, that means assessing the costs and investments at each step of the journalism cycle—staff, technology, materials. How do each of those aspects contribute to the total value created by the organization? Strictly speaking, managers can focus on the newsroom as a cost center with no direct return, but most recognize that without high-quality content, a news organization offers little long-term value to its community. The difficulty is in translating the value of journalistic quality and impact into tangible success measures.

Another common method of locating a competitive sweet spot is identifying your organization's internal strengths and weaknesses, and external opportunities and threats through a SWOT analysis. Though this type of analysis can be unfocused and broad in scope, it can also serve as a useful tool for identifying top-of-mind positives and negatives for an organization among its leaders and managers.

Strengths and weaknesses focus on the organization's internal capabilities. For a news organization, this process involves an honest assessment of those in the newsroom: Where are the staff's abilities and shortcomings, especially in terms of the latest competencies such as data journalism, audience engagement, interactive design, and app development? Are there individuals who can think creatively about new products and ways to tell stories? Are they open to involving the audience more directly throughout the reporting process?

Reviewing opportunities and threats forces an examination of the external environment in which the organization operates. Are there particular areas of growth on the horizon? What does the regulatory/legal landscape look like? Does the analysis of the competitive landscape reveal the potential for strong profit margins and growth? Or has the market matured?

ASSESSING YOUR CAPABILITIES AND OPPORTUNITIES

Once the competitive landscape has been analyzed, Porter describes three potential strategies for positioning an organization: cost leadership, differentiation, focus.[11] Companies can become *cost leaders* by providing the best value at the lowest cost, or they can use *differentiation* to provide a distinctive value offering to the marketplace that distinguishes them from the mass of competitors. The third option is taking cost leadership or differentiation and *focusing* them on a narrow market niche.

A cost-leadership strategy based solely on cutting costs and streamlining operations can eventually be mimicked and duplicated, unless the value chain itself is distinctive. In today's fragmented environment, some successful organizations seek to differentiate themselves by focusing on a narrow, clearly defined niche to connect with a passionately invested audience. As media economist Robert Picard noted, in today's information-saturated environment, journalists need to identify what they can provide that is distinctive and special.[12] News organizations rightfully complain about slender budgets, but at the same time, many outlets duplicate coverage, essentially offering the same content from the same big events such as the National Collegiate Athletic Association Final Four basketball games, he pointed out. His prescription: People will pay for uniqueness, locality, and specialization, and news organizations need to build their strategies with those traits in mind.

Successful online ventures such as FiveThirtyEight, Politico, and Vox Media (with brands such as SBNation, The Verge, and Recode) have followed this approach, pursuing niches and delivering information and entertainment to specific audiences through online content, podcasts, and live events. Vox has used these strategies in its decision-making, as it works to develop communities around authentic, authoritative content. As of 2020, the privately held company reached about 125 million people via its sites per month.[13] Axios has also pursued a strategy in which it focuses on building authority on particular subjects, developing products like newsletters that can showcase the expertise of individual reporters, such as the popular Axios Media Trends, written by media reporter Sara Fisher.[14]

One of the most successful examples of diversifying sources of support is the Texas Tribune, a nonprofit newsroom focused on covering Texas politics and the state legislature. With $4 million in seed funding from donors, the organization launched in 2009 combining journalists with programmers to develop a variation on news delivery that used data and events to complement and expand traditional coverage delivered via website. Over the next decade, the organization had established itself as a vibrant news force in the state, with more than 1.9 million unique visitors per month visiting the site and $10.1 million in annual revenue from a variety of sources, including 6,900 memberships and an annual event attendance total of more than 13,000.[15]

The leadership brought its stated mission to life by investing in staff and operations, and today it has the largest statehouse reporting operation of any news organization in the country. It had remained financially in the black since 2012, when its annual revenue pushed above the $5 million mark for the first time, and by 2019, it was employing 80 full- and part-time employees.[16] Each year in its annual report, the organization reviews its commitment to its journalism-first strategy as a primary part of assessing its performance. Nonprofit status doesn't alter the need for a consistent strategy to guide decision-making, and news startups considering pursuing this model should recognize that some foundations are, unfortunately, constantly looking to fund something new, rather than rewarding consistent skills and abilities; staying true to long-term goals often requires nurturing a variety of sources of funding.[17]

In 2018, in addition to its annual report, the organization developed a strategic plan outlining a path for 2025 that reiterated its journalistic commitment: "Our editorial north star remains unchanged: to produce original journalism of consequence on politics and public policy in Texas, in service to the state's diverse population."[18] With this guiding statement, the report details several new avenues and pathways that spread from that foundation, including expanded video and audio products, fundraising galas, and a focus on memberships.

Part of that strategic plan also included an imperative to diversify the newsroom as an effort to reach a wider, more diverse swath of Texas's population. The overall statement of "double and diversify"— to double its audience in seven years and diversify its reach in the process—includes a specific tactic of incorporating diversity and Spanish-language skills as part of its hiring.[19] In 2020, the organization turned words into action, publishing the demographic breakdown of its newsroom in its annual report, and noted what steps it had taken toward achieving that stated strategic goal.[20]

Strategy is an integral part of the change process because it helps organizations stake their position in the external environment and evaluate progress toward goals. It is a way of thinking that lies between the unconscious stabilizing power of culture and the immediate imperative of innovation. In this age of necessary experimentation, it's easy to dismiss traditional strategy as too slow and deliberative to respond to the dynamic market; however, a well-articulated strategy—one that reflects the organization's underlying cultural assumptions—can provide guiding principles to navigate uncertain terrain. It defines your organization's distinctive place in the landscape and establishes a plan for capitalizing on its unique value. A meaningful strategy builds on how organizational members conceive of their identities in the context of work life and explicitly reinforces those underlying assumptions as it outlines organizational goals. Any tactic that veers too far from an organization's cultural values will ultimately fail.

A well-defined strategy also helps diverse segments of an organization pull in the same direction. Even though the editorial and business sides of news organizations have historically been kept separate to avoid compromising credibility, each depends on the other for survival and needs to be able to share information and broad goals to avoid working at cross purposes. For example, in Milwaukee, some of the business-side leaders we spoke to felt that information they had about readers that could have helped editors serve them better was not widely shared. One said:

> Where newspapers fall down is that research and the newsroom should be working together, but are not. If I go into the newsroom, some people may want to hear it; some may not. Some of it is tradition. There are some old-school people in the newsroom who believe that marketing should not be involved in any way. I just had an editor tell me, 'The market tells me what it wants every day, but it's not about what they want; it's my decision.' I'm in a tough spot. I would think the research would be relevant. I view the newsroom as a bunch of land mines.[21]

DEFINING YOUR MISSION

Successful organizations have clear, succinct mission statements, the kind that rank-and-file employees can embrace, recite, and use to guide their daily responsibilities. But eloquent epigrams alone are not enough. Organization members should be able to see the mission lived out in the day-to-day decisions made by leaders and managers. When employees sense a disconnect, it can affect morale and the willingness to embrace change efforts, an aspect we will explore more deeply in Chapter 6.

Gannett is an example of a company that has shifted its stated mission and strategy frequently over the years. While consistent adaptation and reinvention are necessary, changes have to be rooted in a shared mission, backed by a commitment in resources, training, and support, and affirmed by tangible, visible successes, to move people into a new direction. Without those components, constantly shifting strategies over time may foster a culture of discontent and skepticism, especially if those changes deviate too much from the organization's culture.

Over the past decade, as it evaluated the competitive landscape, Gannett joined Tribune Co. and Scripps-Howard in spinning off its newspaper operations into separate companies, leaving its profitable broadcast operations as standalone enterprises. Gannett later bought Scripps-Howard's spinoff, Journal Media Group, in 2016 but struggled to lift its annual profit margin above 1%.[22] In November 2019, Gannett itself was bought by New Media Investment Group, which owned the GateHouse Media newspaper chain.

The new giant, which kept the Gannett name, announced plans to refocus its efforts on digital marketing through its more than 250 daily newspapers and several hundred weekly publications.[23] "Our mission is to connect, protect and celebrate our local communities," Paul Bascobert, tapped to lead the Gannett Media Corp. operating company, said at the time. "Great journalism really is the core of that mission. The question really becomes, what's the sustainable and exciting business model that powers that mission?"[24] But how to turn that broad vision into an executable reality remained unclear in early 2020 as the company trimmed employment rosters around the country.[25]

In the months before its merger with GateHouse, Gannett stated its purpose on its website: "To be a next-generation media company that empowers communities to connect, act and thrive."[26] But there was an overriding priority: maximizing profits to create shareholder value, a primary goal for for-profit companies, especially ones whose stocks are traded publicly. For years, Gannett had focused on cost-cutting and profit targets as priorities well before many of its competitors.[27] As a result, the newspaper giant appealed to investors, and its stock price grew steadily throughout the 1990s and 2000s.

Like other media stocks, though, it suffered after the financial crisis of 2008. Gannett announced new plans for the "newsroom of the future," which included several new job titles and descriptions meant to push people to think more consistently about online.[28] Some observers noted that Gannett's editorial strategy wasn't the first time it had developed a "newsroom of the future" approach. In a 2006 memo, then-CEO Craig Dubow had described a plan that called for creating "Information Centers" that would gather information around the clock and distribute it when, where, and how the audience wanted it. "It is the essence of our Vision and Mission and a key element of our Strategic Plan," he wrote at the time.[29] It became the focus of newsroom managers until Dubow stepped down in 2011.

By 2015, under the "Our Purpose" section of its website, Gannett listed a purpose ("to serve the greater good of our nation and the communities we serve"), mission (providing trusted news and information), vision (seeing the communities the company serves grow and thrive), and a values statement, with seven stated values including "Results driven: Be accountable. Deliver."[30] By the time of CEO Bob Dickey's retirement in May 2019, the "Our Purpose" page had changed again. Within months, the deal between Gate-House parent New Media Investment Group and Gannett would be struck, leading to yet another revision of the "About Us" page on Gannett's website.

Gannett Blog, a now-defunct blog that had been maintained by former Gannett journalist Jim Hopkins, built a community for current and former Gannett employees to share information about the newspaper giant, especially with regard to cost-cutting initiatives and layoffs. It served as an outlet for staffers to vent their anger and frustrations. Hopkins' signoff in February 2014—about six-and-a-half years after he had begun the volunteer enterprise—elicited scores of comments from supporters. Several noted their frustrations with the company, especially with regard to layoffs, and thanked him for providing a deeper look over the years. Wrote one:

Thank you, Jim, for all of the work that you have done on this site.
I have followed this blog since it's [sic] inception and it has been
a very valuable tool in knowing what is going on with this terrible
company because they always leave their workers in the dark.[31]

AFFIRMING MISSION THROUGH ACTION

Gannett stands in contrast to the *Washington Post*, which was purchased
by Amazon founder Jeff Bezos for $250 million in 2013.[32] In an inter-
view at the Business Insider Ignition conference after buying the paper,
Bezos noted the potential of the combination: "I didn't know anything
about the newspaper business, but I did know something about the
Internet. That, combined with the financial runway that I can provide,
is the reason why I bought *The Post*."[33] Over the next three years, the
organization focused on content over advertising, adding 140 reporters
and expanding its technology team; by 2016, Bezos said the *Post* was
profitable.[34] The investment in content was rewarded with continued
support from news consumers, as the site hit 87.9 million visitors
during January 2020.[35]

These gains in visitors and profitability did not, however, alter its
commitment to journalism or the consistency of its mission. In 2020,
the *Post* still carried the original "seven principles for the conduct of
a newspaper," originally penned in 1935 by owner Eugene Meyer,
on its website.[36] Among them: "The newspaper's duty is to its
readers and to the public at large, and not to the private interests of
its owners."[37]

It does not require being a national or international brand to allow
a journalistically-driven strategy to guide an organization's decisions.
WTXL, a Scripps Media-owned station in Tallahassee, Florida, decided
after years to shut down its "Mugshots" section, which featured pictures
from the Leon County Sheriff's Office booking report each night. In
a post explaining the decision, General Manager Matt Brown noted the
feature was usually among the top-five most visited pages on the website, but the questions about its overall value had sparked much discussion in the newsroom: "Are arrests for minor crimes newsworthy? Does
publishing these booking reports make our community a better place?
Are we simply pandering to lurid curiosity? Are we ruining people's
lives or shaming people in our community for minor mistakes?"[38]

Brown explained the goal behind removing the mugshots: "We hope that this decision helps make our community a better place."[39]

HOW DO YOU CREATE VALUE?

The essence of strategy is value creation. How do you align your resources most effectively to generate a meaningful return on investment? As we have mentioned, the push toward the Internet has complicated that proposition greatly for media companies, as audiences have become fragmented, and online advertising generates far less revenue than ads in print or broadcast media.

As Facebook, Craigslist, and Google have ascended as major media players, news has become a commodity in abundance.[40] The historical value of newspapers and news programs—with information also fulfilling an entertainment need—has shifted in an environment rich with content options and multimedia. Turning information into meaningful revenue has become the challenge. News organizations that embraced search engine optimization strategies like *Forbes* and the *Christian Science Monitor* have seen diminishing returns on third-party and banner advertising that depended upon page views, especially with the advertising dominance of the big online platforms. As this book went to press, the coronavirus crisis had further devastated online advertising.

One example of a clear and specific strategy grounded in an understanding of the changing external environment was developed by Penelope Muse Abernathy, a former *Wall Street Journal* and *New York Times* executive who is the Knight Chair in Journalism and Digital Media Economics at the University of North Carolina. Her book, *Saving Community Journalism*,[41] outlines the following priorities for community newspapers:

- Reduce legacy media costs so that more can be invested in digital opportunities.
- Build community across all platforms. Develop the kind of reader loyalty that enhances both willingness to pay for content and the kinds of sustained attention and engagement that command higher advertising rates. Focus not only on how to make local news more relevant, but how to serve special interests and passions within your community. Use social media and other tools to nurture this

community, facilitate conversation, and learn as much as possible about what people need most.

- Develop new revenue streams by looking beyond core news functions. Advertisers, like their editorial counterparts, can utilize storytelling skills as a unique value proposition in the marketplace, not only to create compelling pitches but also to build the kinds of relationships with consumers that increase return on investment.

These strategic priorities are based on extensive consumer and market research, and could be used to prioritize projects and resource allocation.

Ultimately, whatever products or services you build have to create value for your audience and community. That's where the innovation level of our model is most useful—it is the most outwardly focused, and forces you to focus on your customer, your audience, to ensure what you are creating and developing fulfills a need, beyond your initial suppositions and speculations about the market's desires. But those efforts have to be grounded in meaningful, executable strategy.

One difficulty in today's fast-moving environment is allotting enough resources to research and develop new products that often may fail. To some degree, organizations have to be willing to take on some risk (an idea that we'll discuss further in Chapter 4) and invest in nascent ideas that align with the company's strategic goals.

Chapter 2 focused on looking inward, on understanding who you are as an organization. Those values are key to outlining how the organization will face the marketplace, which has become ever more cut-throat in the digital age. Without that foundation, most planning will go for naught as the internal culture overpowers change efforts that don't mesh with the way people make sense of their world and accomplish work in a way that fits with that world view. Strategy moves from the nebulous nature of cultural identity to the more concrete level of execution.

We've highlighted examples from the nonprofit news sector, largely because they often have a more singular focus on mission than some corporations driven by the profit imperative. However, some would argue that nonprofits, too, have conflicting loyalties, to the foundations, grantors, and donors that fund them.

Still, financial structure often dictates strategy. A singular focus on short-term bottom-line imperatives from shareholders can hamper the ability to do meaningful but costly work, especially if everything is framed in terms of return on investment. Part of thinking strategically requires a pragmatic focus on the bottom line, but it should not be the only consideration for decision-making, especially when it comes to developing long-term competitive advantage. As the coronavirus crisis began to upend American life and media fortunes in spring 2020, The Atlantic lifted its paywall for its pandemic coverage; it was rewarded for this commitment to readers with 36,000 new subscribers and a surge in traffic that was more than double the previous one-month record.[42]

NOTES

1 Ken Doctor, "The Newsonomics of Gannett's 'Newsrooms of the Future'," *Nieman Lab*, August 25, 2014, www.niemanlab.org/2014/08/the-newsonomics-of-gannetts-newsrooms-of-the-future/.

2 Voice of San Diego, "What We Stand For," Voice of San Diego, n.d., www.voiceofsandiego.org/about-us/what-we-stand-for/.

3 Voice of San Diego.

4 Michael Porter, *Competitive Advantage* (New York, NY: Free Press, 1998), 4–5.

5 Stephen Lacy, David C. Coulson, and Hugh J. Martin, "Ownership and Barriers to Entry in Non-Metropolitan Daily Newspaper Markets," *Journalism & Mass Communication Quarterly* 81, no. 2 (2004): 328.

6 Alan Albarran, *Media Economics, Understanding Markets, Industries, and Concepts*, 2nd ed. (Ames, IA: Iowa State Press, 2002), 148–149.

7 Robert Picard, "The Economics of the Daily Newspaper Industry," in *Media Economics, Theory and Practice*, ed. Alison Alexander et al. (Mahwah, NJ: Lawrence Erlbaum, 2004), 113.

8 D. Verklin and B. Kanner, *Watch This, Listen Up, Click Here: Inside the $300 Billion Business Behind the Media You Constantly Consume* (Hoboken, NJ: John Wiley and Sons, 2007), 45–47.

9 Pew Research Center, "Newspapers Fact Sheet," July 9, 2019, www.journalism.org/fact-sheet/newspapers/.

10 Porter, 63.

11 Porter, 11–15.

12 Teresa Mioli, "Screens, Not Physical Media, Dominate Culture, Robert Picard Tells ISOJ Audience," ISOJ, April 18, 2015, http://isoj.org/2959-2/.

13 Vox, Home page, n.d., www.voxmedia.com/a/vm.

14 Jarrod Dicker, Sara Fischer, and Caroline Guerrero, "Smart Revenue Model Diversification in Media," Panel Discussion, Newmark Graduate School of Journalism, New York City, February 19, 2020.

15 *Texas Tribune, The Texas Tribune 2019 Annual Report*, 2020, https://static.texastribune.org/media/files/27687dd795d6aa7c250e829bc3933a56/TT-2019-Annual-Report-021220.pdf?_ga=2.217700816.757394961.1583614142-1331699377.1583614142.

16 *Texas Tribune Annual Report*, 14.

17 Dicker, Fischer, and Guerrero.

18 *Texas Tribune*, "A Strategic Vision for the Texas Tribune's Future," September 5, 2018, www.texastribune.org/about/texas-tribune-strategic-plan/.

19 *Texas Tribune*, "A Strategic Vision."

20 Corrie Maclaggan, "T-Squared: The Texas Tribune's 2020 Diversity Report," *Texas Tribune*, February 13, 2020, www.texastribune.org/2020/02/13/texas-tribune-diversity-report-2020/.

21 Confidential interview, personal communication, March 24, 2008.

22 Gannett, "Company Profile," n.d., www.gannett.com/who-we-are/.

23 Nathan Bomey, "CEOs of New Gannett: 'Pivot' Needed for Digital Transformation as Merger Is Completed," *USA Today*, November 29, 2019, www.usatoday.com/story/money/2019/11/19/gannett-new-media-investment-group-merger-gatehouse-media/4203820002/.

24 Bomey.

25 Barbara Allen, "Gannett Layoffs Underway at Combined New Company," Poynter, February 27, 2020, www.poynter.org/business-work/2020/gannett-layoffs-underway-at-combined-new-company/.

26 Gannett, "Our Purpose," n.d., www.gannett.com/who-we-are/.

27 Ken Doctor, "10 Takeaways from Gannett's Blockbuster Announcements," *Nieman Lab*, August 5, 2014, www.niemanlab.org/2014/08/ken-doctor-10-takeaways-from-gannetts-blockbuster-announcements/.

28 Jim Romenesko, "Here Are the Job Descriptions for Gannett's 'Newsroom of the Future'," August 8, 2014, http://jimromenesko.com/2014/08/08/here-are-the-new-jobs-being-offered-to-gannett-journalists/.

29 Jim Hopkins, "Text of Craig Dubow's Information Center Memo," Gannett Blog, November 2, 2006, http://gannettblog.blogspot.com/2006/11/text-of-craig-dubows-information-center.html.

30 Gannett, "Get to Know Us," n.d., www.gannett.com/article/99999999/WHOWEARE/130426001/Our-Purpose.

31 Anonymous, "Goodbye: After Six-Plus Years, I'm Calling It Quits," Gannett Blog, February 8, 2014, https://gannettblog.blogspot.com/2014/02/goodbye-after-six-plus-years-im-calling.html?showComment=1391865332152#c1272038143152032841.

32 William Laudner, Christopher S. Stewart, and Joann S. Lublin, "Jeff Bezos Buys Washington Post for $250 Million," *Wall Street Journal*, August 5, 2013, www.wsj.com/articles/SB10001424127887324653004578650390383666794.

33 Mike Isaac, "Amazon's Jeff Bezos Explains Why He Bought the Washington Post," *New York Times*, December 2, 2014, https://bits.blogs.nytimes.com/2014/12/02/amazons-bezos-explains-why-he-bought-the-washington-post/.

34 Matt Rosoff, "Jeff Bezos Has Advice for the News Business: 'Ask People to Pay. They Will Pay'," CNBC, June 21, 2017, www.cnbc.com/2017/06/21/jeff-bezos-lessons-from-washington-post-for-news-industry.html.

35 *Washington Post* PR, "Nearly 88 Million People Visited the Washington Post Online in January 2020," *Washington Post*, February 19, 2020, www.washington post.com/pr/2020/02/19/nearly-88-million-people-visited-washington-post-online-january-2020/.

36 *Washington Post* staff, "Policies and Standards," *Washington Post*, January 1, 2016, www.washingtonpost.com/news/ask-the-post/wp/2016/01/01/policies-and-standards/?utm_term=.f5de55daab43#missionstatement.

37 *Washington Post* staff.

38 Matt Brown, "Why We Shut Down the 'Mugshots' Page," WTXL.com, May 23, 2019, www.wtxl.com/news/local-news/why-we-shut-down-the-mugshots-page.

39 Brown.

40 Robert Picard, "Journalism, Value Creation, and the Future of News Organizations," Working Paper Series (Harvard University, 2006).

41 Penelope Muse Abernathy, *Saving Community Journalism: The Path to Profitability* (Chapel Hill, NC: University of North Carolina Press, 2014).

42 Sarah Scire, "For Its Must-Read Coronavirus Coverage, The Atlantic Is Rewarded with a Huge Surge of Digital Subscriptions," *Nieman Lab*, April 6, 2020, www.niemanlab.org/2020/04/for-its-must-read-coronavirus-coverage-the-atlantic-is-rewarded-with-a-huge-surge-of-digital-subscriptions/.

Four

Too often, we've made changes and then breathed sighs of
relief, as if the challenge had been solved. But the pace of
change is so fast that solutions can quickly seem out of date,
and the next challenge is right around the corner.[1]

New York Times Innovation Report, 2014

Since the advent of the Internet for commercial use, the New York Times
has experimented with different strategies to cultivate digital audiences. It developed a large online operation apart from its primary
newsroom. It tried a tiered paywall approach with Times Select,
which offered exclusive op-eds, archive searches, and personalized
email newsletters for $7.95 a month.[2] Although that experiment
failed, the organization came back with one of the industry's first
successful metered paywalls.[3] In the summer of 2015, the Times
blocked its employees' access to its homepage for one week, forcing
them to use mobile in order to foster more innovative thinking about
this increasingly dominant medium for news consumption.[4]

But as the quote from the internal innovation report at the beginning of the chapter revealed, even with its enviable resources and
global reach, the Times had faced the same struggle as other legacy
news organizations in the digital era: *How do we innovate consistently?* Ultimately, the Times proved successful in its digital transition, in part thanks
to its many fast-moving experiments and the "Trump bump" in subscriptions as interest in news spiked following the 2016 presidential
election.[5] It was doing so well in the beginning of 2019 that it
"could pay for the newsroom two times over with just digital
money," as Joshua Benton wrote for *Nieman Lab*. Overall, 2019 was a
record-breaking year for adding new subscribers, and it generated
more than $800 million in digital revenue well before its initial

target date of late 2020.[6] But even now, there's no such thing as stasis as industry conditions and technologies continue to evolve, such as the rise of smart speakers and the need to consider how best to deliver news for that platform.[7]

As legacy news organizations lost ground to the upstarts-turned-behemoths like Facebook and Google, the need for innovation popped up with regularity, so much so that the word hardly has any specific meaning in our tech-infatuated society. But the reality is that news organizations don't need a one-time fix. They need to develop their capacities to adapt and learn rapidly, continuously, routinely.

As we've shown, changes wrought by technology and consumer behavior will disrupt well-established cultures and the daily practices that have become ingrained through past successes. But established theory on organizational learning offers insights into how to encourage innovation in your organization. We'll also draw on some lessons from technology entrepreneurs and design-thinking professionals from inside and outside the media industry that can help teams iterate quickly and learn from mistakes.

ORGANIZATIONAL LEARNING

Scholars Chris Argyris and Donald Schön have identified two types of organizational learning.[8] The first kind, *single-loop*, occurs when an organization changes a policy or practice to achieve a desired result but does not rethink any fundamental assumptions in the process. For example, in the early days of the World Wide Web, many news organizations' digital efforts amounted to little more than "shovelware," basically a cut-and-paste job of content they'd already produced for the legacy medium plopped onto the web with little thought for what the new medium could offer.[9] It wasn't that newspapers were totally unwilling to try new things; in the 1980s and early 1990s, many newspapers grasped the coming impact of new technologies and jumped into videotex, but they did so in a way that remained so tethered to the fundamental assumptions of print that they failed, as scholar Pablo Boczkowski found in his case study of three early efforts by newspapers to embrace new media forms.[10]

The second kind of learning Argyris and Schön identified, *double-loop*, goes beyond simple modifications in behavior. It occurs when organizations *do* fundamentally question assumptions, values, and constructs that do not appear to be matching up well with their fundamental goals or purposes. A news organization that exhibited double-loop learning in its digital transition would be more likely to reconsider its entire editorial process and assumptions about the best ways to present news, taking advantage of the greater inter-activity and potential for multimedia presentation offered by the online medium.

Each of these forms of learning is associated with certain approaches toward problem solving. Single-loop learning is characterized by a desire to "win" by vanquishing the problem quickly and then carrying on with work as usual, minimizing negative emotions—to preserve others' feelings, people avoid saying what they mean. This form of learning often relies on untested attributions of the intentions of others and limits the ability of an organization to learn from its mistakes. Double-loop learning, on the other hand, is characterized by a commitment to learning and change as an explicit mandate. It prizes valid information, which includes the bad but important news that must be communicated even if it is difficult to do so, creating informed choices for the group and for individuals.[11]

Scholars like Argyris and Schön note that double-loop learning is notoriously hard for any organization to achieve.[12] This struggle is especially true for organizations that, like traditional media and newspapers in particular, were long characterized by monopoly conditions and a "past" orientation,[13] or a period of "stable equi-librium" that has eroded their capacity to learn effectively.[14]

Indeed, none of the organizations we have studied reached this level of learning on a consistent basis. But some of the newer non-profit news organizations are developing cultures that encourage double-loop learning processes. Just four years after its founding, City Bureau's leaders spent several months re-examining their mis-sion and processes anew, getting input from stakeholders, reviewing academic literature on defining and measuring the impact of news on communities, and writing publicly about their work.[15] Through this process, they developed 12 principles to guide their work toward the organization's larger strategic goal: "a future in which all people are equipped with the tools and knowledge to effect change in their communities."[16] Each of these principles is supported by 20 key metrics that will be continually collected and assessed.

Other researchers also emphasize the vital connection between communication and organizational learning. Andrew Brown and Ken Starkey, who study organizations from a psychodynamic perspective, argued that organizational learning is linked to organizational identity.[17] Organization members often seek to preserve their sense of self, a phenomenon that affects the organization's ability to learn. The key, Brown and Starkey say, is to cultivate an identity that reflects and embraces learning as part of the routine.

Fortunately, innovation theorists and technology entrepreneurs have developed specific processes for embedding the process of learning and iteration in the organization so that it becomes part of its identity.

LEARNING FROM THE LEAN STARTUP MODEL

Eric Ries, author of *The Lean Startup*, offers a variety of suggestions on developing a culture in which what he calls "validated learning" is the most essential ingredient.[18] Essentially, he argues that you need to gather feedback as early and often as you possibly can in the process of developing a new product or service, allowing you to constantly tweak your process or features to reflect what people actually want and need. Like Argyris and Schön, Ries emphasizes the importance of erecting systems and tests that will reveal feedback you'd rather not hear and avoid "vanity metrics" that can make efforts appear more successful than they actually are. The most critical element of "validated learning" for Ries is starting with what entrepreneurs call an MVP, or minimum viable product. Identify a few top-priority features and build something simple first. Test it with some early adopters, and also begin to hone your internal processes.[19]

When BuzzFeed was developing its news app that launched in June 2015, its editorial team tackled a big story, the Federal Communications Commission vote on net neutrality, to test its processes.[20] Team members were assigned different roles, from curating social feeds to providing context and background, and they documented what they learned in a shared Google Doc and used the office-messaging app Slack to work through the steps they would use when the app actually went live. According to Aaron Edwards, who was then a reporter and curation editor at BuzzFeed, they learned the best methods for internal communication and developed a "wish list" of features for the app's developers. He wrote: "It might feel awkward and kind of frustrating to go through the motions of these workflows without a complete product, but the lessons learned can be invaluable during the early stages of development."[21]

The MVP concept can be especially hard for journalists because it means releasing something before it has been perfected. In a business in which getting a fact wrong can cost you your credibility and your job, this proposition can be scary, although one could compare it to a breaking news situation in which the paper is rapidly publishing what it knows and adding details to better complete the story as they are uncovered. In a world of scarce resources and strong competition, not only from other news sources but from Facebook, Google, and other companies that vie for screen attention, news organizations can't afford to pour resources into an app or service that consumers don't want.

Starting the testing process early and developing a system for regularly incorporating feedback is critical to test the kinds of assumptions that can block learning. Often, people have a hard time thinking through their feelings or needs for a product or until they actually try it out, Ries writes.[22] And capturing good feedback involves talking to and observing people, not just reviewing quantitative metrics. If you really fear your MVP may do damage to your brand, one option some companies use is launching a new product under a different name.

Ries' advice also parallels organizational theory in its description of the importance of learning over optimization. Just as organizations with undeveloped, single-loop learning styles don't question their fundamental assumptions, "if you are building the wrong thing, optimizing the product or its marketing will not yield significant results," Ries says.[23] In other words, organizations may blame a lack of execution when the real problem is that the plan was flawed in the first place.

More recently, as newsrooms are shifting to member revenue sources to support their work, they are learning the importance of identifying the right kinds of data they can use to convert more people to be subscribers. Damon Kiesow, the Knight Chair in Digital Editing and Producing at the University of Missouri's School of Journalism, wrote a detailed report that lays out the steps newsrooms must take to pivot to reader revenue, with a greater emphasis on building trust.[24] Much as Ries and others recommend, this process involves constant testing and measuring the performance of a subscription program so that each aspect of it can be optimized.

UNDERSTANDING INNOVATION

The foundation of innovation is challenging the status quo, a trait that doesn't come naturally to most people, especially in the established culture of a successful organization. Professionals and organizations define themselves in terms of their successes, and as a result, they use those past experiences as their frames for solving problems. That's why it is so vital to understand your culture in organizational change efforts.

Innovative thinking calls for questioning all processes and routines. *That's the way we've always done it* should not be justification enough for continuing with a routine, product, or service. In a news context, it requires thinking about situations from the perspective of the audience, rather than from the viewpoint of the creator. For decades, editors and producers have decided what's important—the news that's fit to publish, broadcast, and post. Today, it is no longer enough to create a product with the hopes of the audience finding it; content creators must find ways to fulfill the communication needs of the audience.

In the 1990s, Harvard business professor Clayton Christensen examined the notion of disruption by pursuing one primary question: Why do successful companies such as Sears and Western Union fail? Through his research, he identified a common thread among them, detailed in his book *The Innovator's Dilemma: When Technologies Cause Great Firms To Fail*: Companies become victims of their own successes.[25] Early in their organizational lives, businesses are often scrappy and creative, driven by strong, passionate founders. They are willing to accept any level of profit as they take risks and experiment to discover what works in the marketplace. Once they become successful, however, routines become set into place, and they fail to adapt to changing circumstances in the market.

They do, however, continue to improve their products and services with sustaining innovations, becoming better and better at what they do.[26] Eventually, financial stakeholders—especially in publicly traded companies—demand certain profit margins. At this stage, managers are rarely encouraged to take risks that could result in lower margins or losses; instead, they are rewarded for guaranteed successes. In this environment, they continue to improve their already successful products and services to a point where they exceed customers' expectations and needs. Christensen argues that once a segment of products and services are consistently reliable, customers begin searching for alternatives that are cheaper or customizable to fulfill their "jobs to be done."[27]

The smaller, more nimble upstarts with little to lose then enter the market, with lower-priced products of lesser quality that still effectively solve the jobs to be done. When Craigslist hit the market with an alternative selling platform for consumers, it fundamentally disrupted the traditional classified advertising model for newspapers. It accepted far lower margins than what newspapers had come to expect, and the giant media companies dismissed it—until Craiglist had become too big and powerful to be uprooted.

Christensen has his share of critics, who argue that his theories lack predictive power[28] and don't fully capture the complexity of the choices involved in trying to figure out which new technologies are going to rise to become a legitimate threat to an established business.[29] And no theory of innovation matters if an organization's culture blocks the changes necessary to adjust, as described in Chapter 2; a journalism project based on disruptive innovation theory, Newspaper Next, largely failed for this reason. As Christensen himself put it, "the [Newspaper Next] report was consumed at the level of the brain and not the heart."[30] Still, his theory is helpful for journalists to understand the bigger picture in which they operate and what kinds of threats they need to be more attuned to.

In later work with Michael Raynor, Christensen expanded his framework to include disruptions that broaden the market to consumer segments that were historically uninterested in the product or service category.[31] For example, with its simple controllers and graphics, the Nintendo Wii newly appealed to non-gamers who previously wouldn't have been in the market for a gaming console. For entrepreneurial strategists, it is useful to consider these opportunities that are outside traditional core targets for potential growth.

Consider CNN. At the time of its launch in 1980, no U.S. networks provided round-the-clock information to consumers. Founder Ted Turner spent years pursuing and refining his vision, investing more than $77 million in the venture; it did not turn its first net profit until 1985.[32] In the process, CNN discovered a new market for 24/7 news, especially during major news events such as the Challenger disaster and the first Gulf War, among consumers who desired information beyond the usual 5, 6, and 10 p.m. newscasts.

Writer Steven Johnson adapted scientist Stuart Kauffman's term "the adjacent possible"[33] to describe this kind of advancement. How can you combine existing technologies, knowledge, and skills in creative ways to develop new innovations?

For example, the nonprofit Texas Tribune has long gone beyond producing stories in order to achieve sustainability, leveraging its journalistic skills to produce topical and informative events. Its annual Texas Tribune Festival capitalizes on its journalists' interviewing skills and brings in money from tickets and sponsorships; by 2014, it had brought in $700,000 in revenue.[34] The organization also developed paid newsletter products and began experimenting with different ways of presenting sponsored content.

IDENTIFYING THE "JOBS TO BE DONE"

Innovation can come in many forms: content, platform, competency. In a news context, organizations must identify their audience's communication "jobs to be done"—whether advertising or editorial or a new adjacent-possible hybrid—and satisfy those needs when, where, and how the audience wants them satisfied. Sometimes, that solution takes the shape of delivering content in a different format, such as through smartphone notifications or email newsletters. It can also mean developing new types of content that expand or even change the traditional notion of "news."

A recent example is the nonprofit Outlier Media in Detroit. Founder Sarah Alvarez knew that low-income communities were not being well served by traditional media sources, and were therefore largely not consuming the journalism that was produced locally, even when it was relevant to their interests. By focusing on how to cover issues not only for and but also with low-income news consumers and learning about their needs and "jobs to be done," she found that tangible, individualized information delivered by text message was the best way to reach people.[35] Drawing on city and county public sources of data, Outlier can offer specific, targeted information about homes and rental properties. It is opening up a new market for news in a creative way. Its model is now being expanded to Milwaukee, and it is combining forces with MuckRock, a 10-year-old nonprofit that focuses on public records and accountability journalism.[36]

Over the past few decades, mass communication researchers have developed an area of theory called uses-and-gratifications that helps identify these jobs to be done. It posits that people are not passive consumers of media; instead, they choose and use media to satisfy certain communication needs.

One focus of uses-and-gratifications researchers has been what motivates media usage.[37] Some people are surveying the landscape for information to help them make decisions. Others desire entertainment or diversion from everyday responsibilities. Still others use it as a way to connect with society or fulfill certain emotional needs.

Esther Thorson and Margaret Duffy tapped into this perspective to develop the Media Choice Model, a framework for helping news organizations understand how to connect with their audiences more effectively.[38] Their model begins with thinking through the four primary communication needs that media consumers desire: *information, shopping, entertainment*, and *connectivity*. The first two are rational and practical; historically, news organizations have built their brands on fulfilling these cognitive needs. The latter two inspire deeper emotional reactions within audiences. Content creators that connect on those emotional levels are more likely to create deeper engagement to build communities around their content, an idea we will discuss more fully in Chapter 5.

According to the Media Choice Model, strategists should think about the primary things people look for in choosing media to satisfy those needs:[39]

- *Features.* What form do users desire the content to be in, and which features are most desirable? Do they want multimedia? Do they need it to be searchable or customizable? Should it be mobile or frequently updated?

- *Voice.* Are users seeking a particular kind of voice for their content? The model posits four voices: authoritative/expert, the traditional voice of journalists; created, or the voice of the amateur/public; opinionated; or collaborative, which offers a combination of the professional and the amateur.
- *Aperture.* What are the contexts in which users come to the content? Are there specific times of the day that are best for reaching them? How deep is their investment in the quality of the information they seek?

The key to applying the model to your own circumstances is remembering that different audience members seek different ways to satisfy their needs. Develop personas of key audience targets, and think about how each may come to your content. What will they be looking for? What will be their level of interest and attentiveness? What will be the circumstances in which they will be connecting with your content?

LEARNING IS UNCOMFORTABLE

In *The Lean Startup*, Ries acknowledges that building a learning culture is difficult because it is messy and frustrating, often threatening to those with well-established competencies.[40] This insight reflects the reality of newsrooms, long siloed by expertise. Staffers were primarily responsible for focusing on an area of expertise—reporting, taking photographs, editing, shooting video. Developing a news product by learning how people respond to your work is a much less tangible goal that requires constant rethinking and revision. Having your productivity and worth suddenly valued in a new way is threatening and produces a lot of anxiety. Doing high-quality work by a well-established and fairly objective standard is no longer enough—journalists are increasingly asked to incorporate feedback from others into their processes and output, which is inevitably challenging and sometimes confusing.

One interviewee in Milwaukee articulated how difficult it can be to learn new skills late in one's career:

These people are just really good at what they do; they are at the expert level. ... And I think it's especially hard for those people to go back to being a beginner again, to have to learn. I've tried to pull people in, talked to them about what we are doing ... but some people are just not open to it, and they won't be. ... It is really hard to learn something new. Usually you are in school when you are at square one. But if you are here, at a good paper, you are at the top of your game. It's hard to go back to being at the bottom again.[41]

We have seen this phenomenon time and again at newsrooms we have studied, and "more training" is often one of the top requests we hear when we talk to staffers. Even at the journalism schools we've worked at and attended, one of the hardest parts of transitioning to digital and mobile has been the reluctance of or difficulty for faculty members to develop new multimedia skills late in their careers.

Scholars of organizational change agree that learning anxiety is a primary reason change is so hard, and they argue that organizations most successful at learning operate under conditions of constant tension between stability and instability, "at the edge of chaos."[42] To be creative, people need both constraints and freedom. People need to feel comfortable with each other and confident in themselves but also enough pressure and competition to go beyond their comfort zones. Think about those fun-but-challenging competitions elementary-school students often participate in during their science classes to build creative problem-solving skills: dropping an egg out of a second-story window without breaking it or building a bridge out of toothpicks. The same fundamental idea applies. Constraint and competition married with a supportive atmosphere are what create the most interesting and unexpected solutions to problems.

Leading an organization in a way that balances between these competing tensions isn't easy, but understanding why people may behave the way they do can help. In some news organizations we've studied, capacity for change was largely seen as an individual trait some people possess. This view avoids the more important ways in which groups respond to change and how people working together have a greater capacity for creativity than individuals alone.

A better approach: Look at what kinds of innovation your systems and processes are facilitating—or blocking.

BUILDING INNOVATION INTO YOUR ROUTINES

Since the 1970s, scholars who have studied newsrooms have documented the routines that allow news to be produced consistently and reliably on deadline.[43] Most newsrooms traditionally operated like a factory, with content changing hands systematically at appointed times throughout the day. To ensure a steady supply of stories to fill space, reporters often rely on bureaucratic sources that can be consulted regularly and can generally be expected to produce something newsworthy.[44] In the past, the audience had few easy avenues to talk back aside from letters or phone calls, so the judgment of editors and news directors about what was important was paramount. The meetings at which they decided what stories to pursue and highlight were key elements of the average day. Deadlines were strict but predictable. This deeply ingrained system is not one well-suited for reflection or the unpredictability of a 24/7, interactive media environment in which news can be posted as soon as it is produced and verified.

Fortunately, tech entrepreneurs, developers, and organizational learning scholars have some daily habits that work better in a fast-changing environment. Newsrooms can adopt these practices, as many have.

Brian Boyer brought agile development techniques common to programming to the news apps teams he has led at places such as the Chicago Tribune and Spirited Media.[45] These routines helped his teams iterate quickly, avoided wasting time on projects that users don't want, and facilitated cooperation between editorial and technology-focused staffers. "Everything we do is about transparency, both inside the team and outside the team, every part of the process," Boyer said. "There are always interesting problems to solve, and we need to be marching together to solve them."[46]

Some of the practices he and other journalists use include:

1 The scrum. A short meeting (from five to 15 minutes) at the beginning of the day in which each participant talks about what they are working on, next steps, and potential obstacles.[47]

2 *The sprint.* Any big project gets broken into small pieces. The most important features or tasks are prioritized, and the team then works on these for a short, intensive time period. When this period is over, the team reconvenes to assess how it went and begins testing with potential users. Feedback is then incorporated into the next sprint.[48]

3 *The manifesto.* A one-line statement that sets the direction for the entire project that keeps the team focused and on track.[49]

4 *Weekly meetings with all stakeholders.* Break down organizational silos, especially between editorial and business, and be sure everyone has input and buy-in early on in the process while there is still time to make adjustments.

5 *Put people from different silos who need to collaborate physically close to one other in the newsroom, and use Slack to encourage ongoing conversation.* Create a kind of embed program in which staffers can spend time with a different group.[50]

6 *Hold demo days or open houses to show new products or ideas to the whole newsroom, or hack days in which a larger group can participate in the process.*[51]

Processes such as these help increase the likelihood teams are engaging in double-loop learning, which is facilitated by regular, open communication. Feedback is incorporated regularly, not at the end of a long and arduous slog. Teams that have invested a relatively small amount of time creating something are generally less sensitive about making changes to it than one that has committed itself to months or even years of toil, reducing the defensive reactions that block learning and change. And having what Boyer calls the "manifesto" can help discourage a higher-up from suddenly suggesting a major add-on or change in direction late in the process.[52]

Organizational learning can also be facilitated by making it easier for newsrooms to get and interpret feedback from their audiences. A full discussion on the merits of specific news metrics is beyond the scope of this book, but many organizations are working on how to give greater context and value to the metrics they collect, helping not only executives but also reporters and front-line staff interpret them and extract meaning. For example, when Melody Kramer was a digital strategist at National Public Radio, she helped build an analytics dashboard that would help journalists understand how their content was spreading and who was sharing it, making it easier for people who were already busy to identify sources and develop greater reach for their work.[53] She and others shared larger lessons and victories with the rest of the newsroom through its "Social Sandbox," which began as an email listserv and later became a blog.[54] The Sandbox helped to promote a culture of sharing information and also allowed them to praise people who were experimenting and doing innovative work, giving people further incentives to try new things.

Another technique Ries advocates to continually evaluate your processes and priorities and identify sources of problems is called the "Five Whys."[55] When confronted with a problem, bring your team together and ask the simple question: Why? Take the answer and ask why again. Repeat for a total of five times. The key: Everyone on a team must be included in this process, or the person left out is likely to be blamed. The problems tackled should also be small and specific, and the attitude should be one that is tolerant of mistakes the first time they happen, with an aim toward preventing them in the future.

The "Five Whys" often means confronting unpleasant truths, but as organizational scholars Argyris and Schön say, this process is critical to learning. They recommend consulting with experts who can help people recognize their own defensive behaviors that prevent valid information being shared; often, awareness is half the battle.[56] Another technique that works involves bringing your team together to discuss case studies of poor communication and how to improve it at other organizations. By taking this discussion out of a personal context, it becomes more palatable and yields internal insight. Exercises like this might seem like an elaborate waste of time, but consider how much time can be lost dealing with political rivalries and other barriers in meetings if these issues aren't addressed.

HOW INNOVATIONS SPREAD

Everett Rogers has spent his career investigating how and why innovations spread. In *Diffusion of Innovations*, he writes about diffusion as a communication process: People within a social system show and share an innovation; if it doesn't mesh with their identities or culture, it won't be embraced, no matter how many advantages it may provide.[57] The paradigm provides a well-tested framework for making sense of how organizations adopt or reject innovations.

Innovations are adopted at different rates by organizations, depending upon how individuals perceive the innovation's advantages and compatibility with the existing system, as well as its complexity. Other critical factors, Rogers found, are trialability, or how simply an innovation may be experimented with, and observability, or how easily those in the organization can see the results of the innovation.[58] Interpersonal relationships are a key part of this diffusion: A *change agent* enters the existing system to introduce the innovation, and spreads the innovation throughout the organization with the help of *opinion leaders*, people well respected and admired by their peers.

Rogers frames the innovation-decision process among individuals and units as a five-step process: *knowledge*, or learning about the innovation; *persuasion*, or understanding the perceived characteristics of the innovation; *decision*, or adopting/rejecting the innovation; *implementation*; and *confirmation*.[59] In the implementation and confirmation stages, old routines are modified, and new ones develop. Box 4.1 has specific steps to developing a learning-focused organization.

As Jeff Sonderman and Tom Rosenstiel wrote in a report for the American Press Institute: "It is important to avoid seeing 'innovation' as a goal in itself. It is more of a byproduct: innovation is what happens while you're busy creating your future by solving problems."[60]

BOX 4.1 STEPS TO DEVELOPING A LEARNING-FOCUSED ORGANIZATION

- Question assumptions, values, processes, and routines on a systematic, regular basis. Jettison those that don't match up with your mission.
- Create a system for sharing all kinds of information, including the bad but important news that must be communicated even if it is difficult to do so.
- Gather feedback as early and often as you possibly can in the process of developing a new product or service, allowing

you to constantly make tweaks to your process or features that reflect what people actually want and need.

- Identify your audience's communication "jobs to be done" and satisfy those needs when, where, and how the audience wants them satisfied.
- Think through how your products and services fit four core needs in the Media Choice Model: information, shopping, entertainment, and connectivity. What kinds of specific features will help you meet those needs? What style of voice are people seeking?
- Develop personas of key audience targets, and think about how each may come to your content. What will they be looking for? What will be their level of interest and attentiveness? What will be the circumstances in which they will be connecting with your content?
- Try a scrum: a short meeting (about five minutes) at the beginning of the day in which each participant talks about what they are working on, next steps, and potential obstacles.[61]
- Do a sprint. Any big project gets broken into small pieces. The most important features or tasks are prioritized, and the team then works on these for a short, intensive time period. When this period is over, the team reconvenes to assess how it went and begins testing with potential users. Feedback is then incorporated into the next sprint.[62]
- Break down organizational silos, especially between editorial and business, and be sure everyone has input and buy-in early on in the process while there is still time to make adjustments.

NOTES

1 Joshua Benton, "The Leaked New York Times Innovation Report Is One of the Key Documents of this Media Age," Nieman Lab, May 15, 2014, www.nieman lab.org/2014/05/the-leaked-new-york-times-innovation-report-is-one-of-the-key-documents-of-this-media-age/; Meredith Broussard, "The J-School Scrum: Bringing Agile Development into the Classroom," MediaShift, January 14, 2014,

http://mediashift.org/2014/01/the-j-school-scrum-bringing-agile-develop ment-into-the-classroom.

2 *New York Times*, "What Is TimesSelect?" n.d., www.nytimes.com/products/time sselect/whatis.html; Michelle Levander, "Agile Storytelling: The Brian Boyer Way," *Reporting on Health*, September 23, 2011, www.reportingonhealth.org/blogs/2011/09/23/agile-storytelling-brian-boyer-way.

3 Ken Doctor, "The Newsonomics of the New York Times' Paywalls 2.0," *Nieman Lab*, November 21, 2013, www.niemanlab.org/2013/11/the-newsonomics-of-the-new-york-times-paywalls-2-0/.

4 Eric Wemple, "Editor Cites Successes of Weeklong Homepage Deactivation at New York Times," *Washington Post*, June 23, 2015, www.washingtonpost.com/blogs/erik-wemple/wp/2015/06/23/editor-cites-successes-of-weeklong-home page-deactivation-at-new-york-times/.

5 Rick Edmonds, "Continued Digital Subscription Surge Carries New York Times Co. to Another Strong Quarter," Poynter, February 8, 2018, www.poynter.org/business-work/2018/continued-digital-subscription-surge-carries-new-york-times-co-to-another-strong-quarter/.

6 Sarah Scire, "Readers Reign Supreme, and Other Takeaways from the New York Times End-of-Year Earnings Report," *Nieman Lab*, February 6, 2020, www.nie manlab.org/2020/02/readers-reign-supreme-and-other-takeaways-from-the-new-york-times-end-of-year-earnings-report/.

7 Laura Hazard Owen, "'Here's What Else You Need to Know Today': The New York Times Launches a Flash Audio Briefing and Other Voice Stuff for Alexa," *Nieman Lab*, January 11, 2019, www.niemanlab.org/2019/01/heres-what-else-you-need-to-know-today-the-new-york-times-launches-a-flash-audio-briefing-and-other-voice-stuff-for-alexa/.

8 Chris Argyris and Donald Schön, *Theory in Practice: Increasing Professional Effectiveness* (San Francisco, CA: Jossey-Bass, 1992).

9 Pablo Boczkowski, *Digitizing the News: Innovation in Online Newspapers* (Boston, MA: MIT Press, 2015).

10 Boczkowski.

11 Argyris and Schön.

12 Argyris and Schön, 12.

13 Edgar Schein, *Organizational Culture and Leadership*, 4th ed. (Edison, NJ: Jossey-Bass, 2010), 126.

14 Ralph Stacey, *Complexity and Creativity in Organizations* (San Francisco, CA: Berrett-Koehler, 1996), 102.

15 Darryl Holliday, "Metrics to Match Our Mission: Measuring City Bureau's Impact," *City Bureau*, February 12, 2020, www.citybureau.org/notebook/2020/2/12/metrics-to-match-our-mission-measuring-city-bureaus-impact.

16 Holliday.

17 Andrew D. Brown and Ken Starkey, "Organizational Identity and Learning: A Psychodynamic Perspective," *Academy of Management Review* 25, no. 1 (January 1, 2000), 102–120.

18 Eric Ries, *The Lean Startup* (New York, NY: Crown Business, 2011), 8–9.

19 Ries, 62.

20 Aaron Edwards, "Creating Editorial Process before a Finished Product," *Buzz-Feed*, March 26, 2015, www.buzzfeed.com/aaronedwards/app-app-app-like-you-dont-care#.ggbN7zQP3N.

21 Edwards.

22 Ries, 42–44.

23 Ries, 126.

24 Damon Kiesow, "What It Really Means to Shift to Reader Revenue," American Press Institute, October 2, 2018, www.americanpressinstitute.org/reader-revenue/what-it-really-means-to-shift-to-reader-revenue/.

25 Clayton Christensen, *The Innovator's Dilemma: When Technologies Cause Great Firms to Fail* (Boston, MA: Harvard Business School Publishing, 2016).

26 Clayton M. Christensen and Michael E. Raynor, *The Innovator's Solution: Creating and Sustaining Successful Growth* (Boston, MA: Harvard Business School Press, 2003), 32–35.

27 Christensen and Raynor, 74–75.

28 Andrew A. King and Baljir Baatartogtokh, "How Useful Is the Theory of Disruptive Innovation?" *MIT Sloan Management Review*, September 15, 2015, https://sloanreview.mit.edu/article/how-useful-is-the-theory-of-disruptive-innovation/.

29 Amar Bhidé, "Clay Christensen's Theories are Great for Entrepreneurs, but Not Executives," *Quartz*, October 9, 2014, https://qz.com/278155/clay-christensens-theories-are-great-for-executives-but-not-entrepreneurs/.

30 Millie Tran, "Revisiting Disruption: 8 Good Questions with Clayton Christensen," American Press Institute, January 24, 2014, www.americanpressinstitute.org/publications/good-questions/revisiting-disruption-8-good-questions-clayton-christensen/.

31 Christensen and Raynor, 45–46.

32 Steve M. Barkin, *American Television News: The Media Marketplace and the Public Interest* (Armonk, NY: M.E. Sharpe, 2003), 110.

33 Steven Johnson, *Where Good Ideas Come from: The Natural History of Innovation* (New York, NY: Riverhead Books, 2010), 30–31.

34 Ellis, Justin, "The Texas Tribune Is 5 Years Old and Sustainable. Now What?" *Nieman Lab*, November 3, 2014, www.niemanlab.org/2014/11/the-texas-tribune-is-5-years-old-and-sustainable-now-what/.

35 Christine Schmidt, "By Mass-Texting Local Residents, Outlier Media Connects Low-Income News Consumers to Useful, Personalized Data," *Nieman Lab*, March 1, 2018, www.niemanlab.org/2018/03/by-mass-texting-local-residents-outlier-media-connects-low-income-news-consumers-to-useful-personalized-data/.

36 Christine Schmidt, "Text-for-Housing-Data Service Outlier Media and Muck-Rock Combine to Close More Information Gaps Around the Country," *Nieman Lab*, January 27, 2020, www.niemanlab.org/2020/01/text-for-housing-data-service-outlier-media-and-muckrock-combine-to-close-more-information-gaps-around-the-country/.

37 Alan M. Rubin, "Uses-and-Gratifications Perspective on Media Effects," in *Media Effects: Advances in Theory and Research*, eds. Jennings Bryant and Mary Beth Oliver (New York, NY: Routledge, 2009), 165–184.

38 Esther Thorson and Margaret Duffy, "Newspapers in the New Media Environment," Presentation to the NAA Marketing Conference, Orlando, Florida, March 22, 2005.

39 Thorson and Duffy.

40 Ries, 140.

41 Confidential interview, personal communication, May 9, 2008.

42 Stacey, 13.

43 Michael Fishman, *Manufacturing the News* (Austin, TX: University of Texas Press, 1980); Gaye Tuchman, *Making News: A Study in the Construction of Reality* (New York: Free Press, 1978).

44 See Tuchman; Pamela Shoemaker and Stephen Reese, *Mediating the Message in the 21st Century* (New York, NY: Routledge, 2014); Michael Schudson, *The Sociology of News* (New York, NY: W.W. Norton & Co., 2003), among others.

45 Erin Kissane and Brian Boyer, "NPR's Brian Boyer on Building and Managing News Apps Teams," *Source*, November 6, 2013, https://source.opennews.org/en-US/articles/boyer-interview/.

46 Kissane and Boyer.

47 Broussard.

48 Levander.

49 Levander.

50 Jeff Sonderman and Tom Rosenstiel, "A Culture-Based Strategy for Creating Innovation in News Organizations," American Press Institute, May 27, 2015, www.americanpressinstitute.org/publications/reports/white-papers/culture-based-innovation/.

51 Sonderman and Rosenstiel.

52 Levander.

53 Jay Rosen and Melody Kramer, "Jay Talks to Melody Kramer, NPR's Social Media Strategist," *Studio 20*, NYU, December 4, 2014, https://nyustudio20.wordpress.com/2014/12/04/jay-talks-to-melody-kramer-nprs-social-media-strategist/.

54 NPR Social Media Desk, https://socialmediadesk.tumblr.com/.

55 Ries, 183.

56 Argyris and Schön, xvi–xvii.

57 Everett Rogers, *Diffusion of Innovations*, 5th ed. (New York, NY: Free Press, 2003), 18–19.

58 Rogers, 15–16.

59 Rogers, 169.

60 Sonderman and Rosenstiel.

61 Broussard.

62 Levander.

Part Two – Page Views Are Not Enough

The sound of a bell ringing, followed by a smattering of applause, echoed in the usually quiet *Monitor* newsroom during our 2012 visit—a muted celebration that csmonitor.com had once again hit 1 million page views in a single day.

In many ways, the early transition to being digital-centric had been a resounding success. Traffic goals had been met or exceeded, catapulting the *Monitor* into a much more prominent position in the national news landscape. By December 2011, the newsroom had hit 30 million page views in a month, well above the original 25-million-per-month goal. A large screen in the newsroom tracked real-time traffic to the site for all to see, serving as a constant reminder that digital audience growth was the top priority.

The newfound sense of relevance had helped create at least some buy-in among even the most reticent of curmudgeons. It built confidence that the newsroom could achieve its goals through experimentation and testing, which was empowering, even though many still worried about the costs to quality and sanity.

But these early feelings of efficacy and hopefulness soon began to fade. About three years after the web initiative had begun, the payoff had yet to come, that hoped-for moment when revenue from increased traffic would allow the newsroom to expand or at least feel more secure in its financial footing. The focus on metrics had allowed the organization to track its strategic goals more precisely. But those numbers revealed a persistent struggle to move visitors from drive-by consumers to engaged members of the *Monitor*'s online community.

And if page views alone weren't enough to bring in needed revenue from advertising, the *Monitor* would have to develop a new strategy to build loyal readership. The struggle opened the door to discussions about engagement, an idea that would require a deeper focus on understanding audience needs. Although less dramatic than killing off the daily print edition, this transition would prove harder, as it required a more fundamental rethinking of the role of journalists to a frame that prioritized the needs of news consumers over a reporter's instincts.

There remained a cultural struggle over identity. On the one hand, the drive for page views had already made *Monitor* staffers more conscious of their readers than they had been during the print era, an important step toward change. But a push for engagement and loyalty required more effort and a more nuanced approach than, say, ensuring that search keywords appear in a headline. There was no simple recipe for producing results.

Even some of those who had initially resisted the push to use strategies such as search engine optimization (SEO) to drive traffic missed the "instant gratification and barometer of success watching the page-view numbers jump when we hit something just right," one said.[1]

As one staffer reflected on a later visit:

> The page views are kind of like a heroin high, you know? We were moving the financial needle as we never had moved it before. ... It was attractive because it was a metric, it was something, it was a lever that you could pull. I pull this; this comes out.[2]

From a cultural perspective, change is hard, but continuous change is even harder, producing fatigue and doubt, even in a newsroom that has come to value experimentation. Once *Monitor* journalists had finally become accustomed to chasing page views and being rewarded for growing them, it was hard to pivot to a different goal.

A NEW STRATEGY OF DISTINCTION

Newsroom management had developed a new strategic document that highlighted a guiding principle for the organization
moving forward: "We need to sharpen the visible brand distinction of the *Monitor* in a way that builds audience."[3]

This guiding principle included five chief goals for
csmonitor.com:

1 Redesigning the home page.
2 Improving the visibility of distinctive *Monitor* content and
  features, such as the solutions-oriented People Making
  A Difference.
3 Changing traffic-driving commodity content to better
  reflect the *Monitor*'s historic mission.
4 Developing a new brand marketing message.
5 Connecting the audience with the staff.[4]

Among the other imperatives identified: subscriptions, new
referral mechanisms beyond Google, and new profit niches
such as verticals—niches of content focused on specific topic
areas that could be sold to sponsors.

A closer review of website analytics sought to identify which
visitors might become immersed beyond a single story. But
it wasn't easy. A preliminary analysis found that those who
came back nine or more times a month—the visitors whom
the organization had historically classified as the most loyal
users—were interested in the same content that also drew
the drive-by audiences, or those visited once or twice
a month. "We have not yet carved out an explicit reason why
readers should come back to us," one editor told us in 2012.
"We're in the process of trying to do that."[5]

The newsroom put together a "home page team," which
included leaders from editorial and publishing, to determine
how to communicate the brand's distinctiveness more clearly
and quickly on the landing page of csmonitor.com. This kind
of collaboration across the traditional "wall" was becoming
increasingly common; although newsroom leaders were

careful to ensure that advertisers couldn't influence the content of stories, they recognized that internal communication across these traditionally-separate departments in pursuit of common goals was vital. One interviewee told us, "You know, it's a marriage of survival. It's what you have to do."[6]

In a May 2012 team meeting, one of the managers explained the home-page strategy:

> Here's two things, two assumptions we want to test, right? One,
> that this [home-page content] is our most distinctive content. This is
> the right content to use to differentiate us. And two, that making
> a more obvious home page will draw return business.[7]

It was an example of the test-and-prove mindset that had begun to take hold. In 2009, the home page averaged about 40,000 page views per day. By 2012, the home-page average had edged upward to 50,000 per day—a level below what the staff had expected.[8] Some initial experiments for building brand loyalty offered hope, though. An in-depth magazine cover story on prisons that took about four months to put together scored thousands of page views after being posted on the home page.

The newsroom had also begun experimenting with Visual Revenue, a tool to recommend story placement on the home page to improve click-through rates. As page views had filtered into the lexicon, the newsroom had become more comfortable quantifying some aspects of layout and topic choice, incorporating algorithms and analytics into a process that had previously been the sole purview of editors.

Loyalty—defined by the *Monitor* staff as how often people returned to the site in a month—was now viewed as a key metric. Data systems are critical for strategic accountability, and the *Monitor*'s had been lacking when it came to generating a clear understanding of what specific actions would make readers more likely to return. Though the analytics system helped the newsroom see how people were accessing their content, it had limitations. For example, the inability to track people who had reached the website through social media made it difficult to discern how the investment of time and resources into the platforms was helping.

The talk of improving brand distinction also revealed a need for a clearer focus, one easily understood by all. As one staffer told us in 2013:

> What was frustrating for me ... was that we didn't have, like, a vision. I wasn't really clear where we were going. We were just sort of stumbling around—actually, *stumbling*'s too harsh—but this organization needs to make money.[9]

Although experimenting with a multi-pronged approach made sense, trying so many tactics at once left some wondering about the clarity of the overall strategy. It was the type of disruptive polychronic shift that Edgar Schein describes.[10] At the *Monitor*, it made it difficult for individuals to tease out priorities for their own work. As one editor told us in 2014,

> For management, that's really difficult to say, 'Now we have four engines of revenue we're trying to drive, and we need to drive them all, you know?' ... It's hard for people ... to get more than one idea going. It's tough.[11]

ENGAGING THE AUDIENCE TO BUILD LOYALTY

The *Monitor*'s leadership recognized that building loyalty and trust required greater connection with the audience, and therefore a deeper commitment to listening to readers and allowing them to participate in meaningful ways in the news process.

Here, the newsroom had struggled. Even more than other news organizations, it had long prided itself on being above the media noise, offering a more cerebral and dispassionate take on the day's news. In the fall of 2010, the newsroom turned on unmoderated comments for all stories. Comments on the site, run through the Disqus system, were not visible immediately; users had to click through to see them. By December 13, 2010, there were 3,640 commenters,

13,500 comments, and 41,000 "likes" on comments. Staffers—especially bloggers—were advised to check the comment threads shortly after posting, but interviews indicated that few did so regularly.

No formal guidance was given for integrating comments into the everyday workflow. As with so many items in the digital age, new tasks that aren't considered journalistic don't necessarily translate into "work." It is instead seen as another task to be added to the growing list of daily duties. When innovation feels piled on, it sparks resistance among those on the front line who are already uncomfortable because they have to learn new routines.

Several *Monitor* journalists said they saw themselves as too busy to review audience feedback and generally had a negative attitude about comments: "Every once in a while, we'll get the golden platonic example of what a comment should be—but not that often," one writer said, echoing the sentiments of several colleagues. "And so, because of that, and because of my own bias against online comments, I have not been impressed by any critical mass of comments, nor what's actually said in them."[12] Staffers were reluctant to become referees moderating arguments or fact-checking mistaken assumptions among commenters.

One editor told us:

> When I think of our mainstream reader—certainly like our print
> subscriber—they're not going to go on there and think, 'These are
> my people. This is my community.' They're gonna think, 'Who are
> these wackos?' ... It's not worse than anywhere else. They're just
> people, you know. Most of the people who comment are largely kind
> of polarized people, and everything quickly dissolves into just
> a general ideological thing.[13]

Although staffers would review comments flagged by users as offensive, the overall hands-off approach to comments gave readers little incentive toward civility or meaningful contributions. Research on commenting has found that there is little point to having comments if journalists ignore them;

offering readers a space for feedback and conversation without proper cultivation breeds distrust.[14]

By September 2012, the newsroom had changed its approach to comments on the website: The function would be off by default; a blogger or writer had to turn on the commenting feature intentionally. "We've made this change after extensive analysis of the comments our articles have received over the past two years," editor John Yemma explained in a blog post. "Some have been thoughtful. Some have added useful information or pointed out our mistakes. Thank you for those. But many comments have been non-productive."[15]

Essentially, audience engagement through interaction was an afterthought. The *Monitor* periodically gestured at the idea in its strategic memos and emails, but it ultimately was treated as secondary. The key measure was readership, not participation. With such an emphasis, it would remain difficult to move the audience down the path of increasing loyalty.

THE STRUGGLE WITH SOCIAL MEDIA

Social media provided another opportunity for engaging with the audience, but this, too, was not prioritized by the newsroom as a whole, even though training on how to best use the platforms was offered.

Since Jimmy Orr's tenure, the online department's traffic-growth strategy included several social media platforms such as Facebook, Twitter, LinkedIn, YouTube, and Digg. By our May 2012 visit, the organization had at least 80,000 fans on its institutional accounts, 56,000 of whom were connected to the *Monitor*'s primary Facebook page,[16] and the online department had begun working more closely with the business side to improve its effectiveness in social spaces. Lane Brown had taken a newly created position of social media manager to oversee strategy across publishing and editorial, and she worked closely with Pat Murphy, of the newsroom's online department, to co-manage the Facebook page. The team also had help from a consultant who conducted a weekly analysis of social media analytics and offered recommendations about posts and promotions. Although the information offered a fresh external perspective, managers questioned and dismissed recommendations that they felt did not jibe with cultural norms.

More broadly, Brown—who had worked as a public-relations professional before coming to the *Monitor*—had begun training the staff to think more deliberately about social media, with tutorials on Twitter and Facebook. The team also encouraged people to become early adopters of Google+ as a way to drive traffic to the site. But widespread, consistent social media use by the majority of individual writers and editors did not take hold. Even as many individual reporters at places like the *New York Times* embraced social media to build their personal brands and interact with audiences, only a few *Monitor* reporters jumped in enthusiastically. And instead of being conversational, most social media use across the organization was primarily promotional. Such an approach can help boost traffic, but it is less valuable for building loyalty and trust.

In April 2012, 3 million page views came in from Facebook alone,[17] and as the home-page team was trying to encourage repeat visitors, so, too, was the social media team trying to build a community on the Facebook page. In fact, some considered the Facebook presence an extension of the home page.[18] The Facebook audience, however, offered a different kind of feedback; the conversation started to reveal cracks in the page-view strategy, as some readers vented their frustration about the multi-screen galleries, quizzes, and lists.

There were some deliberate efforts to interact and ask the audience for feedback on content, particularly on Facebook. Every Wednesday, for example, the social team offered a "caption post," which featured a news photo for the audience to caption.[19] It did active monitoring on the Facebook page, adopting a three-strikes-and-you're-out policy.[20] But these efforts stayed mostly siloed off from the rest of the newsroom.

With a smaller newsroom, the requests to participate on social media fell upon some who felt there were too many innovations to try, too many demands that pulled away from the core task of reporting, writing, and editing news stories.

VENTURING INTO OTHER CONTENT AREAS

The newsroom also experimented with new blog formats to try to connect with audiences in a more collaborative way. In April 2012, the *Monitor* launched Modern Parenthood, a blog written by correspondent Stephanie Hanes that would eventually bring in thousands of page views via Facebook. Hanes shared the blog's collaborative mission on the inaugural post:

> A few of us at the *CS Monitor* decided recently that we wanted to try something different. We were talking about some of the stories we had worked on in the past months about kids and families. ... We started talking about you, as well. Yup, *you*. All of you readers—and there were just tons of you—who shared your own stories, argued with us, asked questions, and wanted more. More stories that explored parenting and family culture and growing up, but with the *Monitor*'s signature approach of reporting with compassion and diligence; reporting that was global in both spirit and practice.
>
> We realized we wanted to keep the conversation going. And so we decided to start this blog as a community for parents, grandparents, friends—anyone, really—who believes in raising compassionate and engaged global citizens.[21]

Despite the use of the word "conversation" in Hanes' inaugural post, many in the newsroom maintained a gatekeeper mentality, describing their role as explaining the world to its audience.

In addition to blogs, newsletters had become a bigger part of the strategy because they provided a way to push content to readers in a more convenient way. A BizTech newsletter had close to 24,000 subscribers by May 2012, although the click-through rate was not high—about 1,000 people would click on something within the newsletter. A popular post might get 5,000 page views through the newsletter.[22]

One of the most important parts of the new strategy was the push to develop verticals. With the growing realization that additional revenue from on-page advertising would require an endless treadmill of effort without a commensurate payoff, a new innovation team worked to develop data-driven content ideas that could be monetized more efficiently.

On the organizational chart, a new position to bridge the worlds of editorial and publishing had been carved out to lead the verticals push: new ventures editor. Matt Clark, a former international editor who had begun pursuing an MBA, moved into the new post and began working with Abe McLaughlin, a former correspondent who had moved to the publishing side in 2008 after earning his MBA. The duo effectively became R&D for content products as an innovation team.

That team reviewed 509 stories about politics and elections from 2011, and discovered that during the last quarter of that year, posts that explained a political topic or issue garnered the most page views.[23] They decided to build an explainer product using the already established *Monitor* brand DC Decoder, which had begun as a column by Peter Grier, a veteran Washington reporter who had been with the *Monitor* since 1979. Over the next year, several reporters contributed explainers under the DC Decoder umbrella, and the effort won some loyal fans. A 2013 analysis found that 30% of the column's readers online were loyal readers who read more stories than average visitors to the site.[24] By August 2013, the DC Decoder newsletter had about 9,000 subscribers with an email open rate of 35%.

The goal was to generate more such wrappers for content sections, with niches on national security (August 2013) and the economy (November 2013). For the newsroom to buy into the verticals concept, journalists had to see these ventures go beyond mere plays for sponsors.

One vertical, Energy Voices, prompted some conflict. It concentrated on energy issues and showcased *Monitor* content alongside clearly designated "Sponsor Content" from such groups as the American Coalition for Clean Coal Electricity, an advocacy group of coal producers, distributors, and utility companies.[25]

One business-side manager told us at the time:

> You have a disconnect between the business model, which is a low-
> revenue and therefore it's gotta be low-cost business model, and
> the reality of your talent pool, which is they're experienced and
> expensive. So what we're trying to do now ... is build a business
> model that supports the experience and the knowledge that our
> staff has and takes advantage of it, and gets people to pay for it.[26]

DIVERSIFYING REVENUE

The innovation team had also discovered that professionals were using the *Monitor* as a source for international information while at work, and staffers began to think about more verticals that would satisfy those needs. In 2013, some *Monitor* staff compiled a "global security" forecast that analyzed the top three threats in several regions around the world. It provided the report for free in exchange for completing a survey, and half of the survey's approximately 2,500 respondents reported using the *Monitor* to help do their jobs more effectively.[27]

These initiatives sought to leverage the *Monitor*'s more experienced writers who did not necessarily write about topics with wide appeal to mass audiences. "If there's not a traffic model for those people writing about those more spinach-y topics, what do you do?" one staffer asked during an interview. "You either stop doing them, or you find ways to get paid for them."[28]

In the summer of 2013, the newsroom began talking with third-party resellers such as Nexis and EBSCOhost about providing premium content from the *Monitor*'s pool of staff writers and 190 correspondents. The staff also started tinkering with building a premium business-to-business (B2B) news product along the lines of the Economist Intelligence Unit, a part of the Economist Group devoted to research and analysis targeting the business sector. The new service, called World Business Monitor, would provide on-the-ground reports from various countries around the world to help businesses assess risk.[29] Another product, called Frontier Markets Monitor, began with specialized, forward-looking reports examining social-responsibility risks, political and security implications, and the business environment in West Africa and South Asia. In the initial stages, the *Monitor* relied on freelancers to put together these prototypes.

But these experimental initiatives revealed a flaw in the organizational structure. The management-by-team approach required a consensus among publishing and editorial leaders before major projects could gain backing and traction. For example, with DC Decoder, not a single point person in either editorial or publishing was accountable for its success or failure; it was seen as a joint experiment. As one staffer told us:

> There's no one person in charge. ... It's hard to sort of read the tea leaves, or understand what level of backing there is for certain things. Or one person does back it and the others don't, or they could change their mind; there's not one person saying, 'Here's where we're going, and here's what it is.'[30]

So while many new products and experiments were being launched, it wasn't clear that any of them would receive the kind of sustained backing needed for success, particularly since most new ventures require some time and consistent effort to build a significant audience. This type of frequent experimentation without extended commitment can also produce a kind of innovation fatigue among staffers inured to the excitement of new announcements and unsure where to place their efforts and hopes. Some also wondered whether such experiments strayed too far from the organization's original mission.

As 2014 began, the newsroom shifted even more resources toward the B2B initiatives, and reallocated two positions to cover cybersecurity for a vertical product. Despite the investments in the B2B product and other efforts at distinctiveness, financial results remained below targets. And the specter of layoffs loomed. Full-time positions had dropped below 70, although interns and temporary positions helped fill in the gaps.

CHANGE AT THE TOP

The end of 2013 brought another shock to the newsroom: After five years as the driver of the *Monitor*'s web-first transformation, Yemma told the newsroom that he was stepping down as editor in January 2014 to focus on writing. "Together with our partners on the publishing side, we've applied intelligence, energy, and creativity to a strategic shift that has preserved the values of *Monitor* journalism, expanded the *Monitor*'s reach, and strengthened it financially," Yemma said at the time.[31] "The humane, internationally-minded journalism envisioned by Mary Baker Eddy when she founded the *Monitor* in 1908 is on firm footing." The financial future, however, was anything but certain.

The Christian Science Board of Directors tapped managing editor Marshall Ingwerson as Yemma's replacement. Ingwerson, who had been with the organization since 1979 and had served as managing editor since 1999, had worked closely with Yemma, and long-term strategic initiatives begun under Yemma continued. Ingwerson left his previous position vacant; instead, he had the primary editors for international news, national news, online, and the weekly magazine serve as a management team.

Although Yemma's departure was a major cultural shift, some in the newsroom said they had become somewhat disillusioned with his leadership. Some noted in our interviews he was not communicating as regularly with the staff about the newsroom's direction as he had earlier in his tenure. Some staffers also felt there was a gap between his public pronouncements of success and the ongoing internal tension following the realization that the paper's bet on massive audience growth might fail.

Ingwerson's promotion showed that the board wanted the paper to continue in a similar vein; instead of hiring an outsider or someone with a reputation for boat-rocking, they went with a soothing pick for many of the long-time staffers who were Christian Scientists themselves, a leader with a strong connection with the paper's traditions and history. Besides his long tenure as an editor, Ingwerson had served as a foreign correspondent in Moscow and a national reporter in Washington, D.C. While managing editor, he led the team in 2006 that worked to get correspondent Jill Carroll out of harm's way after she had been kidnapped by Sunni insurgents in Iraq. Although almost eight years had passed, it remained one of the newsroom's high-profile success stories, one that people would draw upon as an example of the *Monitor*'s resilience.

Continuity is important to provide a sense of stability. At media chains where newsroom leaders are moved regularly, journalists learn to ride out the latest whims of the current leader while maintaining their own trusted routines for accomplishing work. But at the same time, long-time editors can sometimes lack the visionary ideas necessary to continue to push change along and may themselves be so deeply entrenched in the culture's underlying assumptions that they have a hard time executing on their strategies.

When trying to identify cultural markers, it is important to consider opinion leaders. The assertive Orr had left the newsroom, which caused the power to swing back toward some of the long-time newsroom stalwarts. As Dave Scott took over the online editorship, he adopted an experimental mindset but one firmly rooted in how the *Monitor* saw its core values, and his appointment signaled to the rest of the newsroom that there was no inherent contradiction between a web-first ethic and what it saw as high-quality journalism. But some wondered if he would push hard enough for continued innovation.

In 2014, the newsroom also suffered another leadership shock. Soon after our 2014 visit, national editor Cheryl Sullivan passed away after a short illness. Her obituary, subtitled "Epitome of leadership with grace," highlighted her career of more than three decades in the newsroom and noted, "Sullivan was a dynamic, kind leader who helped usher in the *Monitor*'s Web-first era."[32] Indeed, she had led the largest staff contingent in the newsroom and was admired throughout the news department for her ethical, hard-working approach to the news.

It was not clear what the long-term implications of losing Sullivan would be. But she had been a respected advocate for change during the web-first era, one whose decisions were rooted in the values of the journalistic craft with the acceptance of the need to adapt to this reality. As leaders, it is important to not underestimate how profoundly such a loss can affect the organizational psyche.

THE LOSS OF TRAFFIC

As the *Monitor* shifted more of its focus to verticals, its traffic to the more mainstream content began to decline. For example, as the business-news staff now contributed toward Monitor Global Outlook, the new iteration of the global intelligence product, they did not post as often on csmonitor.com. Fewer posts meant less traffic.

A redesigned *Monitor* website, launched in June 2014, had less emphasis on boosting depth of visit and page views, and more on improving user experience. It included a section of "editors' picks" on the home page to give readers a hand-selected guide to the headlines. But with fewer links to quizzes and galleries in the new design, page views dipped further, without a major improvement in bounce rate.[33] The team focused its resources on updating the desktop version of the site and did not optimize the *Monitor*'s mobile site. That choice proved to be a problem as smartphone users became a growing part of the visitor mix.

Other factors contributed to an overall drop in traffic in 2014. As part of its "Think. Share. Do" strategy, the *Monitor* had struck a deal with a small third-party vendor to promote taking action on *Monitor* stories, such as contacting members of Congress or contributing to causes, another nod toward distinction. "I think we'll be serving a fairly small universe," one editor told us. "But ... it signals that we're trying to be different in some way, and there'll be some percentage of readers that care about that."[34]

Google, however, initially viewed that tool as an improper way to spread links and downgraded csmonitor.com. By the time the *Monitor* clarified the issue with Google, it had lost page views and revenue. "One of the takeaways is that when you experiment with a small company that may not have the robust tech staff, you run some risks," a manager told us, "and that's what we saw."[35]

Visitors dropped to about 9 million per month.[36] Google changed its algorithm, making it more difficult for news organizations to use SEO to reach the top of search results. New, web-savvy competitors like Mic and Vox had also arrived on the scene and likely were siphoning off traffic as well, some newsroom staffers speculated.

APPLYING THE MODEL

A few years into the web-first transition, it was clear that achieving sustainability was going to be far more complex than expected. During the initial shift, when SEO was the top priority, new leadership combined with the threat of lay-offs shocked the culture out of its traditional mindset, and the page-view successes helped embed new routines in the newsroom. In 2012, the managing board made a rare visit to the *Monitor* office to congratulate the staff on the best financial performance in decades, reinforcing the historic nature of the changes.

But despite the improved financial picture, surpassing the 25-million-page-view target had not reaped all of the promised rewards, breeding suspicion among some staffers we talked with that leaders, particularly those on the business side of the organization, did not have a solid plan.

The new strategy, focused on loyalty and distinctiveness, seemed more palatable to those concerned with high-quality journalism. But it was also much less straightforward and required viewing the audience in a new way, one that required journalists to adopt a more humble posture when it came to their own news judgment—not an easy task. One reporter told us:

I have mixed feelings about it. On the one hand, as a journalist, it's always annoying that you can't just do whatever you want, or whatever you think is important or interesting. On the other hand, the readers are important.[37]

An editor offered an analogy:

You're at a dinner party, and someone says, 'How about the Somali pirates?' And, you could start—you could launch in and say, 'Yeah, I just wrote about that today. They're really cool and this is what happened today. They attacked an oil tanker today; it's the second this week.' Or, what we run into with some of our writers is, 'I wrote about that last month. I don't want to talk to you about that. Go read my story.' And that's sort of the old-school newspaper mentality that sometimes you run into with our writers—when you say you need to do another pirate story, and the writer says, 'I wrote about that last week, or last month.' You know, well, if you're at a dinner party, you never tell somebody, you know, 'Go read my story. Don't bother me.' …

So, for the first time … the readers are in our face like at a dinner party, saying, 'This is what I'm interested in. Tell me about it.' And as a reporter you can ignore them and tell them they're wrong, go read my other story. Or you can respond to them. So that's the adjustment. For the first time, I think, we are having to adjust to the reader in a way that we haven't had to before.[38]

Eventually, the newsroom's real-time analytics dashboard, a billboard amplifying the focus on traffic, was taken down, and the newsroom dispensed with "batting average" reports for individual staffers that focused on their most popular stories. In some ways, these changes were a relief to staffers, but some journalists had become accustomed to having such a clear indicator of the success or failure of a given story. Other metrics felt fuzzier and less satisfying.

Despite the effort to create a distinctive brand vision, most of the rank-and-file journalists did not see a single unifying thread to pull the disparate strategic ideas together. While the *Monitor* staffers have an enviable awareness of mission—they often reference it unprompted—"bless all mankind" is ambiguous, especially to people outside the faith. The mission affects how audiences and potential sponsors respond, many of whom are not familiar with the *Monitor* and mistake it for a religious publication.

One long-time staffer who is also a Christian Scientist told us: "What we've stood for is what we aren't. We aren't sensationalized."[39] But, as another interviewee noted, being defined by what you aren't makes it hard to establish a niche in a competitive digital information landscape.

Shortly before her death, Sullivan had spoken to a meeting of Christian Science church members in southern California about the *Monitor* and the overwhelming nature of world news. During her talk, she recalled driving with her husband to the airport to catch the flight for the church meeting. As she scanned the sky, dark clouds littered the horizon. Her husband pointed out one rimmed in silvery sunlight. "I thought, 'Wow, that is kind of an interesting way of thinking about the *Monitor*'," she told the group.

> It is the only newspaper on this planet that, yes, tells you that the dark clouds are out there, but insists that there is a sun, and sunlight of truth, behind it. ... When we do our coverage, our motive is always to have that insistence that the truth is shining in that dark place.[40]

Sullivan's vision was a lofty and ambitious one. But unless readers believed this too and showed a willingness to support the *Monitor* with their dollars and sustained attention, the organization would struggle to fulfill it.

NOTES

1 Confidential interview, personal communication, July 7, 2010.
2 Confidential interview, personal communication, March 17, 2015.
3 Confidential interview, personal communication, May 23, 2012.
4 Organization document, August 2013.
5 Confidential interview, personal communication, May 21, 2012.
6 Confidential interview, personal communication, December 1, 2009.
7 Confidential interview, personal communication, May 21, 2012.

8 Confidential interview, personal communication, May 21, 2012.

9 Confidential interview, personal communication, August 9, 2013.

10 Edgar Schein, *Organizational Culture and Leadership*, 4th ed. (San Francisco, CA: Jossey-Bass, 2010), 128–129.

11 Confidential interview, personal communication, August 6, 2014.

12 Confidential interview, personal communication, May 24, 2012.

13 Confidential interview, personal communication, May 21, 2012.

14 Natalie Jomini Stroud, Emily Van Duyn, Alexis Alizor, Alishan Alibhai, and Cameron Lang, "Comment Section Survey Across 20 News Sites," Engaging News Project, January 12, 2017, https://mediaengagement. org/wp-content/uploads/2017/01/Comment-Section-Survey-Across-20- News-Sites.pdf.

15 John Yemma, "A Word about Comments on CSMonitor.com," *Christian Science Monitor*, September 5, 2012, www.csmonitor.com/Commentary/ upfront-blog/2012/0905/A-word-about-comments-on-CSMonitor.com.

16 Confidential interview, personal communication, May 22, 2012.

17 Confidential interview, personal communication, May 22, 2012.

18 Email, February 9, 2012.

19 Confidential interview, personal communication, May 23, 2012.

20 Confidential interview, personal communication, May 23, 2012.

21 Stephanie Hanes, "Welcome to Modern Parenthood," *Christian Science Monitor*, April 9, 2012, www.csmonitor.com/The-Culture/Family/ Modern-Parenthood/2012/0409/Welcome-to-Modern-Parenthood.

22 Confidential interview, personal communication, May 24, 2012.

23 Confidential interview, personal communication, May 25, 2012.

24 Confidential interview, personal communication, August 6, 2013.

25 Evan Tracey, "EPA Regulations Will Raise Your Electric Bills, Threaten the Grid," *Christian Science Monitor*, September 10, 2012, www.csmonitor. com/Environment/Energy-Voices/2012/0910/EPA-regulations-will-raise- your-electric-bills-threaten-the-grid.

26 Confidential interview, personal communication, August 6, 2013.

27 Confidential interview, personal communication, August 5, 2013.

28 Confidential interview, personal communication, August 4, 2013.

29 Confidential interview, personal communication, August 4, 2013.

30 Confidential interview, personal communication, August 5, 2013.

31 David T. Cook, "New Editor Named to Lead the Christian Science Monitor," *Christian Science Monitor*, December 16, 2013, www.csmonitor. com/USA/2013/1216/New-editor-named-to-lead-The-Christian- Science-Monitor.

32 Staff, "Cheryl Sullivan: Epitome of Leadership with Grace," *Christian Science Monitor*, August 13, 2014, www.csmonitor.com/Commentary/ 2014/0813/Cheryl-Sullivan-Epitome-of-leadership-with-grace.

33 Confidential interview, personal communication, August 6, 2014.

34 Confidential interview, personal communication, August 6, 2014.

35 Confidential interview, personal communication, August 6, 2014.
36 Confidential interview, personal communication, August 6, 2014.
37 Confidential interview, personal communication, November 29, 2009.
38 Confidential interview, personal communication, December 1, 2009.
39 Confidential interview, personal communication, July 21, 2010.
40 Christian Science Publishing Society, "Meeting Excerpt, Cheryl Sullivan," n.d., http://dl.cdn.csps.com/am/2014/CSBD-scott_preller_ca_meeting-excerpt-140813.mp3.

Five

In 2017, the "whisper network" became a roar.

Women who had long confined their stories of sexual assault and harassment to private conversations with other women took to social media, using the hashtag #MeToo to share their experiences with powerful men like Harvey Weinstein, whose abusive behavior was exposed by the *New Yorker* and the *New York Times*.[1]

The Me Too movement began long before hashtags, under the leadership of Tarana Burke.[2] But when the social media floodgates opened, a long overdue national conversation began, and, as it had with #BlackLivesMatter, the power of the audience to drive media attention was again revealed. The Pew Research Center found that the #MeToo hashtag had been used more than 19 million times on Twitter since actress Alyssa Milano's October 2017 tweet urging victims to share their stories, through September 30, 2018.[3] *Time* magazine named Me Too activists Persons of the Year.[4]

Of all the changes journalists have grappled with over the past couple of decades, the increasingly participatory, two-way nature of news is among the most profound. New technologies and platforms allow users to broadcast their own messages, images, and videos to the world, and they can interact with, participate in, and even drive the news process. This transformation has made it all the more obvious that—as critics have long noted—journalists' reliance on official, bureaucratic sources limits their knowledge of the ways in which issues affect people's daily lives, particularly those who lack institutional power or who have been marginalized due to their gender, race, or class.

Acknowledging the crucial nature of nonprofessional voices in news is also one of the most disruptive changes *within* the newsroom itself. The increasing power of the audience to set the news agenda and engage in conversation both with each other and with the media upends the power of journalists as gatekeepers. *The Guardian* of London tracked this phenomenon during the 2011 London riots.[5] Analyzing more than 2.6 million tweets, researchers discovered the power of community influencers to affect understanding of rumors and information in breaking news. Many of those influencers were not journalists, just as Burke and other leaders of the Me Too movement were non-journalists who influenced coverage and national conversation for months and even years. These changes often bring a welcome array of new voices and perspectives that have long been left out of national and local news coverage. But they can also present challenges to newsrooms adapting in this new environment.

Digital business models demand closer listening to communities, as news organizations become increasingly reliant on subscribers, members, and regular visitors to their websites. In this landscape, journalists have to think differently and change their processes to engage members of the public and respond to their needs more deliberately. But this change in perspective does not come easily or quickly. The deeply embedded cultures at legacy organizations make it difficult to move toward a more audience-centric approach to news.

In this chapter, we will apply our model to this challenge facing so many newsrooms today as an example of how to think at the cultural, strategic, and innovation levels simultaneously. We will dig deeper into how you can use our model of change to shift your culture to one that embraces building deeper relationships with your audience and producing impact. It's also a good subject for a deeper dive because one analysis found that newsrooms that embraced audience participation were also more likely to embrace change generally.[6]

WHAT DOES ENGAGEMENT MEAN?

A key step in any meaningful change effort is fully understanding the change itself, whether it be technological, psychological, or industrial. Unfortunately, engagement remains a fluid concept with varying definitions in both academic and professional circles,[7] and each news organization will have to develop its own definition to guide its work. But over time, many engaged journalism practitioners have developed and tested some useful conceptions of engagement.

Joy Mayer, a full-time engagement strategist who runs the Trusting News project, offers this holistic definition: "a focus on, respect for and enthusiasm about the role of the audience."[8] In interviews with journalists, she found three primary kinds of engagement: *community outreach, conversation, and collaboration*. Community outreach goes beyond hoping the audience will find your work; it is taking your work to them, as well as identifying and meeting community information needs. Conversation involves engaging in dialogue, and convening forums and discussions with the community. Collaboration requires soliciting and utilizing user-generated content and actively involving users in editorial decision-making.

For example, Mayer worked with 14 newsrooms to test different ways of engaging via conversation on social media platforms to find out what strategies best build trust.[9] The organizations identified best practices, including not asking for more intimacy than you have earned, and being sure you are listening and taking action on the answers to any questions you posed. They learned the importance of respecting audience interests when choosing topics to chat about and recognizing that people come to different platforms with varying motivations. Journalists cannot force dialogue if the audience isn't interested.

Another useful definition comes from Lindsay Green-Barber, the founder and CEO of Impact Architects, a strategic consulting firm that incorporates entrepreneurial thinking into its work:

> Engaged journalism is an inclusive practice that prioritizes the information needs and wants of the community members it serves, creates collaborative space for the audience in all aspects of the journalistic process, and is dedicated to building and preserving trusting relationships between journalists and the public.[10]

Engagement isn't new; it builds on philosophies about the role of journalism in a democratic system that go back decades. In 1927, philosopher John Dewey wrote about how journalists need to engage the public to be active participants in democracy rather than passive recipients of information whose role was restricted to voting.[11] In the 1990s, the public or civic journalism movement garnered foundation support for newsrooms that engaged citizens in a variety of ways, such as through community forums that informed election coverage with a better understanding of the issues most important to voters. But these efforts largely faltered, and few news organizations changed their routines or coverage priorities outside of their participation in these occasional events.[12]

Engagement journalism is gradually growing in acceptance and practice in newsrooms. A 2011 survey of more than 500 newspaper leaders named audience engagement as a top priority, and over the next decade, organizations began focusing on this area. Job ads with titles such as "community engagement editor" or "audience engagement editor" have been increasingly appearing for news organizations of all kinds.[13]

Despite that progress, some of the same forms of resistance that stalled public or civic journalism remain. How do you coax your organization's naysayers? How does engagement fit into a larger strategy for sustainability, and how can you continually test and improve your efforts? Incorporating culture and strategy into your innovation efforts is key.

OVERCOMING CULTURAL RESISTANCE TO ENGAGEMENT

As we outlined in Chapter 2, any change requires that you first take the time to surface your organization's deep-seated values and underlying assumptions. What are you proposing that might threaten the identities of people in the newsroom?

In the case of engagement, cultures in news organizations often default to a professional perspective that privileges the journalist over the community. Even though the Internet effectively destroyed the gatekeeping model in which journalists alone decide what issues deserve public attention, it is hard for them to relinquish that authority because it contributes to their sense of professional efficacy and worth.

Detailed interviews with 67 journalists at two dozen leading national newspapers in 10 Western democracies revealed a profound ambivalence and conflicting attitudes toward audience participation in news.[14] While many journalists said contributions from their audience made their work more accurate, inclusive, and complete, many also noted the difficulty in verifying audience-provided information and moderating/limiting inappropriate or abusive statements. Many also worried that engagement efforts would drive journalists to pander to the lowest common denominator. In one study, just 14% of news workers surveyed in a mid-sized Midwestern city felt that community members should be considered a part of the news team, and many expressed skepticism about new job titles such as "community builder."[15]

Two-way information flow also means that to some extent, journalists are revealing something about the person behind the byline, a vulnerable position that can challenge professional norms of detachment. It is not a matter of just stepping back to let the readers contribute what they will; some mutual sharing is implied in a journalism in which building relationships and trust is the goal. For example, allowing comments on stories is just one step; fostering meaningful contributions over the long term means responding to comments and using them to inform future work. And hosting events to elicit input on issues of importance or concern to community members requires mutual exchange and conversation. It goes well beyond the traditional reporting task of attending a meeting and taking notes.

None of these process changes means compromising a journalist's independence, but nevertheless, they can prompt nervousness because standing apart from the story has long been the mantra of reporters seeking to avoid perceptions of bias. These habits are hard to break because journalists at some organizations have been punished for violating these norms.

Engaging and listening to communities can also be a blow to journalists' egos at times, and it is human to deflect criticism, especially in professional contexts.[16] Many reporters and editors have endured long hours and low wages because they believed their work was vital to uncovering wrongdoing and protecting their communities; indeed, their work often does drive better public policy or prevent corruption. But it can be demoralizing to learn that the work can sometimes be extractive—or even harmful—or hear that their slogans may be patronizing to many communities whose neighborhoods are often portrayed as violent or hopeless. Such evaluations can prompt defensiveness.

True engagement takes time. It is not easy or simple to achieve. Many reporters are overworked and rightfully suspicious of being asked to take on new tasks, especially if it takes time to see positive results, but that investment is necessary for engagement efforts to succeed. Understanding the sources of resistance to a new initiative is a key first step to overcoming it. Although we have identified common ways many newsrooms that we have studied resist engagement, uncover the specifics in your own newsroom. Each organization is different.

Think of ways to mesh with people's existing identities and underlying assumptions, especially when promoting new ideas. Start by framing engagement in the context of reporting, and show journalists how it can make the work they are already doing better. Instead of trying to sell people on a large philosophical shift, frame new ideas in the context of the existing work. Instead of pitching engagement as a completely new style of journalism, help reporters see it as a useful tool for finding story ideas or developing new sources.

ProPublica offers many examples of how building community relationships leads to new perspectives, more diverse sources, and ultimately better reporting. It regularly engages its readers as participants in its work, and it has won multiple Pulitzer Prizes and other accolades.[17] For example, students at two high schools helped ProPublica tell the story of resegregation in Tuscaloosa, Alabama, where nearly 1 in 3 black students attend a school that would have seemed more typical of the Jim Crow South.[18] Students at an integrated school and an all-black school documented their experiences with race and education with photos and six-word stories, with guidance from journalists. There was lasting impact: After the project, students proposed an exchange program to their superintendent that would allow them to continue to interact more with students from outside of their school.

In your own organization, look for pockets in the newsroom that have embraced aspects of engagement. In one newsroom we studied, we found pockets of innovation in the sports and photography departments, but those lessons were not being shared because those areas operated in silos apart from the rest of the newsroom.[19] In your organization, be sure to highlight and share engagement successes.

Be explicit about how new efforts reflect core values. In the case of engagement, one of the core principles of journalism Bill Kovach and Tom Rosenstiel identified in *The Elements of Journalism* was the need to make important news interesting and relevant.[20] The public needs entry points that help them understand how an issue affects their lives and why they should pay attention.

An example used regularly in the Committee of Concerned Journalists' newsroom training based on Kovach and Rosenstiel's book was how a property tax hike affects apartment dwellers. A dry report chronicling the back-and-forth of a city council meeting addressing this issue doesn't do much to engage non-insiders, and younger people who don't own homes yet are especially likely to wonder why this matters to them. But a journalist who listens to and engages the community at all points in the reporting, publication, and post-publication process is most likely to understand how to make this story relevant to readers of all demographic stripes.

In other words, community engagement can offer a way out of the classic conundrum of giving people what they want versus what they need. If you understand what information is most relevant to people's lives, you can earn their attention without resorting to cats or the Kardashians.

THE PROCESS OF INTEGRATING ENGAGEMENT

The connection between engagement efforts and core values needs to be communicated clearly and frequently. People should be encouraged to raise concerns and hash out ways to make new initiatives most successful in the context of your organizational identity. In most of our work with newsrooms, we have found a consistent disconnect between how much bosses felt they had communicated and what their staff heard. Leaders should not be afraid to repeat key points because people need multiple opportunities to understand what is desired from them and how it fits with their own goals and workflow.

All internal stakeholders should be involved early on in engagement projects. When American Public Media attempted its first iteration of a community-based platform called the Idea Generator to discuss social issues, it chose its Marketplace program as the first place to try the new engagement tool. But people involved with that program had not been involved in the early planning stages, and at launch time, they told us they struggled to see how it fit in with their mission of delivering a daily radio show about business.[21]

Leaders should reinforce the strategic importance of the shift to engagement in their organizations through recalibrated routines and incentives. In another newsroom we worked with, editors said they wanted all reporters to have blogs and update the website regularly, but leaders provided no guidance to help reporters figure out how to incorporate that work into the daily routine of writing for the print edition.[22] The reporters had to take it upon themselves to have an after-hours meeting to brainstorm. A meeting with reporters *and* editors at the beginning of the process that focused on how to incorporate engagement into the daily workflow would have been better.

HOW DOES ENGAGEMENT FIT INTO YOUR STRATEGY?

In addition to overcoming internal resistance, it's also important to assess how your innovative engagement efforts will fit into your larger strategy and your organization's position in the competitive landscape. For example, building the kind of trust and loyalty necessary to garner subscriptions or memberships also fosters readers who are more engaged in content and ads—a win for all departments.[23]

Even as news organizations are continually forced to cut costs, they must invest in serving communities if they hope to differentiate themselves in an increasingly fragmented media landscape.[24] Many news organizations like the *Huffington Post* and BuzzFeed are turning to membership programs instead of subscriptions for a new revenue stream that relies even more on building relationships with the audiences.[25] *The Guardian* made money for the first time in its recent history with its focus on memberships, which required careful testing of its pitch for contributions with readers as well as understanding that many donors want a less transactional relationship with news organizations.[26] For example, the organization learned that many members were motivated by keeping the journalism free for others to read rather than getting exclusive access.

As Jeff Jarvis argues in his book *Geeks Bearing Gifts*, chasing a mass audience is an increasingly unappealing strategy for all but a few media behemoths as ad rates online and on mobile remain low and the use of ad blockers is surging.[27] Content that is replicated across the web or derivative of others' work doesn't pay online, where distribution costs are nil and the supply of "good enough" journalism—journalism that satisfies the basic need-to-know of the audience in the way they want it—is high. Therefore, he argues, the key to economic sustainability lies in building relationships and treating news not as a product to be consumed passively, but as a service that helps people do things.

Building community across platforms is also one of three strategic priorities for community news organizations outlined by University of North Carolina's Penelope Abernathy, a former *New York Times* and *Wall Street Journal* executive, in her book *Saving Community Journalism*.[28]

For people to pay for news, organizations have to explain why their audiences should care and how they can use the information, argues Abernathy. Segment your readers into groups/communities and understand the precise value each is getting—or wants to be getting—from the news, and then show how the organization is actually delivering on this promise. Treat people as more than just sources for stories to find out what their concerns or passions are. Rachel Davis Mersey of Northwestern University argues that the web has ushered in a shift in priorities from communities defined by geographic location to communities brought together by individual interests; the key is being closely connected enough with your readers to know what those interests are.[29]

Abernathy writes:

> The challenge for editors trying to build community based on geographic identity is getting readers to "care about" the journalism. In contrast, when building communities based on social interests, the journalistic challenge is figuring out how best to connect readers with the content, each other, and the newspaper, as well as with advertisers who want to reach them.[30]

A loyal, engaged audience also allows you to make a better argument for higher digital advertising rates. Advertisers increasingly realize that interruption and repetition aren't as effective and are looking to engage in spaces where the audience is already accustomed to interacting with a trusted brand.[31]

ENGAGEMENT AS A REVENUE GENERATOR

The *Arizona Daily Star* created an independent digital startup, *This is Tucson*, to serve women in Tucson under 40, a poorly reached market segment for its work. Led by Irene McKisson, the team interviewed a diverse group of around 30 women to understand their information needs and how and when they typically accessed news.[32] They developed a detailed persona of their target audience members' characteristics and identified her biggest problem: finding relatively inexpensive things to do with kids in the city.

Just three-and-a-half years after it launched, *This is Tucson's* audience reach hit 300,000 people a month, in a city of around 500,000. With a staff of six, it is set to break even near the end of the year. Because its ads are also tailored toward its well-researched target persona, they have high click-through rates as well as success with content sponsorships. Even as the pandemic shut down events and activities in early 2020, the team's deep knowledge of its audience served as a guide to creating lists of vital resources and meeting people's more immediate needs.[33]

News organizations that connect closely with their audiences and discuss topics in approachable, engaging ways also reduce the mental load associated with news consumption, researchers have found.[34] While people may say in surveys they are interested in stories on government and politics, dense pieces tailored to insiders lead them to skip these stories for lighter fare. The answer isn't to necessarily offer them lighter fare; it is to find ways to reduce cognitive burdens by producing content that is easier to grasp quickly.

Engagement also isn't just for smaller news organizations or non-profits. In a strategy memo to staff in October 2015, the *New York Times* emphasized the importance of engaging readers as a key piece of its goal to double digital revenue by 2020.[35] Unlike other newsrooms that were doubling down on volume to juice ad revenues, the *Times* declared it was more focused on building a loyal audience that was more likely to subscribe. The paper's success in accomplishing this goal in the ensuing years—and its concurrent growth in digital revenue—points toward the validity of this strategy even at organizations with a broad audience.[36]

HOW CAN YOU CONTINUE TO EVOLVE?

The cultural and strategic levels help you keep the internal and external big pictures in mind as you think about how to incorporate engagement efforts into the newsroom. The innovation level helps you identify how to learn continuously about the best ways to make engagement work in your community.

Any engagement effort starts with listening. Understanding community information needs and developing relationships involves spending time talking to people outside the context of reporting or interviewing for a specific story. There are numerous models for doing this well. The Listening Post Collective advocates beginning with a walk around a neighborhood to see where people congregate and how they share information by analog means; it has also developed a set of specific questions to assess information needs, and advocates setting up listening posts at parks or community centers with prompts inviting people to share their concerns.[37]

Listening is not a one-and-done proposition, however, and there is no simple recipe for engagement. For example, social media platforms and their level and type of use among different demographic groups are evolving continuously, and your processes and techniques will need to change accordingly. And each community has different needs and past relationships with your organization.

Can you create a system that will allow you to quickly test different approaches to, say, a crowdsourcing effort? Could you conduct an A/B test to evaluate different word choices on a pitch for a recurring membership? Instead of waiting for a comprehensive engagement plan, what can you start doing today that you can then quickly assess and tweak as you go along? Social media and engagement editors pay close attention to many data points to see how readers are responding, from the wording of a headline on Facebook to the results from a community dialogue in a physical space, and rapidly assess each tweak's efficacy.

As we talked about culture, we discussed identifying respected employees in your organization who understand the need for transformation and are open to new ways of accomplishing work. These are the opinion leaders whose voices will help innovations spread throughout your organization, the people who will experiment with engagement and share their successes and failures with the rest of the staff.[38] They are the keys to innovation taking hold.

News organizations are also learning more about how to track qualitative metrics like impact to measure the efficacy of engagement efforts; continuous improvement requires a way to systematically assess progress. Green-Barber, formerly of the Center for Investigative Reporting, built the open-source Impact Tracker that helps news organizations easily record the changes associated with their work and track their progress over time.[39]

A SEQUENTIAL MODEL FOR ENGAGING A COMMUNITY

Philip Napoli, professor of public policy at Duke, developed a sequential model for understanding how audience engagement moves from cognitive awareness to tangible behavior and action. We like Napoli's model because it breaks down the large and intimidating goal of developing a more engaged audience into discrete stages; each one can be strategically tackled. His multi-phase path follows a psychological, emotional progression that establishes a connection between audience and organization. It begins with awareness of the brand and moves through interest, exposure, attentiveness, loyalty, appreciation, emotion, recall, attitude, and, finally, behavior.[40] In advertising circles, the *behavior* stage is often seen as conversion in the form of purchasing or embracing a product or service; for news organizations, it could be subscribing or becoming a member.

Using Napoli's model as a guide, we have created a modified path to engagement specifically for content-driven organizations that integrates elements from his model with ideas from media-usage and user-experience research. As we noted earlier, Everett Rogers' work has shown that embracing an innovation is a social communication process that requires understanding how people fit new ideas into their lives.[41] We believe that process is also at work when someone adopts a source into their informational lives. Some researchers have documented the importance of habit strength in media choice: Once users have decided on a particular device or media outlet they are going to go to regularly, they will stick with it because they don't want to make that choice over and over.[42] Integrating those ideas inspired a five-stage path toward building engagement.

Creating a social journalism community

By being *authentic* and *transparent* with their journalism, news organizations can establish *credibility* and earn *trust* to build community.

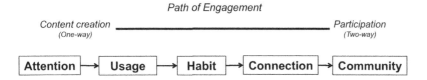

Figure 5.1 The path of engagement

Attention

With the explosion of competition from websites, social media, and apps, it has become ever more difficult for media creators to connect with distracted, fragmented audiences. In the past, news organizations had a built-in advantage; in local markets, they were one of few options for information and entertainment, a competitive advantage driven by the fact that few people had access to a printing press or broadcast tower. Today, legacy brands still have name recognition, but they must foster a sense of openness to connect with younger generations who have grown up participating in social media throughout their lives on more personalized devices.

The first stage of engagement, as Napoli notes, is making sure your organization is heard in the crowded media environment. While basic metrics of exposure such as page views aren't enough to denote a loyal and engaged audience, you have to see whether people are finding your work in the first place. Questions to ask at this moment: Is your brand cutting through the noise of the marketplace? Are people discovering and viewing your content? And perhaps most important, what are the contexts in which people are coming to your content to satisfy their communication needs?[43] Answering these questions means digging into your metrics beyond page views, and also conducting interviews or observations of people in your community.

For most organizations, seizing attention involves adopting search engine optimization and social-marketing strategies. Yes, you have to adapt your content so it can be discovered on the web and connect with audiences in the myriad online spaces where they live. But engagement also means listening to your audience and learning more about what their needs are.

Connecting with audiences in social spaces requires authenticity. Credibility studies have shown that commercially-oriented messages can make users suspicious and question credibility; in fact, users are more likely to depend on nonprofessional cues like user review systems for valid information.[44]

Usage

Once the audience has discovered your content, the content must be easy to use, especially in today's user-centric media environment. As usability expert Jakob Nielsen has written, "Users are selfish, lazy, and ruthless."[45] If they can go somewhere else that solves their problem faster and more easily, they will. Witness the popularity of Wikipedia, which provides easy-to-digest summaries of information in a standardized format. It's not solely because the site appears at the top for many topic searches; its posts have an easy-to-navigate structure and are written in a consistent style.

In an industry where so much emphasis has been put on crafting a story or editing a well-told package, it is often difficult for journalists to think about new ways to present information. But organizations are experimenting with new forms, such as interactive data visualizations, long-form multimedia narratives, and live blogs of major events. Some see journalism becoming a process, where a "story" is no longer the discrete unit; instead, journalists and the community contribute a rolling series of related pieces—whether they be online posts, photographs, or social updates contributed by journalists and the community—where the "story" emerges from the flow of information and insights.[46]

Making news that requires little effort to consume is the best way for news organizations to become reliable sources of information in users' busy lives and cluttered home screens. The difficulty at this stage is having the audience begin to recognize the organization's name in the cluttered information stream. Your content and your journalists' voices have to be distinctive enough to emerge from the mass.

In the *This is Tucson* example we described earlier, the team's interviews with women in their target demographic led it to develop a distinctive "news from a smart friend" tone.[47] It learned that members of its audience have no time for clickbait. They like positive surprises about their community and are looking for news that helps them be the expert in their friend groups.

Habit

Distinctive content that is easy to access helps to create a media habit. Over the years, media scholars have focused on the importance of connecting with readers and viewers in a way that your product or service becomes a part of their everyday lives, where usage becomes automatic. One of our studies found a significant link between how often one used a medium for news and whether that medium was one's primary source for news.[48] Some researchers have found a link between credibility and familiarity: Once users embrace a particular site, the more likely they are to continue to use it and deem it credible.[49] Without credibility as a foundation, it's difficult to create an authentic connection with your audience.

Historically, news organizations have looked at their audiences primarily as a mass, aggregated mainly by geography or large demographic swaths. But online offers so many choices that it is more difficult to connect with sizable clusters of the audience consistently.

Instead, Chris Anderson's conception of the Long Tail can be helpful.[50] Historically, businesses often depended on the top 20% of customers who provided 80% of the revenue. But digital can alter this calculation. Rather than focusing on one large aggregated mass, news organizations should think about connecting with a number of smaller niche audiences—the other 80% down the long tail—to construct their audience. This process can involve developing networks of smaller news organizations that collaborate by sharing content or skill sets to better scale serving niche audiences, like the New Jersey News Commons based at Montclair State University.[51] With funding from the Dodge Foundation, sites that belong to the NJ News Commons can now come together for business and journalism training, collaborative reporting projects, a Story Exchange for sharing content, and legal help.[52]

Connection

Establishing a meaningful connection with the audience means inspiring an emotional attachment. As we've mentioned, four communication needs typically lead to media use: information, shopping/consumption, entertainment, and connectivity.[53] Historically, news organizations have had little problem connecting on the first two needs, which are more rational in nature; unfortunately, they don't inspire as deep an emotional reaction and connection as the last two needs. As a result, many organizations—trying to adhere to a mistaken interpretation of objectivity by focusing on information only—fail to make a personal connection with their audiences.

Often, they use what we've dubbed "engagement-light" techniques: a soft online-poll question, a half-hearted appeal of "send us your photos," limited participation from staff journalists in comments and social media. Although they can be a place for organizations to get started, such efforts to inspire a deeper emotional connection can fall flat because there is little authenticity behind these requests, and users are not likely to feel connected or be entertained by such hollow, self-serving measures.

A number of strategies can inspire a connection with the audience. People want to connect with *people*, and often, the personalities behind the news drive and sustain the popularity of particular news brands. Talk shows on television and radio rose to prominence because their personality-driven approach helps cut through the firehose of information in an entertaining, easy-to-digest way that inspires trust in the audience.

For example, the *Detroit Free Press* has experimented with using greater voice and personality on social media.[54] The organization has found that being more fun and snarky on Twitter helps it connect with people in a more intimate way. Similarly, the *Dallas Morning News* created a Facebook group for its subscribers, giving them special perks and direct access to reporters and editors. It also connects these paying customers with each other.[55]

Community

In the final stage of the engagement process, we see the formation of community, a space where the organization and its audience come together as partners, or where the news organization is able to add value to already existing communities in a non-transactional way. In news organizations, it can manifest as participatory journalism: Does the audience feel strongly enough about a particular news organization and the community it serves that it will *participate* in the journalism process, through comments, story ideas, contributed content, social sharing, and event attendance? From our perspective, the most engaged audience members are the ones who offer meaningful contributions or additional information, seeking to improve the community they care about. In a truly participatory newsroom, the community becomes part of the journalistic process on a consistent basis.

Amanda Zamora, the co-founder and publisher of The 19th, similarly argues that it is a common misconception in newsrooms that engagement happens primarily after a story is written.[56] Instead, staffers should be constantly coming up with creative strategies to turn the audience into collaborators instead of passive consumers at all stages of the reporting process. She wrote: "To dismiss the audience editor's creative capabilities is to dismiss the audience's creative capabilities."[57]

These efforts take time to nurture. Minnesota Public Radio, one organization we have worked with, spent years connecting with its audience through its Public Insight Network project.[58] Through a series of town-hall meetings and online initiatives, it built a network of more than 34,000 who voluntarily contribute their time and expertise to the organization to help with stories and coverage.

Another project we studied involved WellCommons, a collaborative community health site sponsored by the *Lawrence Journal-World* that launched in April 2010. In the months leading up to the official kickoff, developers created an advisory board of about 40 community volunteers from the local health community to help build and design the site.[59] Some came from nonprofits and public entities such as Lawrence Memorial Hospital and the Douglas County Public Health Department. Others were citizens who were advocates for buying and growing food locally, or who did not have health insurance. When the site went live, members of the public could post alongside the journalists without editing from the professionals. The effort quickly proved popular in the city of 88,000 people. By December 2010, the site had received 78,000 unique visitors, with posts, comments, and photos from 700 different people in the community.[60] The site was soon paying for itself, but because it wasn't adding additional revenue, the paper's commitment flagged. The project's internal champion, Jane Stevens, left the paper in 2012.

More recently, ProPublica collected nearly 5,000 stories of women who had died or nearly died in childbirth for its award-winning story, Lost Mothers. Creativity was required by the engagement team to fill a gap they noticed in the stories they were receiving: black mothers were underrepresented. The strategy they found that resonated most was asking if women wanted to talk with their own mothers or daughters about their personal experiences with childbirth. Given that it is a profoundly intimate and often difficult experience, this gave potential participants a greater sense of security than talking to a journalist. ProPublica offered questions but allowed these interviews to be relatively unstructured, and they captured a rich array of new information for the database they were building and increased the diversity of participation.[61]

This engagement model, derived from Napoli's research, is only one way to conceptualize the process of building greater participation with audiences, but we hope that it offers one specific, concrete path forward that you can customize to your organization.

NOTES

1 Nadia Khomami, "#MeToo: How a Hashtag Became a Rallying Cry against Sexual Harassment," The Guardian, October 20, 2017, www.theguardian.com/world/2017/oct/20/women-worldwide-use-hashtag-metoo-against-sexual-harassment.

2 Sandra E. Garcia, "The Woman Who Created #MeToo Long Before Hashtags," New York Times, October 20, 2017, www.nytimes.com/2017/10/20/us/me-too-movement-tarana-burke.html.

3 Monica Anderson and Skye Toor, "How Social Media Users Have Discussed Sexual Harassment Since #MeToo Went Viral," Pew Research Center, October 11, 2018, www.pewresearch.org/fact-tank/2018/10/11/how-social-media-users-have-discussed-sexual-harassment-since-metoo-went-viral/.

4 Dalvin Brown, "19 Million Tweets Later: A Look at #MeToo a Year after the Hashtag Went Viral," USA Today, October 13, 2018, www.usatoday.com/story/news/2018/10/13/metoo-impact-hashtag-made-online/1633570002/.

5   Alastair Dant and Jonathan Richards, "Behind the Rumours: How We Built Our Twitter Riots Interactive," *The Guardian*, December 8, 2011, www.theguardian.com/news/datablog/2011/dec/08/twitter-riots-interactive.

6   Jane B. Singer, Alfred Hermida, David Domingo, Ari Heinonen, Steve Paulussen, Thorsten Quandt, Zvi Reich, and Marina Vujnovic, *Participatory Journalism: Guarding Open Gates at Online Newspapers* (Chichester: Wiley-Blackwell, 2011).

7   Philip Napoli, *Audience Evolution: New Technologies and the Transformation of Media Audiences* (New York, NY: Columbia University Press, 2010), 96–98.

8   Joy Mayer, "What 'Engagement' Means to the Guardian's Meg Pickard," Reynolds Journalism Institute, December 1, 2010, http://rjionline.org/blog/what-engagement-means-guardians-meg-pickard.

9   Joy Mayer, "How Building Trust with News Consumers Is Like Dating," Reynolds Journalism Institute, February 23, 2017, www.rjionline.org/stories/how-building-trust-with-news-consumers-is-like-dating.

10 Lindsay Green-Barber, "Towards a Useful Typology of Engaged Journalism," Impact Architects, October 18, 2018, https://medium.com/the-impact-architects/towards-a-useful-typology-of-engaged-journalism-790c96c4577e.

11 John Dewey, *The Public and Its Problems* (Denver, CO: Alan Swallow, 1927).

12 Carrie Brown, "The Challenges and Opportunities of Public Journalism: An Evaluation of the Philadelphia Inquirer's Efforts to Better Serve a Diverse Community," Master's Thesis, Annenberg School for Communication, University of Pennsylvania, 2001.

13 Elia Powers, "The Rise of the Engagement Editor and What It Means," MediaShift, August 19, 2015, http://mediashift.org/2015/08/the-rise-of-the-engagement-editor-and-what-it-means/.

14 Singer et al.

15 Brian Ekdale, Jane B. Singer, Melissa Tully, and Shawn Harmsen, "Making Change: Diffusion of Technological, Relational, and Cultural Innovation in the Newsroom," *Journalism & Mass Communication Quarterly* 92, no. 4 (July 24, 2015), 938–958.

16 Chris Argyris, *Knowledge for Action: A Guide to Overcoming Barriers to Organizational Change* (San Francisco, CA: Jossey-Bass, 1993).

17 ProPublica, "Awards and Honors—ProPublica," www.propublica.org/awards/.

18 Amanda Zamora, "Student Perspectives on Race and Education in Tuscaloosa," ProPublica, May 17, 2014, www.propublica.org/article/student-perspectives-on-race-and-education-in-tuscaloosa.

19 Jonathan Groves, "Understanding the Change to Integration: An Organizational Analysis of a Small Newspaper," Doctoral Dissertation, University of Missouri-Columbia, 2009.

20 Bill Kovach and Tom Rosenstiel, *The Elements of Journalism: What Newspeople Should Know and the Public Should Expect*, 3rd ed. (New York, NY: Three Rivers Press, 2014), 191.

21 Carrie Brown and Jonathan Groves, "New Media, Enduring Values: How Three News Organizations Managed Change in an Age of Uncertainty," *Electronic News* 4, no. 3 (2010), 131–145, http://enx.sagepub.com/content/4/3/131.

22 Jonathan Groves, "Understanding the Change to Integration: An Organizational Analysis of a Small Newspaper," Doctoral Dissertation, University of Missouri-Columbia, 2009.

23 Napoli, 90–91.

24 Penelope Abernathy, *Saving Community Journalism: The Path to Profitability* (Chapel Hill, NC: University of North Carolina Press, 2014).

25 Christine Schmidt, "HuffPost Is the Latest Digital Media Company to Give Membership a Shot," *Nieman Lab*, April 17, 2019, www.niemanlab.org/2019/04/huffpost-is-the-latest-digital-media-company-to-give-membership-a-shot/.

26 Joshua Benton, "Want to See What One Digital Future for Newspapers Looks Like? Look at The Guardian, Which Isn't Losing Money Anymore," *Nieman Lab*, May 1, 2019, www.niemanlab.org/2019/05/want-to-see-what-one-digital-future-for-newspapers-looks-like-look-at-the-guardian-which-isnt-losing-money-anymore/.

27 Jeff Jarvis, *Geeks Bearing Gifts: Imagining New Futures for News* (New York, NY: CUNY Journalism Press, 2014).

28 Abernathy.

29 Abernathy; Dana Levitz, "10 Tips for Understanding Your Audiences and Targeting New Ones," American Press Institute, July 23, 2013, www.americanpressinstitute.org/publications/reports/white-papers/10-tips-understanding-audiences-targeting-new-ones/.

30 Abernathy, 134.

31 Abernathy, 48.

32 Personal interview with Irene McKisson, April 24, 2020.

33 Ibid.

34 Rachel Davis Mersey, "Reducing the Cognitive Burden of News," *Nieman Lab*, December, 2014, www.niemanlab.org/2014/12/reducing-the-cognitive-burden-of-news/.

35 Ravi Somaiya, "Times Co. Outlines Strategy to Double Digital Revenue," *New York Times*, October 7, 2015.

36 Joshua Benton, "The New York Times Is Getting Close to Becoming a Majority-Digital Company," *Nieman Lab*, February 6, 2019, www.niemanlab.org/2019/02/the-new-york-times-is-getting-close-to-becoming-a-majority-digital-company/;
Sarah Scire, "Readers Reign Supreme, and Other Takeaways from the New York Times End-of-Year Earnings Report," *Nieman Lab*, February 6, 2020, www.niemanlab.org/2020/02/readers-reign-supreme-and-other-takeaways-from-the-new-york-times-end-of-year-earnings-report/.

37 Listening Post Collective, "Playbook," accessed April 22, 2020, www.listeningpostcollective.org/playbook.

38 Everett Rogers, *Diffusion of Innovations*, 5th ed. (New York: Free Press, 2003), 222–223.

39 Lindsay Green-Barber, "CIR's Impact Tracker: How to Use It and Why You Need It," *Reveal at the Center for Investigative Reporting*, September 22, 2016,

www.revealnews.org/article/cirs-impact-tracker-how-to-use-it-and-why-you-need-it/.

40 Napoli, 89–91.

41 Rogers, 6.

42 Matthew S. Eastin and Robert LaRose, "A Social Cognitive Theory of Internet Uses and Gratifications: Toward a New Model of Media Attendance," *Journal of Broadcasting & Electronic Media* 48, no. 3 (2004), 358–377.

43 Esther Thorson and Margaret Duffy, "A Needs-Based Theory of the Revolution in News Use," Reynolds Journalism Institute, (2006).

44 Miriam J. Metzger, Andrew J. Flanagin, and Ryan B. Medders, "Social and Heuristic Approaches to Credibility Evaluation Online," *Journal of Communication* 60, no. 3 (2010), 413–439.

45 Jakob Nielsen, "Information Foraging: Why Google Makes People Leave Your Site Faster," Nielsen Norman Group, June 30, 2003, www.nngroup.com/articles/information-scent/.

46 Sue Robinson, "Journalism as a Process: The Organizational Implications of Participatory Online News," *Journalism & Communication Monographs* 13, no. 3 (September 22, 2011), 137.

47 Personal interview with Irene McKisson, April 24, 2020.

48 Jonathan Groves, "Understanding the News Habit: An Exploration of the Factors Affecting Media Choice," paper presented at the Association for Education in Journalism and Mass Communication, Boston, MA, 2009.

49 Miriam J. Metzger, Andrew J. Flanagin, Keren Eyal, Daisy R. Lemus, and Robert M. McCann, "Credibility for the 21st Century: Integrating Perspectives on Source, Message, and Media Credibility in the Contemporary Media Environment," *Annals of the International Communication Association* 27, no. 1, 293–335.

50 Chris Anderson, *The Long Tail: Why the Future of Business Is Selling Less of More* (New York, NY: Hachette Books, 2008).

51 Jarvis.

52 Molly de Aguiar and Josh Stearns, "How We Are Working with Universities to Strengthen Local Journalism," Local News Lab, July 22, 2015, https://medium.com/the-local-news-lab/how-we-are-working-with-universities-to-strengthen-local-journalism-646814a4383a.

53 Thorson and Duffy.

54 Joseph Lichterman, "These Tweets Are Fire: How the Detroit Free Press Created a Unique Social Media Voice," *Solution Set*, April 25, 2019, www.lenfestinstitute.org/solution-set/2019/04/25/these-tweets-are-how-the-detroit-free-press-created-a-unique-social-media-voice/.

55 Joseph Lichterman, "How the Dallas Morning News Builds Subscriber Loyalty with a Facebook Group," *Solution Set*, January 24, 2018, www.lenfestinstitute.org/solution-set/2018/01/24/dallas-morning-news-builds-subscriber-loyalty-facebook-group/.

56 Amanda Zamora, "I'm Not (Just) Your Paperboy," *Medium*, September 21, 2015, https://medium.com/crowd-powered-news/i-m-not-your-damn-paperboy-3d4634fdb2dd.

57 Ibid.

58 Minnesota Public Radio, "Public Insight Network," n.d., www.americanpublic media.org/public-insight-network/.

59 Jane Stevens, "Kudos and Thanks to our Advisory Group," WellCommons, May 26, 2010, http://wellcommons.com/groups/about-wellcommons/2010/may/26/kudos-and-thanks-to-our-a/.

60 Jonathan Kealing, "Closing the Books on WellCommons 2010," WellCommons, December 22, 2010, http://wellcommons.com/groups/about-wellcom mons/2010/dec/22/closing-the-books-on-well/.

61 Adriana Gallardo, "How We Collected Nearly 5,000 Stories of Maternal Harm," ProPublica, March 20, 2018, https://www.propublica.org/article/how-we-collected-nearly-5-000-stories-of-maternal-harm.

Six

In the previous chapters, we outlined a three-tiered model for helping you think about change. But this framework is not a panacea. The psychology of transformation is such that resistance will arise because new initiatives challenge the accepted view of the world, and it is natural for people in the organization to trust their own experiences above the uncertainty of change. This chapter goes into greater detail to help you understand the underlying reasons why resistance to change forms and what leaders can do to help their staff push past it.

It's important for leaders to understand their key role in moving their organizations forward. Too often in our work, we have heard top managers complain about cultural unwillingness to change without recognizing their own role in blocking change. In an interview with researchers from the Pew Research Center, one news executive exemplified this attitude:

> Probably the most difficult thing is to change a corporate culture because you don't really have the power to do it. You can change CEOs, executive VPs, digital VPs. You can wave this magic wand all you want. But at the end of the day, the troops in the field hunker down. From our company—and I would venture for other organizations as well—the most difficult thing to do is change it.[1]

Contrary to what this executive and others say, failure to change is often as much the fault of leadership as it is others in the organization. Change isn't either top-down or bottom-up; it's a complex interplay of both managers and staffers finding ways to set the framework for success.

In many ways, leadership during a time of tumultuous industry-wide change is a balancing act. The news industry needs dexterous leaders at a time in which the pace of technological change leaves little opportunity to tease out the potential outcomes of a new initiative and limits the ability to plan, discuss, and collaborate. But the more quickly leaders respond, the more resistance they are likely to face from within, especially as people raise valid concerns about unintended consequences. Do not underestimate the ability of key employees to recognize and resist knee-jerk reactions from above.

Fast or deliberative, each approach has its downside:

- *Change agents* can be people who by personality are more willing to try new things and can often inspire others to do so as well by unlocking the imagination for what's possible. However, change agents can be under pressure from shareholders or corporate expectations. Their changes can spark quick results, but those successes often fade after the initial burst of enthusiasm. Within a few months, key personnel will often leave or sidestep new policies and procedures by finding subtle ways to revert to their old, comfortable methods of working.
- *Consensus builders* want to ensure everyone is on board to build a foundation for true transformation. But this approach often stretches the planning process beyond the timeline of innovation; leaders fail to make decisive strategic moves in a timely enough fashion to make a difference. It creates a less combative climate but moves too slowly to keep pace with the fast-changing environment.

The challenge is finding the right spot for your organization between those approaches, respecting and nudging the organizational culture forward while disrupting the internal environment enough to bring about meaningful change in the unique context of your organization.

Like culture, resistance is not unchanging. Even under the threat of organization-ending scenarios, people see situations from differing perspectives. The key for leaders is avoiding the dismissiveness that comes too often to justify top-down change initiatives: *They don't want to change; we have to force them.* In addition to having specific reasons why they might not like a particular initiative, some employees in your organization may evaluate risk differently because they occupy a less privileged socioeconomic position and recognize that they have more at stake if something fails than others do.

As with culture, you need to dig into the deeper core elements of resistance to understand the underlying basis of frustration and fear—the fundamental emotions that cause people to resist and block change within an organization.

LEADERSHIP IN A TIME OF CHANGE

The biggest barriers arise when a change effort lacks a connection to the organization's conception of itself. That's why we devote so much time to understanding cultural assumptions. Culture provides a psychological framework for people to understand what group they're part of and their roles within that structure. As we discussed in Chapter 2, when a new initiative with no apparent connection to the organization arises, people are often left confused.

Leaders play a critical role in establishing or maintaining organizational culture, especially through the example they set for others. Leaders communicate their underlying assumptions through rewards and punishments; the direction and intensity of their attention; the measurements used for evaluating success; the allocation of resources; and staff choices in hirings, firings, and promotions.[2] The personality of leaders is particularly important because it can play a constructive or a destructive role in shaping organizational culture and influencing what type of people work at the organization and how they relate to the boss.[3]

For example, a leader who is a "constructive narcissist" is a dynamic, attention-seeking person who seeks affirmation from others and is often idealized by followers as a heroic figure. This form of narcissism is relatively healthy and produces a situation in which the leader may be very successful at inspiring and motivating others and communicating a clear vision,[4] an important aspect of successful leadership.[5] A "reactive narcissist," on the other hand, requires constant admiration, which decreases the likelihood that people will share important but potentially upsetting news with them.[6] These are just two relatively common examples of types of leadership. Others include depressive leaders that struggle to make decisions, or paranoid types that can become overly obsessed with perceived slights or threats.

Published accounts about the rise and fall of *New York Times* editor Howell Raines reveal a classic example of a dramatic, narcissistic leader, and the advantages and disadvantages of having someone with this type of personality at the top of an organization. Raines was widely regarded as a high-energy boss who "had a management style that was very hard-driving" and who was impatient with complaints.[7] When he was appointed to the top job, he talked about how he would "raise the competitive metabolism" of the paper.[8] In some ways, his high personal intensity was contagious, bringing a sense of excitement, and his boldness served him well in leading the paper through its coverage of the 9/11 attacks. In the chaos that erupted in the paper's home city, employees may have especially needed a strong leader to help carry them through. Unabashedly comparing himself to Ulysses S. Grant, Rainey comforted distraught staffers and organized the paper's comprehensive coverage, which eventually won several major awards for its hard-hitting, thoughtful reporting.

But many staffers alleged that Raines could be autocratic; as one editor put it, "A lot of us were cowed by Howell."[9] The same intensity that served him well on big breaking stories also led him to micro-manage. One reporter nicknamed the stairs separating the newsroom and the upper-level editors as the "DMZ staircase."[10]

This kind of leadership contributed to increasingly poor communication and a climate of fear in the newsroom. As a result, warnings about problems with an otherwise promising young reporter, Jayson Blair, who was well liked by Raines, were ignored. Blair was, of course, later discovered to have been fabricating information, leading to Raines stepping down under pressure.[11]

The demand for quick results, especially in competitive environments that need nimble innovation, wreaks havoc on leaders. Pressures from outside the organization, often beyond the influence of those in charge, often steal the sense of control, and so executives naturally focus on what they *can* control: their own internal environments. They begin crafting plans, issuing edicts, and changing the company, for good or ill. They often do it to provide a sense that they are *doing something*; they can't afford to wait for the answers to bubble up because the organization could cease to exist.

At the opposite end of the leadership spectrum are those who are disengaged, which often results in departments competing for power and resources rather than focusing as a cohesive organization on the audience, and larger editorial and business imperatives.

When it comes to leadership, even the most subtle ways leaders interact with others matter. Scholars have found that good leadership is often characterized by the following factors:

1 Open and honest communication about both the positive and negative aspects of change.
2 A clear, well-articulated vision, with specific goals.
3 Perhaps most importantly, a congruence between rhetoric and reality and a genuine concern for employees' needs.[12]

ORGANIZATIONAL LIFE CYCLES

Where an organization is in its life is critical for understanding how its members work together to attack threats and solve problems. One common framework for understanding group dynamics comes from educational psychologist Bruce Tuckman, who laid out the steps of small-group development as *forming, storming, norming,* and *performing.*[13] In that process, any group of people comes together for a purpose, and in those formative sessions, the participants determine their roles with the group and decide how much of themselves they decide to put into the group's success. They then create structures and routines, establishing norms of behavior and interaction that affect how the group ultimately performs its work. Generally, the more well defined the goal, the more successful the group tends to be.

Startups, which begin small, usually work through the first three steps together, but newcomers to established organizations arrive after the formative group has established the norms that became embedded as "the way we do things around here." From a cultural perspective, new employees must be socialized into this environment to determine where they fit within the organization if they are to remain and become contributing cultural participants. In this process, members are deciding how much of their individuality they are willing to give up to help the group or organization meet its goals.[14]

Established news businesses tend to be at a later stage in their organizational lives, with dozens of years of myths and traditions in their histories. In such instances, history is transmitted rather than experienced; new members are socialized into the organizational fabric and therefore may be less willing to challenge the existing culture, especially if they have embraced it. But even in newer digital news startups, many of the leaders and employees experienced similar earlier career trajectories, and norms are quick to form.

THREATS TO IDENTITY AND SENSE OF SELF

Formal job descriptions help people understand how their position is perceived in the organizational hierarchy, but it is only in practice, through seeing how the position plays out within the actual social structure, that people truly shape their role in the organization. Depending upon their position and their commitment to the workplace, employees' identity and sense of self often arise from their roles—formal and informal—within their organizations.[15]

Because of this psychological identification with their positions, any change in structure can threaten perceptions of self, especially in a knowledge-based profession such as journalism. Threats to their roles become threats to their identities. It is not just changing an organization; it is altering the very identities of those employees, especially if they no longer are positioned in the social order in quite the same way.

Gannett discovered this title–identity connection with its first push toward what it dubbed "information centers" in 2006. Then-CEO Craig Dubow announced the new approach in an email to all employees. As he described the "newsroom of the future,"[16] he noted how people's roles would be changing. Photographers would now embrace video as well. Copy editors would come up with new ways of writing headlines. Reporters and editors would become far more focused on local news.

> Many jobs are transforming to allow for immediacy, multi-platform coverage and greater interaction with the community. People will be asked to perform many new and different functions than they are used to. Schedules are changing as the Information Center becomes a 24-hour operation.[17]

Two years later, those changes had not turned around traffic or revenue at Gannett's sites.[18] Newspaper division president Sue Clark-Johnson had retired, and her successor, Bob Dickey, was developing a plan to refine the strategy. Phil Currie, longtime head of Gannett's news department, tried to ease concerns that the organizational changes were overturning the company's commitment to traditional journalism. But commenters on the much-followed independent site Gannett Blog were not buying it.

Wrote one anonymous contributor:

> How does Currie, or anyone, for that matter, in corporate, in the newsrooms and out on the streets expect any level of hard news and watchdog journalism when most of the reporters are too busy working on rewrites of "local, local" township press releases announcing free hot dog night at the free juggling expo under the stars in the park or the 44 pound cat wandering around Camden County, NJ?. [sic][19]

On paper, Gannett's goals in developing its "information center" model made sense and reflected imperatives felt throughout the industry for greater immediacy, multiplatform news delivery, and engagement with the audience. Some media watchers appreciated the attention to "community conversation,"[20] something not widely embraced at traditional news outlets in 2006. But in reality, making sweeping corporate pronouncements about new job descriptions and ways of doing things without securing buy-in is a recipe for resistance, especially dangerous if employees believe they only have to wait it out until another pronouncement is issued.

It's not just structural or positional issues, either. Threats to identity arise in newsrooms when newcomers try different ways of doing journalism, challenging the routines and methods that have developed as part of the social structure. Though Politico developed as a digital media startup, it was launched with two former *Washington Post* journalists—John F. Harris and Jim VandeHei—in top editorial positions. Its mission, as posted on the Our Story page of its website in 2015, touted the organization's innovative mindset but also contains nods toward journalistic tradition: "none of this works if we ever fall short of that initial promise of delivering nonpartisan news, fast, fair and first."[21]

As an online medium, Politico expects its reporters to connect and converse in social media, a free-flowing environment that demands unfiltered authenticity from its participants. But authenticity in social spaces can often clash with established notions of journalistic objectivity. In June 2012, reporter Joe Williams made observations critical of then-presidential candidate Mitt Romney, noting that Romney was more comfortable in settings such as *Fox & Friends*, where "they are like him, they're white folks who are very relaxed in their own company."[22] Williams also cracked jokes about the candidate on his locked Twitter account.

Williams was soon suspended, with Harris and VandeHei noting he had violated the standard of fairness and judgment expected of the site's political reporters. "Regrettably, an unacceptable number of Joe Williams's public statements on cable and Twitter have called into question his commitment to this responsibility," they wrote in a memo to the staff. "His comment about Governor Romney earlier today on MSNBC fell short of our standards for fairness and judgment in an especially unfortunate way."[23]

In the digital media environment, in social spaces where unfettered conversation is common, such experimental transparency might be welcomed and appreciated.[24] Indeed, it's also an opportunity for long underrepresented voices in the newsroom to speak out about coverage failures. More recently, then-*Washington Post* reporter Wesley Lowery clashed with executive editor Marty Baron over Lowery's tweets, some of which criticized the *New York Times* for a Tea Party retrospective that ignored some of the racist undertones of the movement. Baron felt the comments were too political. Lowery later tweeted:

> Should go without saying: reporters of color shouldn't have their jobs threatened for speaking out about mainstream media failures to properly cover and contextualize issues of race. What's the point of bringing diverse experiences and voices into a room only to muzzle them.[25]

As we noted in earlier chapters, the notion of objectivity has become blurred over the years. In many corners, it has become a deeply

Leading through Change and Resistance

embedded industrial norm to declare that journalists—not just their method of information gathering—should be opinion-free. In her foundational newsroom research, sociologist Gaye Tuchman documented more than four decades ago how important objectivity was to journalists because it was a useful tool for deflecting criticism.[26] Even in a relatively new news organization, it remains a powerful aspect of journalistic identity that can inhibit experimentation.

LACK OF CLEAR DIRECTION

Closely tied to the disconnect between embedded culture and transplanted innovation is a lack of clear direction from the top levels of the organization. As we've noted previously, leaders shape their organizational cultures through their management styles, and a clear connection among resources, training, action steps, and rewards is necessary for a change effort to succeed over the long term.

Some organizations we have worked with have struggled to provide a clear statement of objectives with new initiatives. One newspaper we studied clearly wanted to become a web-first news organization, with investments in a new content-management system and an emphasis on blogging and web updates. But reporters and editors were expected to find ways on their own to squeeze this work around their contributions to the primary revenue generator, the print newspaper. As a result, reporters found themselves adrift, uncertain about how much of their daily routines to commit to blogging and web updates. Most considered the online content as supplementary to their work for the printed product, and if they went a day or two without blogging, editors rarely chastised them. Said one reporter: "I think I'm still at the point where the paper is kind of pre-emptive for me. The tops of my checks say [the name of the newspaper]."[27]

With such change efforts, leaders must construct tangible reward systems and praise web-first work as vigorously as front-page stories and packages that lead the newscast. If digital work is downgraded as an afterthought, only those employees passionate about the task will embrace the innovation, and the rest won't bother.

For legacy news organizations today, change often comes in the form of mandatory mergers and layoffs, which adds to the unease created by the uncertain competitive environment. Although any organization would prefer to avoid a situation in which people lose their livelihoods and those that remain are asked to do more, often, that is the reality. The *Deseret News*, one of Salt Lake City's newspapers with ties to the Church of Jesus Christ of Latter-day Saints, underwent high-profile disruptive changes after CEO Clark Gilbert took the helm in 2009. In 2010, the paper cut its staff by 43% and merged its newsgathering operation with broadcasting partner KSL.[28]

Five years later, news director Doug Wilk described the challenges that had to be overcome:

> [it] offered a management challenge as employees struggled to understand who was in charge, who had decision-making rights over the news and each platform, and provided challenges in maintaining differentiation of the news brands.
>
> This was not an easy task, and there were many missteps. But we learned it required two distinctive traits in managers: trust and cooperation. Those who chose not to work together in search of solutions soon left the company or senior managers made changes. We focused on workflow and understanding the roles in the room—legacy print reporters, legacy TV reporters, Web producers, TV and radio producers, editors for print and editors for TV and a host of other platform-specific functions.[29]

With clearly defined roles and explicit lines of authority, people within the organization eventually adapted to the disrupted environment, Wilk wrote.

UNDERSTANDING POWER AND MOTIVATION

The key to managing transformation successfully is understanding what motivates people to follow, contribute, collaborate, and, ultimately, change. Management researchers often talk of motivators in terms of *extrinsic* (those external rewards and punishments that motivate from outside the person) and *intrinsic* (those driven by employees' own internal desires and wishes). To think of these in a leader–follower context, it's helpful to understand what social psychologists John R.P. French and Bertram H. Raven described as the bases of social power.[30] Here, we apply the original five bases in a workplace environment:

- *Coercive*: the ability to punish someone, through termination or demotion.
- *Reward*: the ability to elevate someone, through public praise, raises, or promotions.
- *Legitimate*: authority emanating from the position or title.
- *Expert*: authority emanating from superior ability or knowledge.
- *Referent*: power given willingly to an individual (not necessarily a supervisor) because of respect, admiration, or other relationship-driven emotions.

Coercive and reward power are connected to extrinsic motivation, and both require close oversight to maintain. The influencing person must be physically present to exert much control. The other three forms are more closely linked with intrinsic motivation, as the respect for those bases of power does not require the physical presence of the leader at all times to ensure compliance. But they also can take longer to develop, as the connection isn't driven by tangible means. It requires an emotional, psychological connection built through trust and commitment.

Referent power is the most powerful and long-lasting because the employee is most willing from a psychological perspective to grant power to the other person. Employees identify with the supervisor in such a way that they seek to model that person's behavior. Often, they strive to emulate the traits of the person they respect and admire.

Legendary *Philadelphia Inquirer* editor Gene Roberts was a leader who published accounts suggest was able to wield referent power. Investigative reporter Don Barlett said of his boss: "If you were a reporter and you didn't love working for Gene Roberts, there was something wrong with you."[31] Roberts was known as an editor who valued talent. "We couldn't attract them with money," he once said. "Instead we offered them a vision that we could be a really excellent newspaper and a congenial workplace." During his tenure, the paper went from being known for corruption to one that people wanted to work at: "Instead of having to woo people, they started wooing us," Roberts said.[32]

So how do you spark that connection? The literature on leadership is expansive and profiles many styles, from authoritarian to laissez-faire.[33] From our perspective, the transformational leadership model offers the best guidance for engendering the referent power best for managing in creative, knowledge-based environments. The four facets of the model for leaders to consider are:[34]

- *Idealized influence.* Inspire respect and admiration by considering followers' needs over your own.
- *Inspirational motivation.* Inspire teamwork by making sure work is meaningful and challenging.
- *Intellectual stimulation.* Inspire creativity by questioning long-held assumptions and encouraging experimentation.
- *Individualized consideration.* Inspire individual achievement through mentorship.

Transformational leaders can guide employees to make sense of a frenetic, uncertain environment by appealing to larger ideals rather than specific tasks. Humans naturally seek order from chaos, but it often doesn't happen as neatly as we hope, especially as the pace of change accelerates in the modern media environment. It is up to transformational leaders to help ease the anxieties of the rank-and-file.

LACK OF RESOURCES

One issue crops up over and over in change efforts: the need for tools and support. In an era of tightening budgets, news organizations are regularly asking newsrooms to do more with less. We realize that for most people in the news business, additional resources are in the category of areas you do not control. But it's important to point out that organizational research shows that investment is required if you are going to adapt to a changing environment. The *Washington Post*, after being bought by Amazon CEO Jeff Bezos, offers a case study of the innovation that can happen with a robust investment in news.

Marty Baron was working as the *Post*'s executive editor when the Graham family had sold the family-owned newspaper company to Bezos in October 2013, and he remained in his role after the purchase.[35] In January 2014, he shared a memo with the staff outlining the way forward. He announced several new hires and highlighted several online blog initiatives, including a commitment to the Fix blog and the paper's well-known political coverage. But he reaffirmed the organization's dedication to the *Post*'s traditional platform as well, with an expanded Sunday magazine and Style & Arts section: "This is a news organization of extraordinary achievement. It is home to journalists of immense talent and dedication. With these initiatives, we can all look forward to a future of great promise."[36]

Those words were backed up by an investment of resources. Unlike many news organizations, the *Post* committed to hiring key employees for new digital initiatives. In October 2015, Bezos publicly reminded everyone of his patience in an interview with CBS's Charlie Rose (emphasis added):

> The *Washington Post* today is a bright light that helps shine light on all of our institutions in this country, and the political process. We know that some of the things that have happened in the past, we wish we had known more about our political leaders and our other powerful institutions in this country, and that's been the role of the Post for a long time. And we're just gonna keep doing that. *We're doing it now with more resources and we have a lot of patience for that job.* We're just gonna keep working at it and make sure that that institution stays strong, so that it can shine a light on all of these important players, especially in Washington.[37]

By November 2015, the *Post* had hit a monthly record for unique visitors—71.6 million—and time spent per visitor reached 15 minutes, up 21% from the previous year's numbers.[38] These figures marked the first time the *Post* had surpassed the *New York Times* in web visits, riding high on its new robust social strategy and efforts to speed its page-loading time.[39] Although the *Times* pulled ahead again in January,[40] the milestone "was (and is) seen as a big deal in the world of journalism since the *Post* has long been the *Times*' little brother in terms of journalistic reach and Web traffic," the *Post*'s Chris Cillizza wrote.[41]

LEADERSHIP AS A BALANCING ACT

Over and over again in research on newsrooms, the need for leaders to constantly strike a balance between extremes comes up. People need to be pushed before they give up comfortable routines, but they also need enough of a sense of security to avoid paralysis. Individuals also need both autonomy and a sense of belonging to perform well.

Organizations are at their most creative when they operate on the "edge of chaos," scholars like Ralph D. Stacey have found.[42] Cooperation and constraints produce creativity when balanced against competition and a sense of limitless possibility. Leaders have to navigate carefully to provide both of these stabilizing and destabilizing forces. Organizations that exist at a kind of "stable equilibrium" become preoccupied with control and the execution of routines that have often been centrally developed. Organizations with what Stacey calls "bounded instability" don't have to reinvent the wheel constantly, but are still motivated to search for new solutions even when it may be painful to do so.[43]

Another set of countervailing but mutually important forces in an organization are what Schein calls the *legitimate network* and the *shadow network* in organizations.[44] The "legitimate" network is composed of bureaucratic structures and ways of doing things prescribed by rules; it is out in the open. The "shadow" network, on the other hand, is the informal social and political environment; it, too, may have its own set of rules and conventions. The two networks must coexist; both are vital for effective organizational functioning. The shadow network is where diversity can flourish and new ideas can grow; concepts developed there may become vital if the organization changes.

Another aspect of balance in leadership is setting a clear vision and imperative for change while securing buy-in early on from all levels of the organization. Resistance comes when people who must implement changes aren't included in the planning and development process for transformation.

This phenomenon can occur with experimental skunkworks ventures designed to spark innovation outside of the organizational mainstream. Though creative ideas can thrive in these off-shoot entities, the learning can remain relegated to those silos of innovation and never filter into the organization proper. The rhythms, structures, and reward systems are often different from the main organization, and it can be difficult to spread that learning to the rest of the workplace because those employees were not part of the original innovation. They're having to adopt someone else's ideas that were created and developed elsewhere, without the input from the people who have to put the innovations in practice.

In 2011, Jim Brady joined the Journal Register Co. to develop Project Thunderdome, a way to standardize digital-production processes and ease content sharing across the chain's news organizations.[45] Thunderdome, located in New York, eventually brought together more than 50 coders, designers, and multimedia journalists to develop and manage content for the news company. Although it was increasing page views and was known for its talented team, three years later, shortly after the full merger of Journal Register and MediaNews Group, the effort was shuttered in a cost-cutting move.

On his well-respected Newsonomics blog at Nieman Lab, Ken Doctor described some of the skunkworks problem:

> Thunderdome wasn't universally received well within the company. Talk to the locals and you heard grumbles. Traffic to the new Thunderdome sections didn't impress them. They didn't like national imposition on local news judgment.[46]

THE MESSY PATH OF INNOVATION

The cycle of innovation–investment–change rarely works neatly and seamlessly. Mistakes and chaos ensue in the uncertainty. Leaders have to win over employees to execute and incorporate innovation, a pathway that communication scholar Everett Rogers calls the "innovation-decision process." It's navigating the sense of uncertainty that comes from examining and testing an innovation to decide whether it's appropriate for your style and culture.[47]

A key part of overcoming the psychological roots of resistance is understanding how individuals and groups perceive the characteristics of innovations and changes.

Using Rogers' framework[48] as a guide, leaders should be able to take employees through these questions:

- How can we test out the innovation and see how well it works in our organization?
- What advantages do the changes provide? How are they better than what we're doing now?
- How compatible are the changes with us, in terms of culture and identity? How does it meet our needs?
- How complex are the changes? Do they meld easily into our organization?
- How can we develop an iterative process to incorporate the best facets of the innovation into our work and discard the incompatible parts?

Using these questions, organizations can begin to learn how to incorporate new ideas into their workflows. Ultimately, you want your organization to stop approaching each new technology or approach as isolated innovations to embrace; your goal should be fostering a culture of innovation, one that provides the training, resources, and reward structure that encourages people to experiment and develop new ways of accomplishing work without the growth demands of traditional, deliberate strategy.

For leaders to bring about long-lasting change, especially in a volatile, challenging financial environment, it's critical to ease employees' concerns as much as possible through constant communication and support. Only when front-line employees understand how changes align with their values and beliefs, and see how they can participate to bring those changes to fruition in the organization can the entire group move forward into the uncertain future, together, as a cohesive unit to confront external challenges.

Leading transformative change is not easy, and it can be frustrating to not have a single outline with specific steps to follow. Just as leaders' personalities differ, so do those of their employees, and any approach requires some tailoring to individual organizational circumstances. But by understanding how leadership can drive or block change, you can develop a plan that fits your style and organization, as well as the specific type of change you hope to achieve.

NOTES

1 Tom Rosenstiel, Mark Jurkowitz, and Hong Ji, "The Search for a New Business Model," Pew Research Center's Journalism Project, March 5, 2012, www.journalism.org/2012/03/05/search-new-business-model/.

2 Edgar Schein, *Organizational Culture and Leadership*, 4th ed. (Edison, NJ: Jossey-Bass, 2010), 219–220.

3 Manfred Kets de Vries, *The Leadership Mystique: Leading Behavior in the Human Enterprise*, 2nd ed. (Upper Saddle River, NJ: FT Press, 2009).

4 Kets de Vries.

5 Schein, 305–306.

6 Kets de Vries.

7 Ken Auletta, "The Howell Doctrine," *New Yorker*, June 10, 2002, www.newyorker.com/magazine/2002/06/10/the-howell-doctrine.

8 Ken Auletta, "Changing Times," *New Yorker*, October 24, 2011, www.newyorker.com/magazine/2011/10/24/changing-times-ken-auletta.

9 Auletta, "Changing Times."

10 Auletta, "Howell Doctrine."

11 Jacques Steinberg, "Executive Editor of the Times and Top Deputy Step Down," *New York Times*, June 5, 2003. www.nytimes.com/2003/06/05/national/05SHELL-PAPE.html.

12 Kets de Vries; Kenneth C. Killebrew, "Culture, Creativity and Convergence: Managing Journalists in a Changing Information Workplace," *International Journal on Media Management* 5, no. 1 (January 1, 2003), 39–46. doi:10.1080/14241270309390017; Schein.

13 Bruce W. Tuckman, "Developmental Sequence in Small Groups," *Psychological Bulletin* 63, no. 6 (June 1965), 384–399. doi:10.1037/h0022100. www.ncbi.nlm.nih.gov/pubmed/14314073.

14 Kenwyn K. Smith and David N. Berg, *Paradoxes of Group Life: Understanding Conflict, Paralysis, and Movement in Group Dynamics* (San Francisco, CA: Jossey-Bass, 1997).

15 William Czander, *The Psychodynamics of Work and Organizations, Theory and Application* (New York, NY: Guilford Press, 1993), 294–297.

16 Jim Hopkins, "Text of Craig Dubow's Information Center Memo," Gannett Blog, November 2, 2006, http://gannettblog.blogspot.com/2006/11/text-of-craig-dubows-information-center.html.

17 Hopkins.

18 Jim Hopkins, "Results Weak, GCI Revamping Information Center," Gannett Blog, July 31, 2008, http://gannettblog.blogspot.com/2008/07/results-weak-gci-revamps-information.html.

19 Gannett Blog, July 31, 2008, http://gannettblog.blogspot.com/2008/07/results-weak-gci-revamps-information.html?showComment=1217516640000#c10041 57526008855540.

20 Amy Gahran, "Crowdsourcing, Community Conversation, and the Journalism Job Market," *Poynter*, November 8, 2006, www.poynter.org/2006/crowdsourcing-community-conversations-the-journalism-job-market/79249/.

21 John F. Harris and Jim VandeHei, "Our Story," Politico, n.d., www.politico.com/about/our-story.

22 Erik Wemple, "Politico Suspends Reporter," *Washington Post*, June 22, 2012, www.washingtonpost.com/blogs/erik-wemple/post/politico-suspends-reporter/2012/06/22/gJQAvvf8uV_blog.html.

23 Dylan Byers, "Politico Reporter Suspended for Remarks," Politico, June 22, 2012, www.politico.com/blogs/media/2012/06/politico-reporter-suspended-for-remarks-126989.

24 Amy Mitchell, Jeffrey Gottfried, and Katerina Eva Matsa, "Millennials and Political News," Pew Research Center, June 1, 2015, www.journalism.org/2015/06/01/millennials-political-news/.

25 Maxwell Tani, "Washington Post Threatened Another Star Reporter Over His Tweets," *Daily Beast*, February 3, 2020, www.thedailybeast.com/washington-post-threatened-another-star-reporter-wesley-lowery-over-his-tweets.

26 Gaye Tuchman, *Making News: A Study in the Construction of Reality* (New York, NY: Free Press, 1980).

27 Jonathan Groves, "Understanding the Change to Integration: An Organizational Analysis of a Small Newspaper," Doctoral Dissertation, University of Missouri-Columbia, 77.

28 Doug Wilk, "The New News Hub: Strategies for Success. Innovation Wire Web site," deseretdigital.com, n.d., http://solutions.deseretdigital.com/innovationwire/doug-wilks-the-new-news-hub-strategies-for-success.html.

29 Wilk.

30 Bertram H. Raven, "The Bases of Power and the Power/Interaction Model of Interpersonal Influence," *Analyses of Social Issues and Public Policy* 8, no. 1 (December, 2008), 1–22.

31 Sydney Finkelstein, "Need to Find, Keep, and Maximize Talent Today? Look to an Old-School Example, Gene Roberts," *Nieman Lab*, February 3, 2016, www.niemanlab.org/2016/02/need-to-find-keep-and-maximize-talent-today-look-to-an-old-school-example-gene-roberts/.

32 Finkelstein.

33 Manfred Kets de Vries, *The Leadership Mystique: A User's Manual for the Human Enterprise*, 2nd ed. (London: Pearson Education, 2001).

34 B.J. Avolio, B.M. Bass, and D. Jung, "Reexamining the Components of Transformational and Transactional Leadership Using the Multifactor Leadership Questionnaire," *Journal of Organizational and Occupational Psychology* 7 (1999), 441–462.

35 Paul Farhi, "The Washington Post Closes Sale to Amazon Founder Jeff Bezos," *Washington Post*, October 2, 2013, www.washingtonpost.com/business/economy/washington-post-closes-sale-to-amazon-founder-jeff-bezos/2013/10/01/fca3b16a-2acf-11e3-97a3-ff2758228523_story.html.

36 Washington Post PR, "Marty Baron: What's to Come in 2014," *Washington Post*, January 29, 2014, www.washingtonpost.com/pr/wp/2014/01/29/marty-baron-whats-to-come-in-2014/.

37   Laura Hazard Owen, "Jeff Bezos Says the Washington Post's Goal Is to Become the 'New Paper of Record'," *Nieman Lab*, November 24, 2015, www.niemanlab.org/2015/11/spacesuit-wearing-jeff-bezos-says-the-washington-posts-goal-is-to-become-the-new-paper-of-record/.

38   Washington Post PR, "The Washington Post Continues to See Explosive Growth, Breaks Yet Another Record with 71.6 Million Users in November," *Washington Post*, December 14, 2015, www.washingtonpost.com/pr/wp/2015/12/14/the-washington-post-continues-to-see-explosive-growth-breaks-yet-another-record-with-71-6-million-users-in-november/.

39   Lucia Moses, "How the Washington Post Leapfrogged the New York Times in Web Traffic," Digiday, December 1, 2015, http://digiday.com/publishers/washington-post-leapfrogged-new-york-times-web-traffic/.

40   Jeremy Barr, "The New York Times Pulls Back Ahead of the Washington Post for Unique Visitors," Adage, February 17, 2016, http://adage.com/article/media/york-times-pulls-back-ahead-washington-post/302720/.

41   Chris Cillizza, "Why the Fight between the Washington Post and New York Times Over Traffic Misses the Point," *Washington Post*, December 1, 2015, www.washingtonpost.com/news/the-fix/wp/2015/12/01/why-the-fight-between-the-washington-post-and-new-york-times-over-traffic-is-stupid/.

42   Ralph Stacey, *Complexity and Creativity in Organizations* (San Francisco, CA: Berrett-Koehler, 1996).

43   Stacey, 97–98.

44   Schein.

45   Megan Garber, "What's Project Thunderdome, You Ask? Inside Jim Brady's New Job at Journal Register Company," *Nieman Lab*, March 29, 2011, www.niemanlab.org/2011/03/whats-project-thunderdome-you-ask-inside-jim-bradys-new-job-at-journal-register-company/.

46   Ken Doctor, "The Newsonomics of Digital First Media's Thunderdome Implosion (and Coming Sale)," *Nieman Lab*, April 2, 2014, www.niemanlab.org/2014/04/the-newsonomics-of-digital-first-medias-thunderdome-implosion-and-coming-sale/.

47   Everett M. Rogers, *Diffusion of Innovations*, 5th ed. (New York, NY: Free Press, 2003), 168.

48   Rogers, 15–16.

Part Three – Retrenchment

By March 2015, traffic to csmonitor.com had hit its lowest level since 2001, and the site's bounce rate was 95%, meaning that despite all of its professed efforts at distinctiveness and engagement, remarkably few of the site's visitors found a compelling reason to stick around. The home page was no longer among the top 200 U.S. sites on Quantcast. Online ad revenue followed suit, falling from its high of $3 million in 2014, and did not appear to be coming back.

Managers were split on the path forward. For busy media consumers to discover the *Monitor*, some argued the organization had to maintain its pursuit of search engine optimization (SEO)/social media tactics to garner attention and continued revenue from advertising. But others saw a different pathway to distinction and ultimately, a loyal audience. For them, cutting through the cluttered chaos of the daily news cycle required returning to the original mission of serving as a beacon of calm, highlighting solutions and progress.

Midway through the shift to web-first, the *Monitor* had developed marketing personas for an audience of 18 million attracted to this type of journalism: a couple in their 50s named Greg and Miranda, who were interested in understanding the world and solving problems. This ideal audience segment reflected about half of the current visitors to the website at the time. It also reflected many in the newsroom itself, including several leaders.[1] But even though these personas were familiar, they didn't spark a newsroom movement toward explicitly serving them; we heard an occasional reference to Greg and Miranda, but there wasn't a clear strategy focused on connecting with those personas.

"Distinction" had been a buzzword among editors since the early page-view success failed to translate into financial sustainability, and the management team sought to identify a way to make the concept more tangible, more measurable. During his time as managing editor under John Yemma, Marshall Ingwerson had been working to develop a qualitative expression of impact. After assuming the editor's chair in January 2014, Ingwerson began working with his five-person management team—national editor Mark Sappenfield, international editor Amelia Newcomb, online editor David Scott, weekly editor Clay Collins, and new ventures director Matt Clark—to distill the essence of the *Monitor* into an actionable mission.

At this moment, the organization was trying to balance all levels of our change model. Could this group—all of whom had worked at the *Monitor* for a decade or longer—articulate a clear vision, remain true to the "bless all mankind" ethos of founder Mary Baker Eddy, *and* put the organization on an innovative path to sustainable revenue from an engaged group of loyal subscribers?

DEFINING A NEW VISION

In the fall of 2014, Ingwerson and the newsroom's management team fashioned a guiding document for the newsroom called "The Core Tasks of *Monitor* Journalism." The memo's preamble laid bare the reality:

> If *Monitor* journalism is not first and foremost good journalism, well grounded in the integrity of its facts, the open quality of its observation, and the transparency of its analysis, then it won't have credibility and it won't have power. It won't matter.
> If *Monitor* journalism is just good journalism, even excellent journalism, without a clear and consistent distinction from many well-funded sources of excellent journalism, then it won't build an audience. And it won't survive.[2]

The succinct document outlined three "core tasks" that each piece of *Monitor* journalism should accomplish: promoting understanding across division, distance, and difference; illuminating ideas or "models of thought" behind the news; and registering progress, to show how thinking has evolved on a particular topic or trend. All three tasks were to spring from strong, credible journalism.[3]

Though the memo did not specifically mention the Christian Science faith, several statements reflected the spirit of church teachings. Under the idea of registering progress, the memo noted: "*Monitor* journalism is about healing, broadly conceived, as in the Jewish concept of 'tikkun olam' or healing the world." Under the concept of "surface models of thought," it noted: "*Monitor* journalism is about elevating human thought," or ways of understanding the world that will lead to positive outcomes. Under "promote understanding of others," it said, "*Monitor* journalism at its best is animated, at some level, by love for one's fellow humankind."[4] Especially among the longer-tenured employees, the document resonated with the *Monitor*'s deepest cultural values.

The memo was not sent to the entire staff.[5] Instead, the section editors used it as a guide in planning discussions with reporters about how a *Monitor* story could distinguish itself from the mass of reporting on current events and issues. In the newsroom, the shorthand became "UMP," a mnemonic for *understanding, models of thought,* and *progress.*

In the morning editorial meetings, the top editors would review stories to see how well they met the UMP ideal. In one meeting during our March 2015 visit, a story on the home page about Hillary Clinton's prospects for the presidency had "zero distinction," Ingwerson told the editors; it did not succeed in achieving the UMP tasks.[6] Reporting on an important topic wasn't enough; perspective, context, and approach mattered.

Another story focused on the shooting of an unarmed teen by police in Madison, Wisconsin.[7] That 944-word post passed the UMP test, as it focused on progress on the issue of race relations after a volatile community situation, and promoted understanding among disparate groups. Despite the story's distinction, however, an editor noted that it had performed poorly in page views—908 as of 9 a.m.

By contrast, a story that failed to meet the UMP criteria, an article about Senate Majority Leader Mitch McConnell holding up a vote on an attorney general candidate, had 17,000 views in the same time span. Someone suggested that the Madison headline undersold the story. One editor responded: "Culturally, we're not built to be provocative. We're built to undersell."[8] The organization was struggling to align its culture values with the audience's "jobs to be done."

CONTINUING THE SOCIAL MEDIA PUSH

Amid the focus on distinction and loyalty, there was an effort to stem the fall in traffic. In the fall of 2014, online editor David Scott—one of the five pillars of Ingwerson's management team—created a "social first" team of interns to focus on generating referral traffic through trend-related posts driven by popular topics on social media. Team members would generate two or three posts a day—some reported, some curated—with specific traffic goals.[9] During its first three months of existence, the team met its goals, with some posts scoring as many as 10,000 page views in a day, but its success had slowed in the first quarter of 2015. By March 2015, overall traffic had dropped from 10 million unique visitors per month to about 7 million,[10] and the business side worried that if the number of unique visitors fell too far, selling advertising on the site would become even more difficult.

New faces were willing to embrace new routines. Laura Edwins, a graduate of New York University's Studio 20: Digital First program,[11] became social media coordinator, and as with her predecessor, her position was split between editorial and business, as she reported to both Scott in the newsroom and Sue Hackney, vice president of marketing and strategy.

As part of the social media push, Edwins had begun "Social Media Tuesdays" to highlight well-performing *Monitor* posts on social media identified by Spike, a monitoring tool from NewsWhip. On these days, a series of hourly emails were meant to inspire story-sharing by newsroom staff on their own Twitter and Facebook accounts. For example, the first email of the day on March 17, 2015, was sent at 8:55 a.m. It began:

> Good morning! Here are three stories from Spike that got lots of shares last night.
>
>   Harry's piece did especially well on Twitter.
>
>   Robert Durst and "The Jinx": a true crime classic, both for the tale and the telling of it http://www.csmonitor.com/USA/Justice/2015/0316/Robert-Durst-and-The-Jinx-a-true-crime-classic-both-for-the-tale-and-the-telling-of-it-video@HarryBruinius (Robert Durst is trending)
>
>   Henry has done a great job of tweeting about the trial ... definitely worth checking out this feed: https://twitter.com/henrygass[12]

Over the course of the day, she sent eight more emails, highlighting strong performers from throughout the day so reporters and editors could see what was doing well with the *Monitor*'s social media audience. Some highlighted stories reflected topical fodder reminiscent of the *Monitor*'s SEO heyday: the NCAA basketball tournament schedule, a quiz on Ireland for St. Patrick's Day, the best places to view the Northern Lights, and a rewrite of a Vice interview with President Obama.[13] A few selections, however, seemed more on-brand, including original staff stories focusing on sex-trafficking bills in Congress, McDonald's workers suing the fast-food chain over working conditions, and Russia's unwillingness to relinquish Crimea to Ukraine. Outside of the online team, however, the emails often received little attention. For much of the newsroom, the attention was less on traffic and more toward stories that might better reflect the UMP ideal, a reversion to the culture of old.

Sometimes, a Facebook post on a controversial topic such as gun control might get dozens of comments on the platform itself but would generate few click-throughs to the actual article on csmonitor.com. In other cases, a quiz might get little interaction on Facebook itself but lots of clicks to the site. By March 2015, about 5% to 7% of the csmonitor.com's traffic was coming from social media referrals.[14]

Just as editors had previously reviewed page-view reports during the SEO era, the "social first" team used metrics to guide its work, expanding beyond page-view goals to track number of followers and interaction.[15] The team regularly reviewed Facebook posts for number of comments, shares, and likes to evaluate what content might be gaining traction on social media, which often was different from what was popular via search and what did well on the site itself. "There has to be an emotional appeal to a large group of people in order for people to want to share and engage on social media," one editor told us. "If they don't relate to the story or they feel like it doesn't matter to them, they're not going to share it."[16]

In mid-2015, Facebook instituted a major algorithm change that favored updates from friends and family over news, and news organizations of all kinds saw a massive drop in traffic, further complicating the social team's efforts.

BETTING ON CYBERSECURITY

Despite the conversation around UMP and the *Monitor*'s traditional news content on the home page, the newsroom remained committed to its verticals strategy for developing new revenue streams. By the time of our March 2015 visit, Monitor Global Outlook (MGO) had about 300 subscribers but had not become profitable.[17] Subscriptions ranged from $2,500 to $5,000.[18] Though Ingwerson received updates about the project, he was not involved in the daily management of the experiment, and the site functioned independently of the *Monitor*'s primary news operation; most people we interviewed said they didn't pay much attention to the new product.[19]

MGO had, however, demonstrated the ability to develop topic-specific content for a niche audience with a much smaller staff. Some editors had worried that board trustees who supported the venture might look at MGO's lean framework—built around a couple of editors and freelancers—as a model for slimming down the newsroom. "There's a big difference between doing a one-source freelance thing for business and doing the real editorial general news, where you check with lots of sources, you know, and write a great story,"[20] one editor said.

For some time, the *Monitor* had been bundling its national security coverage under a section of csmonitor.com called Security Watch, an effort that inspired development of a niche site focused on cybersecurity. Modeled after the successful *Texas Tribune*, the experimental project sought to expand beyond web-based content to include a newsletter, podcasts, and live events as part of a multipronged revenue strategy.

During the planning process, the vertical had been built around longtime reporter Mark Clayton, an award-winning journalist who had covered the topic since 2008 and had broken the 2010 story of the Stuxnet attack on Iran's nuclear fuel sites.[21] But Clayton died on August 23, 2014, just as the project's development was in the final stages.[22]

In the spring of 2015, the newsroom unveiled Passcode, a new branded site focusing on cybersecurity that would eventually show the promise of a profitable path forward. Like MGO, it operated independently of the daily operation of csmonitor.com, although its staff was housed in the newsroom.

These independent ventures did not come without risk. "These aren't products that draw page views,"[23] one editor said of MGO and Passcode. "These are products that are targeted for specific niche markets. So we've taken resources away from the website to get more hopefully invested in the richer revenue streams that are more targeted." What wasn't clear was whether the lessons from these ventures would eventually be integrated more fully into the *Monitor*.

PASSCODE'S GROWING PROMISE

Several people in the organization had questioned whether the business-to-business MGO really aligned with the

Monitor's original mission,[24] and by October 2015, when it appeared the project was not going to break even its first year, the newsroom ended the venture, despite the investment of time and resources.[25] Other trims to ease the financial pressure in the newsroom that year came through attrition: Departing journalists were not replaced, leaving five positions vacant.

In another corner of the newsroom, though, Passcode was percolating with innovative energy—and potential new revenue streams—under editors Mike Farrell and Sara Sorcher. From its inception, Passcode was a joint creation of the business and editorial departments, and like MGO, revenue had been central to the planning process. Though Passcode's budget originally came from the newsroom, it had moved to the business side of the ledger by 2015, and the team sought sponsors for podcasts, newsletters, and live events. Instead of focusing on page views, it concentrated on developing a smaller but more valuable audience: cybersecurity experts; people who need to know about cybersecurity, such as chief information officers and lawyers; and the informed consumer.[26]

The vision for Passcode's platform included a more responsive design and a cleaner look that would play better to a tech-savvy crowd than csmonitor.com's more staid appearance. The Passcode team struggled to bend the site's framework to its audio and graphical needs, so—much as Orr had done in the early days of web-first—it sought a platform outside of the main site. Team members won reluctant acceptance from the web technology department to use the multimedia publishing platform Atavist.[27]

Though Passcode springboarded off the familiar *Monitor* brand, it sought to forge its own identity. By March 2015, Passcode's newsletter had 1,000 subscribers, and its live events were gaining traction. The team had put on eight live news events, including four at South by Southwest in Austin, Texas, and half of those had brought in some sponsorship revenue.[28] The first episode of the Cybersecurity Podcast, a joint production with the New America Foundation, featured an interview with Lt. Gen. Edward Cardon, the Army's top cyber commander, and it, too, scored a sponsor—Mach37, a cybersecurity accelerator in the Washington, D.C. area.

Despite the site's niche appeal, some editors saw a high-profile vertical focused on the progress of cybersecurity as a natural fit for the UMP mission. They hoped the new offering would not suffer the same fate as MGO since it aligned more closely with the organization's journalistic goals.

PRESSURE FROM ABOVE

The specter of the church's board of directors and the Christian Science Publishing Society's board of trustees, who ultimately controlled the newsroom's fate, loomed over the various strategies. Those boards operate like corporate boards. They do not necessarily take a hands-on approach to managing the organization, but their overall vision matters, especially since they hold the purse strings. Historically, the boards had had a light touch when it came to editorial operations, but as budgets became tighter, they began to exert more influence.

The board of trustees visited the newsroom for a rare meeting with the *Monitor*'s top managers as the end of the fiscal year approached in April 2015. They listed concerns about the multipronged strategy, especially about initiatives that seemed too far removed from the *Monitor*'s original mission set forth by Mary Baker Eddy. One top manager summarized the board's concerns in a cultural context:

> They have a problem with web traffic because to get web traffic, you have to do stuff that doesn't feel like us, and you have ads that certainly don't feel like us. So they'd rather have a digital product that's very distinct, and they seem willing to sacrifice some of that reach that we've developed if it means that you don't have obnoxious display ads.[29]

During Yemma's reign, when the paper first began its SEO efforts in earnest, top editors had heard some complaints from above about headlines and posts, but by 2015, such conversations had become more frequent. The board wanted content that "uplifts and awakens thought" and could contribute to "helping and healing humanity."[30] The UMP approach was a much closer cultural fit with what the board wanted, but figuring out how to incorporate that vision into tangible journalism was challenging, some editors told us, and writers struggled with exactly how to weave the elements into their stories. Some tried to frame it in a more familiar context. "I'll just make sure I do good explanatory journalism that analyzes the news events, and hopefully, that'll be good enough for whatever the higher-ups are looking for. ... Hopefully, that fits into somebody's category," one writer told us.[31]

UMP reflected some ideals put forth by Solutions Journalism Network,[32] seeking not just to illuminate problems but also to highlight progress on solutions. However, at the *Monitor*, the approach emphasized changing the way people thought about issues—a concept more in line with Christian Science principles—rather than pushing readers to take individual action. One editor explained:

> [The board members] haven't defined it very well, but they're sort of like—they don't care about people taking action like building soup kitchens or building roads or whatever; we care about changing thought. ... Some of the board members say if everyone read an article that, you know, challenged an assumption, a negative assumption about a news development, that everyone that read it could have been impacted and changed their thought. That's the power that they want to have.[33]

Some people we interviewed welcomed the new approach because it favored reporting on weightier subjects beyond superficial trending topics. Ingwerson quoted Steve Jobs, saying it was "how we can make a dent in the universe," and the UMP standard became the primary mechanism by which individual and organizational success would be judged. The approach regularly filtered into conversations between editors and reporters during our March 2015 visit as they tried to incorporate this definition of distinction. An editor explained:

> Our priority has been to figure out how to effectively make a stronger *Monitor* experience on the web so that more people who come to a *Monitor* story through whatever means, by some increment are going to say, 'Who are these guys?'[34]

Another editor framed the struggle in competitive terms:

> The ... problem is a lot of organizations are starting to do solutions journalism in one form or another, and we've kind of been quietly toiling in the fields of solution journalism for, you know—since 1908. So others do it faster, they do it better, they do it bigger, you know. Organizations like *The Atlantic* just have the power to come out and try things, and if they fail, they can bail. We need to kind of marshal a lot of resources, make a commitment, and then come at things in our small, persistent way, which is a really difficult strategy in the current marketplace because you're relying on discovery, and it's hard for us to get that.[35]

The push toward UMP also meant continuing to alter the set of fast-paced digital routines that had by this time become ingrained by page-view successes. One editor suggested that some reporters had gotten out of the habit of making extra phone calls and doing additional on-the-ground reporting during the page-view-chasing era that required faster, shorter posting rhythms.

Schedules also began to shift with the emphasis on a more reflective approach to the news, rather than one driven so much by immediacy. "There used to be more of a push for volume, and we were pushing about 10 to 12 stories a day," one of the editors told us. "But now ... we're focusing more on ... the UMP. Now we're focusing a little bit more on the quality of the stories, and so we won't necessarily have as many."[36]

Another editor noted:

I still think very much about SEO. Keywords are—you know, we're
not as rigid about it as we used to be. There used to be certain very
formulaic ways that you had to get the first two words in the front
of the sentence, if you were going to try and get a Yahoo trend, or
something like that. But a lot of those games are harder to play
now, I think, because the algorithms all adjust accordingly.[37]

Some worried that the church's board was pushing the
Monitor—which had always included a blend of Christian
Scientists and people not connected to the church—to focus
on church members as a primary target audience. "They
don't want to do the news to the exclusion of anyone who's
not Christian Scientist, but ... I guess it's sort of like they
want to get back to the base and serve the Christian Science members more," one manager told us. "So this is
becoming clearer like almost by the day lately. So it leaves
some of us wondering what are the implications of that."[38]

The other big issue: how to monetize UMP. Although
ideally the frame helped to distinguish *Monitor* journalism
from commodity content and therefore in theory would keep
people coming back, metrics revealed uneven results. "The
struggle with that is there's no business model to [UMP],"
one editor said.

That's sort of just do this really good content on whatever you see
as worthy news, and you know, if it takes longer to do, that's OK,
even if you miss a traffic window. It might take you a long time, but
if it's doing the three-core task, it's fine.[39]

At this time, the Daily News Briefing (DNB), an email subscription product that brought in about $150,000 a year,
was becoming an area of focus. In the morning editorial
meeting, editors picked five stories to highlight in the newsletter. After stories went through their final edits, the desk
editors would trim the chosen stories to 250 words for
the DNB.[40]

ANOTHER ROUND OF LAYOFFS

The board had another big concern beyond making sure the *Monitor* was better aligned with its mission: the financial imperative. The newsroom had to find a way to balance the budget without the $3.6 million church subsidy—and do it by April 2018.[41]

Fading membership had taken its toll on church finances, and in the March 2015 meeting with the *Monitor* leadership, the managing board of trustees was clear: The news organization would have to be self-sufficient, like the church's smaller religious publications, *Sentinel* and *Journal*. The $3.6 million subsidy would be cut in half for fiscal 2017. It would be gone by fiscal 2018. The *Monitor* wasn't alone; many entities that depended on the church for financial support were suffering, with the church selling off many of its urban buildings across the country and leasing some of its buildings near the Mother Church in Boston.[42]

With little revenue growth to cover the cut, the organization braced itself for the largest round of staff cuts since the move to web-first. A November 2015 memo to staff about the cuts noted a move toward targeted topics with a focus on protecting front-line writers.[43] The document also noted the continued push toward blended editorial–publishing teams like Passcode's. Leaders formed strategic groups to review four areas of operations: content, audience, staffing, and sustainability. "All of this means carefully considering where we put our resources and learning to work together in new ways," a memo said.[44] "We are convinced we can build a vital and sustainable *Monitor* that attracts and serves a deeply engaged audience, makes a difference, and delivers on its powerful mission."

A major structural change also came to the role of the manager of the Christian Science Publishing Society, who oversees all of the church's publications including the *Monitor*. Historically, the position had focused on finances and operations, but in 2015 the manager's portfolio was expanded to include content and product. At the end of the year, Abe McLaughlin, who had worked for both the editorial and publishing sides of the *Monitor*, was appointed to the position. Though Ingwerson still reported to the church's board of directors as previous editors had, he now had a line on the organizational chart connecting to McLaughlin as well.

After word of impending layoffs spread, at least eight staffers volunteered to leave; in all, 17 positions—just over a quarter of the newsroom—were cut.[45] Some said that the build-up to the layoffs had led to feelings of depression as well as questions about the purpose and direction in the newsroom. But once the layoffs hit on April 1, it was like releasing a pressure valve; the threat was done and over with, and the organization could return to mapping out a strategy with what resources remained. By our May 2016 visit, the newsroom was down to 48 people (including temporary fellowship positions), and some longtime employees, including Matt Clark of the management team, were gone.

One top manager summed up the mood post-layoff this way:

> There's a few dimensions: 'Wow, we survived, and it's not as bad as we maybe thought.' 'Uh, we're all really overworked.' In some moments, 'seeing that this could be better.' I've heard people say, 'Maybe this could be better.' But it's all of those, and the overworked part is a huge thing. … But that's where we are.[46]

That mix of frustration and acceptance was felt throughout the organizational hierarchy. One writer who had been with the organization less than five years noted:

> Not everyone was very comfortable with how it was all handled, I would say—that all those people hadn't necessarily been treated fairly. There was that kind of sentiment. But at the same time, I think there was understanding that it had to happen, and certain people—the responsibility fell on their shoulders, and they had to make decisions.[47]

Fewer resources force hard decisions about what will and won't be part of the coverage mix, and the *Monitor*—like many other news organizations—had to work through that evaluation process in 2016.

DECLINING REVENUE

Monthly traffic to csmonitor.com had continued to dip, to 6 million unique visitors and around 20 million page views per month by May 2016.[48] In the fiscal year that ended April 1, 2014, csmonitor.com had generated $3 million in ad revenue from the website; for fiscal 2016, the annual ad revenue had plummeted to $1.2 million, in part because it had eliminated Adblade, a third-party ad delivery system that sometimes presented ads that were problematic to the board of trustees.[49] For example, ads for prescription or over-the-counter drugs are anathema to Christian Scientists, who believe that prayer is the proper path to healing.

Other revenue streams were not making up the shortfall. Subscriptions at the weekly publication and the DNB email product remained flat, and Passcode's success was not yet enough to make up for the loss of ad revenue, since it had been operating only a short time.

As the leadership team looked forward, it sought to integrate lessons from the experiments of the previous eight years. To build audience and sustain some level of ad revenue, the online unit's "social first" initiative had expanded into a group of 10 interns called the Rapid Response Team, which would produce consistent posts spurred by trending topics but rooted in UMP ideals. The team of interns worked to maintain the site's story count, as the declining number of stories per day had affected the number of unique visitors and page views—and therefore, traffic-based ad revenue. Some wondered if the team could eventually raise enough revenue to cover all of the costs for the newsroom. But not everyone agreed with the strategy, as it maintained some of the traffic-chasing aspects from the *Monitor*'s SEO era.

With fewer employees at the *Monitor*, the national and international desks had merged into a single unit focused in-depth coverage on education, sustainability, and inequality. With the emphasis on "rapid response," the online production team had disbanded by 2016, leaving news editors to take on more of the formatting tasks.

From this point forward, any new effort needed to hew to the mission-centric approach. One editor said:

> That was actually very energizing to me in the sense that I've long
> felt that the perception that mission and sustainability are at odds
> is the inverse of the truth of things, which is that mission and
> sustainability are complementary and connected, and that if we can
> deliver even better on the mission, that will lead us to sustainability.
> And why is that true? Because to deliver on the mission requires
> us to be more distinct.[50]

Tension was building, however, as the smaller staff worked to balance deep-dive reporting in the chosen key topic areas with the breaking news of the day. During our May 2016 visit, the newsroom left the story of the killing of an important Taliban leader to the news wires, a decision that sparked disagreement in the morning editorial meeting. One editor said later:

> On some days, it's like, 'Why don't we have that story?' Well, the
> reason we don't have that story is we don't have any value-add
> there. What makes us distinct? If we can't make it distinct, why are
> we doing it? Just hand it off and either let the wires do it, or let the
> Rapid Response Team do it and add some slight value-add, with
> sort of the sheen of UMP there. But don't waste one of our
> remaining three or four of our correspondents or freelancers—don't
> spend money or their time on something that's not going to be
> a really true value-add.[51]

Scoops—beating peer organizations to report major news developments—are a key benchmark of success among professional journalists. At the *Monitor*, among those who got hired or promoted on the basis of their ability to compete well and break news, it was difficult to let something they had once taken great pride in go. But with a much smaller news organization, it was clear that they had to focus more narrowly.

As with other experiments outside of the main news desk, the Rapid Response Team was located in a separate part of the newsroom. "I do feel so separate, so isolated," one intern told us. "[C]ommunication—there just isn't any, and also physically, we're kind of over there on a little island, and it feels like we're not really part of the news."[52]

Interns on the team had to write two posts a day, and the posts—typically 500 words or less—would follow a similar editing track of other *Monitor* stories: two edits from separate editors and a final review from the writer before publication. At the beginning of a shift, each intern would pitch three or four ideas with an UMP angle to assignment editors, pitches inspired by trending topics on Facebook, Twitter, or Google News. If approved, the stories would be added to the daily news budget. If the post dealt with a topic related to health, biology, or gambling, the story would receive a "needs CS sensitivity review" designation. The church has strong positions related to these issues, and the newsroom wanted to remain cognizant and respectful of those stances when considering story choice and presentation.

On the team's editing checklists, a number of questions focused on fact-checking and grammar, but one stood out from the usual copy-editing list: "Is there a U.M.P. nut graph—within the first 3 grafs—that gives a clear direction or statement of thesis to the story?"[53] And editors doing second reads on the posts were supposed to ensure the content had been optimized for search.

"We've moved away from traffic-chasing kind of stories," one editor explained. "We're doing stories that, yeah, are trending, but we're also trying to make sure they fit with our values and were done in a way that we feel like are *Monitor* UMP stories."[54] Despite that emphasis, the traffic effort still lacked unanimous support from the management team, with lingering worries that trend-driven stories still might damage the brand and draw the ire of the board.

"They're pushing us hard to say, 'Look, you need to stop thinking about the numbers so much'," one editor said of the board. "'You need to think about who we are that makes us distinct and unique, and if you push hard on that, the revenue will come,' which is not exactly a business plan."[55]

ADOPTING INNOVATIVE PROCESSES FROM THE STARTUP WORLD

People throughout the organization evaluated several options to boost revenue: paywalls, micro-payments, donations, paid content, sponsorships—all streams beyond advertising, which had remained a key, if diminishing, part of the *Monitor*'s sustainability formula into 2016. The publishing side had experienced cuts over the years and had about 20 people left by 2016. Funding for the *Monitor*'s outside direct ad sales team had dried up, as resources for traditional ad sales were shifted to sponsorship sales for efforts such as Passcode.[56]

Since 2015, members from the newsroom's online unit and the publishing side had been working together on design sprints (see Chapter 4) to develop and test new ideas and products quickly. The *Monitor*'s model followed the guidelines from the book *Sprint: How to Solve Big Problems and Test New Ideas in Just Five Days* by Jake Knapp (with John Zeratsky and Braden Kowitz),[57] who developed the process for Google Ventures. By 2016, the two units' budgets had merged.

Editors and other staffers involved in each two-week sprint process had to find ways to balance that work with their primary duties. But the process helped test ideas and develop improvements for the *Monitor*'s future. One that emerged from the process was called "the Redirect," a Facebook experiment developed jointly by publishing and editorial to create distinctive, graphically driven videos to expand the brand's reach on social media. Social referrals had consistently brought in less than 10% of the traffic to csmonitor.com; the staff hoped to capitalize on the *Monitor*'s large following to push that number to 15%.

One video, called "Dangerous Times," used crime statistics to dispel the notion that the United States had grown more dangerous. "It's really easy to think we live in dangerous times," the video began as a fever line sketching the U.S. murder rate skipped across the screen. "But here's the reality. The U.S. is safer now than at any point in modern history."[58] The video then highlighted key crime statistics and other reported information to validate the statement, and ended with the tagline: "Fight fear. Change the conversation."

The focus on dispelling unfounded fears fit well with the "changing thought" ethos. It also proved popular on Facebook. The video, shared more than 17,000 times, scored more than 1 million views, and served as a successful prototype for the *Monitor*'s social videos moving forward. "We have this antidote approach to news, and we found initially it played very well within our bubble of loyalists," one editor said, "and what we found the second time we sprinted around the Redirect was that there seemed to be an appetite for it in general, kind of beyond our bubble."[59]

Even though social media was showing the largest potential for audience growth, the organization was investing little money in the effort at this time. And even though the continued Social Tuesdays email effort had led to traffic increases, it typically was the same handful of reporters promoting their stories on their personal Twitter and Facebook accounts. "There's still a struggle to get everyone on board with the act of being social because I think people just get busy, and they don't prioritize it," one editor said.[60] The leadership, however, had not required social media activity among the reporters; it remained an encouraged option. Culturally, most of the staff had not embraced it.

Five sprints that developed out of larger strategic conversations had been completed by May 2016. The goals of building a strong Facebook following and a robust email subscriber list were designed to set the foundation for developing a digital subscription/membership product.

But as we had seen over the years, the various initiatives— the Rapid Response Team, the social media team, Passcode— did not always connect with the larger organization. "I think newsrooms in general struggle with this, but we're still pretty siloed," one editor said. "People work in little units and don't always have the best communication outside of their unit."[61]

THE SUCCESS OF PASSCODE

The year-old Passcode and its hybrid editorial–publishing team met its early revenue targets and had started off 2016 on a strong note. In March, the team returned to South by Southwest in Austin, Texas, and had a 1,000-square-foot booth on the showroom floor. More importantly, the Passcode team had secured a major sponsor, Dell Computer, for the event, raising thousands of dollars in revenue for the newsroom.

Sponsorships came in different forms. In some cases, special "sponsored content" involving only the business-side staff would kick off the events. A sponsor would be allowed 10 minutes for a segment styled like a TED Talk, or the event might feature a short interview with David Grant, director of content strategy, before the main segment. The rest would be dedicated to editorial content, such as a keynote interview or panel.

In April 2016, the Passcode unit was moved into the main news pod, and it was allowed to hire a full-time staff member under a one-year fellowship position named for Mark Clayton to support the team's expanding content portfolio. The Passcode's editorial team participated in all aspects of event planning and execution, including writing stories and managing social media.

The unit focused much of its effort on its newsletter, which came out three times a week. The team would use an algorithm to analyze top tweets from thousands of cybersecurity influencers on social media to help decide what content to highlight, and the newsletter featured an "influencers poll," where the team would regularly survey leading thinkers in cybersecurity on issues of the day.[62] Sara Sorcher, deputy cybersecurity editor, continued to work with the New America Foundation to draw big interview names to monthly episodes of the Cybersecurity Podcast, including Cory Doctorow of BoingBoing, security pioneer John McAfee, and former

National Security Agency and Central Intelligence Agency director Michael Hayden. Though sponsorship was inconsistent, some episodes secured sponsors such as Dell, the Edison Electric Institute, and HackerOne, a security platform.

Much like the tension over the Rapid Response Team, however, a split had emerged over Passcode. Some saw Passcode's financial and audience successes as a way forward; others saw the work as too specialized and narrow for the organization's mission. Did it fit? "That tension is really playing out as senior editors are now trying to shape their own focuses, right?" one editor said. "They're very reluctant to call anything that they do a 'vertical' because they see that as being so specialized that it divorces itself from the mission of the *Monitor*."[63]

"[Church founder] Mary Baker Eddy said that this should be a newspaper for the home, and it should be for all Christian Scientists and as many others as possible," said one editor who was also a member of the church. "And to me, that means it should have a unified purpose and a unified mission, and so far I've not heard any compelling arguments or thought of any on my own of how all of these things tie together."[64]

ANOTHER CHANGE AT THE TOP

As the end of 2016 approached, Marshall Ingwerson went to the church's board of directors and said that he wanted to step down as editor so he could take the chief executive position at The Principia, the nonprofit corporation that runs Principia College as well as a K–12 school for Christian Scientists in the St. Louis area. A December 15 post at csmonitor.com announcing Ingwerson's move ran in the Commentary section. It had been written by the Christian Science Board of Directors.

"We are tremendously grateful for the deep commitment, wisdom, and spiritual sense Marshall has brought to this work and for the progress the *Monitor* has made under his stewardship ..." the board wrote. "As Christmas draws near, we can trust that the light that is always coming into the world will continue to spread the Science that operates unspent, and provide all that is needed for blessing humanity."[65] It seemed to be another sign the church was becoming more closely involved with the *Monitor*'s day-to-day operations.

By March 2017, the board of directors had selected its next editor: Mark Sappenfield, who had spent 20 years at the *Monitor* with assignments in the San Francisco Bay area, Washington, D.C., and South Asia. He had returned to the Boston headquarters in 2009, as the web-first push had begun, where he became deputy news editor on the national desk and later part of Ingwerson's editorial management team. With Abe McLaughlin, manager of the Christian Science Publishing Society, the well-entrenched team developed the plan for the *Monitor*'s next steps.

"Done correctly, journalism can be an agent of healing and hope because it is not about arguing over facts and events but getting to the basic issues that matter so greatly to us all," he said in a staff-written *Monitor* post about his promotion.[66]

A NEW STRATEGIC FOCUS

Despite the revenue successes, the organization halted Passcode and the other verticals in the same month as the leadership change and put all of its energy into the sprint-developed subscription product known as the Monitor Daily. The newsroom would concentrate journalistic effort on five in-depth stories per day to be delivered to subscribers. On March 17, the Passcode staff posted a simple goodbye: "Passcode signs off," the headline read, noting that the offshoot would end March 31. On the @CSMPasscode Twitter account, the staff noted, "Passcode wouldn't have been possible w/o hard work of many dedicated reporters, columnists, contributors. Thank you."[67]

Members of the Passcode team were shocked and demoralized, editors said. Content strategist David Grant became associate publisher at the *Monitor*, but Mike Farrell and Sara Sorcher, the editorial leaders of the unit, moved on, after seeing the growing product abandoned before it could fully realize its potential.

The Rapid Response Team, too, was disbanded, and David Scott had moved more fully into a business role with the title "chief product manager/editor." Indeed, the revised organizational chart now showed business and editorial on the same chart, something that hadn't been seen in previous iterations. Combining the boxes on a single chart reflected a merger in thinking that had been developing over the years. As the new fiscal year began on April 1, 2017, the church—for the first time in decades—did not use any money from its general fund to support the *Monitor*. All money came from the *Monitor*'s endowment, subscription and advertising revenue, and donations.[68]

The board had decided that a significantly smaller organization with lower output focused on its mission was better than a larger one hyperfocused on meeting financial targets. One editor characterized the board's thinking in this way:

> We don't want you to make decisions anymore based on what the bottom line says per se. We want you to produce the best *Monitor* content possible and let that drive your decision-making—this new Daily—and see where that takes you.

Each day, the Monitor Daily would include an opening section about the day's news topics written by an experienced editor. It then highlighted the *Monitor*'s five stories, pieces that fit with the UMP ethic, and the editor would explain why each story was chosen. The Daily also featured an audio version that would hit the website at 6 p.m. each weekday. The model planned for a metered paywall. New visitors could view five stories before they were cut off from further content.

At the time, the DNB had about 1,800 subscribers. Using that base and the magazine subscribers, the team set a goal of about 5,000 subscriptions for the Daily for the first year. The new product launched on May 8, 2017.

The traditional "Page One" editorial meetings, which historically had been a daily conversation among top editors, had morphed in this new environment to become a much larger gathering of disciplines, including reporters, graphic artists, and the social media coordinator. Board members, too, would sometimes visit the meetings. Similarly, the organization had begun to adopt a "scrum" process, a development framework borrowed from the tech sector, using interdisciplinary teams to create product ideas and improvements.

Daily traffic to csmonitor.com had dropped sharply after the dissolution of the Rapid Response Team, from 6 million monthly unique visitors in August 2016 to about 2 million monthly unique visitors a year later. But with the new emphasis on the Daily, such drops were less of a concern. The benchmark was now subscriptions, and within the first three months, the *Monitor* had surpassed the initial goal of 5,000. A new target of 10,000 subscriptions was set, with a long-term goal of 30,000 over three years. The going rate: $9 per month for access to the website and newsletter.

By August 2017, all of the original primary players in the development of the web-first strategy were gone, including John Yemma, Jonathan Wells, Marshall Ingwerson, and Sue Hackney. But several in the top ranks remained from years past, from the *Monitor*'s days as a leading daily newspaper dedicated to national and international news, and a collaborative leadership team that included both business and editorial leaders emerged.

As 2017 came to a close, the organization remodeled a smaller space on the third floor of the Christian Science Publishing Society building to house the *Monitor* operation and abandoned the larger second floor that had been the *Monitor*'s home for years. The tighter quarters brought the editorial and publishing sides closer together physically, further proof that the firewall between the two departments had fallen. Having some people on the publishing side with some editorial experience helped ease the transition, said one editor with more than 15 years' experience.

It's like everybody is just trying to figure it out. And it's almost good to know we have, like, one of our own that is in publishing, instead of feeling like, 'Well, publishing doesn't understand editorial.' Well, yeah, as a matter of fact, they do. That excuse goes away.[69]

The new space was fresher and more modern than the old newsroom, with adjustable desks and a computer-aided reservation system for conference rooms, which came in handy to keep scrum meetings on track. The *Monitor*'s scrum process followed the book *Scrum: The Art of Doing Twice the Work in Half the Time*, by Jeff Sutherland and J.J. Sutherland.[70] All parts in the organization had undergone a three-hour training session to understand the process, whether or not they were part of a scrum team, and several people were sent to more advanced training to become scrum masters to manage teams. The *Monitor* implementation focused on short stand-up meetings in which the interdisciplinary teams would update their progress for development projects, which would be tracked using the online tool Trello. New ideas were tested and refined based upon feedback.

The newsroom had been divided into "pods" to cover specific topics and geographies: U.S. (with four regional reporters), Africa and Asia, Europe, Mideast and Diplomacy, Economy, Education, Politics, and Science. Two reporters were put on a project team as well. The approach was gaining traction among some readers, as the subscriptions had topped 8,700 by February 2018.[71]

In the conference room, a white board mapped out potential stories for the coming weeks. "The idea is, we can't be doing five significant stories from a standing start every morning," one editor explained. "The idea is two to three stories locked and loaded at the beginning of the day."[72] The other pieces could come in response to news of the day. With the Monitor Daily, the newsroom sought to vary the ways stories were told and be more explicit about the ways in which understanding, models of thought, and progress were infused in the journalism of the day.

Some topics called for shorter pieces of 600–800 words; others might be longer, up to 1,500 words. Graphical presentations of stories became part of the mix as well. And there appeared to be a market for this type of subscription product. By June 11, the whiteboard tracking the latest subscriber count showed 10,384, a 17% bump from February. Learning from its previous experiments with video, the newsroom had hired a videographer and incorporated more video storytelling into its coverage.

Beyond subscriptions, the *Monitor* worked through a four-month scrum process to develop a system to measure story impacts that went beyond traffic analytics. Stories were scored internally by editors on their "UMP" and given a "potential subscriber" score that incorporated conversion rates for the newsletter and visits to the subscription page. Each Wednesday, the *Monitor* team would review the analytics to see which stories hit the highest total scores among three categories: current subscribers, potential subscribers, and the internal UMP score.[73] "The bottom line is, are we visible?" one editor said.[74] "Are we getting enough people to buy in?"

A DECADE OF CHANGE

Over the years, most of the *Monitor*'s journalists—especially after the 2016 layoffs—had moved toward the reality of working with the business side for survival's sake, and the 2019 organizational structure fully reflected that combination of publishing (now thought of as product and marketing) and news. Two *Monitor* peers who had moved up together over the years, Sappenfield and McLaughlin, now stood atop this structure. It had taken more than a decade, over many experiments, for a cultural shift to take hold. Such a shift emerges after new successes and failures are woven into the organizational mythos. Our model reflects the differing time horizons among innovation, strategy, and culture; culture cannot change overnight.

Even after all of the *Monitor*'s experiments, trials, and changes, its long-tenured journalists still privileged the deeply embedded newsroom routines. Similarly, with the ties to the church—and so many Christian Scientists working at the *Monitor*—any innovation ultimately had to circle back to a culture that was sensitive to the church and its teachings. The idealized vision of the *Monitor* as a beacon among news organizations was woven into the strategy, and the cultural work involved integrating the old and the new. Even in 2019, during our last visit, that work was far from over, as Sappenfield worked on a new iteration of UMP for the subscription era.

By that time, Passcode and the other verticals were gone, the operations were slimmer, and the focus had sharpened toward solutions-oriented journalism products, driven by the subscription-based Daily newsletter and podcast. The success of the paid newsletter, with more than 10,000 subscribers, inspired a boost of confidence reminiscent of the SEO days. It affirmed the strategic push toward distinction, an idea rooted in the original values of *Monitor* journalism.

But much like discovering a lack of revenue upon reaching the page-view goal, the newsroom hit yet another bump in 2019: Newsletter subscriptions had plateaued after rocketing to 10,000. The organization had discovered a churn problem, with people not renewing after the first year. Also, in February 2019, associate publisher David Grant, one of the *Monitor*'s vocal change agents behind Passcode and the Daily newsletter, left for a product manager position at Facebook.

In times of struggle, people often revert to the Model I defensive behavior described by Argyris. One manager told us in June 2019:

When there's no progress, ... everyone starts to look inward: 'Well, what am I doing wrong? What are they doing wrong? Obviously, I'm doing great content, so it must be the marketing side.' And the marketing side feels like, 'We're doing everything we possibly can; it must be the content.' And that's just the age-old suggestion: I'm doing my job well, so it must be them.[75]

A cross-functional team that included journalists, marketers, and tech developers had developed the metered paywall for subscriptions, a truly integrated effort. But once that project was built, editorial retreated from regular involvement in product teams. Some worried that effort dedicated to the sprints took away from editing and other core journalistic tasks. As the newsroom had shrunk, each minute dedicated to journalism had become more valuable. "Whenever we try something new, there is a lot of resistance," one staffer told us. "There is always this question of, 'Why are we doing this?'"[76]

In 2018, Samantha Laine Perfas had moved from social media editor to producer of the Monitor Daily podcast, and with a deepening interest in audio, she pitched the idea of developing a podcast series with richer production. After a design sprint and user testing, she began work on a limited-run project called Perception Gaps, which focused on the difference between perception and reality on hot-button topics such as crime, guns, and gender. Despite approvals from above, the idea faced some internal resistance, especially since it consumed valuable tech and journalism resources to produce. Still, it proved successful; a free pop-up newsletter to support the podcast had 6,000 subscribers by the time of the 10th and final episode.[77] The success won Perfas a promotion to story team leader, a new position. Her team, which included an engagement specialist and a video producer, went on to experiment with other story forms including an informational stop-action video to explain how to fix Congress. It was another example of a cultural nudge born of reluctant innovation.

By 2019, product testing and user interviews had become part of the decision-making process, and the language of software development continued to filter into the daily jargon. Its organizational structure also reflected this innovation ethic. Clay Collins, who had been part of the sprint that developed the Daily product, moved from daily editor to a newly created post, director of editorial innovation and outreach. Also, a senior product manager with years of experience outside of the *Monitor* working in customer and digital experience roles was hired.

Though the financial pressure from the board had eased, it had not disappeared, and the *Monitor*'s connection to the Christian Science Publishing Society was more keenly felt. Much like the expanding ties between regional newspapers and a corporate hub at for-profit media chains, the *Monitor*'s marketing and technology-development resources had been subsumed into its Christian Science Publishing Society parent, which had publications and products beyond the secular *Monitor*.

CONCLUSION

The *Monitor*, with its ties to the Church of Christ, Scientist, is a unique case among news organizations. But its journalists are much like others we have worked with and interviewed in other newsrooms, and its balancing of the cultural, strategic, and innovative imperatives over a decade of change carries lessons for any news organization. From our vantage point, we witnessed consistent efforts toward innovation over the decade, sometimes strategic, sometimes not. Fear and necessity drove occasionally frantic experiments, especially after the failure of the SEO strategy to generate sufficient revenue to maintain its idealized state as a larger organization with numerous bureaus around the globe. The transition to the UMP era, with a more clearly defined purpose, did help strategically and culturally, but it took the final round of layoffs in 2016 to force the organization to make difficult choices and emerge in its latest focused incarnation.

As we have found with many of the news outlets we've studied, the past is ever-present at the *Christian Science Monitor*. Its deep connection to the church, combined with the fact that so many of its employees are Christian Scientists, was a key contributor to its approach to coping with change.

The *Monitor*'s journalists held long-embedded underlying assumptions about what counts as high-quality journalism— many of them steeped in the long primacy of print-based traditions and routines—that caused them to initially resist new digital strategies or tools like social media. But the removal of the print daily from the equation and the dire nature of the financial situation sparked change, as many felt they did not have any choice. The rapid initial successes in growing page views helped burnish those new strategies and routines, even though many were concerned that they were no longer doing good journalism.

Efforts at distinctiveness and engagement suffered from vague definitions and a resistance among journalists to cede power to the audience. Like many journalists we've interviewed or worked with, *Monitor* reporters and editors were loath to give up the gatekeeping role and let audience information needs shape news judgment. At the *Monitor*, this resistance was even more powerful as the organization had long seen itself as a shaper of thought.

As the financial squeeze continued, the *Monitor* ultimately gave up on the aspirations to maintain its size and broad audience. It exists now as a much smaller organization tightly focused on a narrowly honed mission and more emphasis on serving church members, especially as the church board asserted itself in a way that it hadn't in the past. The original mission was paramount, even if it meant giving up on being part of the national conversation.

UMP, or the idea that stories should bring understanding, change models of thought, and promote progress, took years to embed itself in newsroom routines, but today, UMP is formally integrated into the organization's way of doing business; it is incorporated in daily reviews of content and discussed in regular meetings.

By the time of our last visit, the *Monitor* had fully incorporated the language and rhythm of experimentation into the newsroom processes, although some familiar tensions persisted. Through a mix of strategic changes and trials driven by innovation, the culture has moved. For any organization considering our model during periods of change, the story will be different, but a similar lesson will arise. Cultural values and traditions must inform strategy, and strategic vision must guide innovation efforts. Experiments with little connection to organizational identity, purpose, and value— no matter how successful—will eventually fade and fail to move the culture toward a new identity, a transformed sense of itself.

NOTES

1 Confidential interview, personal communication, March 20, 2015.
2 Memo, "Core Tasks of *Monitor* Journalism," n.d.
3 Confidential interview, personal communication, March 20, 2015.
4 Memo, "Core Tasks of *Monitor* Journalism," n.d.
5 Confidential interview, personal communication, March 20, 2015.
6 Meeting, March 16, 2015.
7 Mark Sappenfield, "How Madison Avoided Becoming another Ferguson," *Christian Science Monitor*, March 15, 2015, www.csmonitor.com/USA/Justice/2015/0315/How-Madison-avoided-becoming-another-Ferguson.
8 Meeting, March 16, 2015.
9 Confidential interview, personal communication, March 17, 2015.
10 Confidential interview, personal communication, March 17, 2015.
11 New York University, "Studio 20: Digital First," n.d., https://journalism.nyu.edu/graduate/programs/studio-20-digital-first/.
12 Confidential interview, personal communication, March 17, 2015.
13 Confidential interview, personal communication, March 17, 2015.
14 Confidential interview, personal communication, March 19,2015.
15 Confidential interview, personal communication, March 19, 2015.
16 Confidential interview, personal communication, March 19, 2015.
17 Confidential interview, personal communication, March 16, 2015.
18 Confidential interview, personal communication, March 18, 2015.
19 Confidential interview, personal communication, March 16, 2015.
20 Confidential interview, personal communication, May 23, 2016.
21 Mark Clayton, "Stuxnet Malware Is 'Weapon' Out to Destroy ... Iran's Bushehr Nuclear Plant?," *Christian Science Monitor*, September 21, 2010, www.csmonitor.com/USA/2010/0921/Stuxnet-malware-is-weapon-out-to-destroy-Iran-s-Bushehr-nuclear-plant.
22 "Ralph Langner on CSM Reporter Mark Clayton's 'Guts to Break the Story'," YouTube, October 28, 2016, www.youtube.com/watch?v=H1ke6NO_qeo.
23 Confidential interview, personal communication, March 17, 2015.
24 Confidential interview, personal communication, March 18, 2015.
25 Confidential interview, personal communication, May 23, 2016.
26 Confidential interview, personal communication, March 20, 2015.
27 Confidential interview, personal communication, March 20, 2015.
28 Confidential interview, personal communication, March 20, 2015.

29 Confidential interview, personal communication, March 18, 2015.
30 Confidential interview, personal communication, April 16, 2015.
31 Confidential interview, personal communication, March 16, 2015.
32 Solutions Journalism Network, "Solutions Journalism," n.d., www.solutionsjournalism.org/.
33 Confidential interview, personal communication, March 18, 2015.
34 Confidential interview, personal communication, March 17, 2015.
35 Confidential interview, personal communication, March 19, 2015.
36 Confidential interview, personal communication, March 19, 2015.
37 Confidential interview, personal communication, March 20, 2015.
38 Confidential interview, personal communication, March 18, 2015.
39 Confidential interview, personal communication, March 18, 2015.
40 Confidential interview, personal communication, March 20, 2015.
41 Confidential interview, personal communication, March 20, 2015.
42 Caroline Fraser, "Dying the Christian Science Way," *The Guardian*, August 6, 2019, www.theguardian.com/world/2019/aug/06/christian-science-church-medicine-death-horror-of-my-fathers-last-days.
43 Jim Romenesko, "Christian Science Monitor Will Cover Fewer Topics but Do So with Authority and Insight," jimromenesko.com, November 25, 2015, http://jimromenesko.com/2015/11/25/christian-science-monitor-well-cover-fewer-topics-but-do-so-with-authority-and-insight/.
44 Romenesko.
45 Confidential interview, personal communication, May 27, 2016.
46 Confidential interview, personal communication, May 27, 2016.
47 Confidential interview, personal communication, May 25, 2016.
48 Confidential interview, personal communication, May 24, 2016.
49 Confidential interview, personal communication, May 24, 2016.
50 Confidential interview, personal communication, May 27, 2016.
51 Confidential interview, personal communication, May 24, 2016.
52 Confidential interview, personal communication, May 25, 2016.
53 "CSM Rapid Response Team Editing Checklists," 2016.
54 Confidential interview, personal communication, May 24, 2016.
55 Confidential interview, personal communication, May 24, 2016.
56 Confidential interview, personal communication, May 26, 2016.
57 Jake Knapp, with John Zeratsky and Braden Kowitz, *Sprint: How to Solve Big Problems and Test New Ideas in Just Five Days* (New York, NY: Simon & Schuster, 2016).
58 "The Redirect," Facebook, April 7, 2016, wwww.facebook.com/ChristianScienceMonitor/videos/10154187706169658/.
59 Confidential interview, personal communication, May 25, 2016.
60 Confidential interview, personal communication, May 26, 2016.
61 Confidential interview, personal communication, May 26, 2016.
62 Confidential interview, personal communication, May 25, 2016.
63 Confidential interview, personal communication, May 23, 2016.

64 Confidential interview, personal communication, May 27, 2016.

65 Christian Science Board of Directors, "Editor of the Christian Science Monitor to Step Down," *Christian Science Monitor*, December 15, 2016, www.csmonitor.com/Commentary/2016/1215/Editor-of-The-Christian-Science-Monitor-to-step-down.

66 Staff, "New Editor at the Christian Science Monitor," *Christian Science Monitor*, March 6, 2017, www.csmonitor.com/Commentary/2017/0306/New-editor-at-The-Christian-Science-Monitor.

67 @CSMPasscode, Twitter, March 31, 2017, https://twitter.com/CSMPasscode/status/847870108592742400.

68 Confidential interview, personal communication, August 17, 2017.

69 Confidential interview, personal communication, June 12, 2018.

70 Jeff Sutherland and J.J. Sutherland, *Scrum: The Art of Doing Twice the Work in Half the Time* (New York, NY: Crown Business, 2014).

71 Confidential interview, personal communication, February 18, 2018.

72 Confidential interview, personal communication, July 31, 2018.

73 Confidential interview, personal communication, June 13, 2018.

74 Confidential interview, personal communication, July 31, 2018.

75 Confidential interview, personal communication, June 26, 2019.

76 Confidential interview, personal communication, June 25, 2019.

77 Confidential interview, personal communication, June 25, 2019.

Throughout this book, we have emphasized the importance of thinking across multiple levels—culture, strategy, and innovation—to bring about lasting change in your organization. Understanding the distinctive aspects of your culture will help you identify where you fit in the competitive landscape and what new value you might provide for your communities. But how do you put this model into practice, under the pressure and grind of the 24/7 news machine?

This conclusion will help you apply our model and approach change efforts from multiple perspectives: culture, which helps you identify the deeply embedded values that affect change; strategy, which guides your organization's big-picture goals; and innovation, which inspires experimentation and allows you to adjust quickly to audience needs.

Thinking through the model is not a linear process. Though we present this road map as an outline, you will find yourself moving among the three levels simultaneously. Each is connected to the others; change at one level inevitably alters another. The key is tempering the pressures of short-term performance with patience for long-term transformation.

CULTURE: DIAGNOSE YOUR CULTURE

You may feel as though you already understand your organization's culture—after all, you work there. But the research is clear: You must actively set aside your own assumptions to decipher the true underlying, unspoken aspects of the collective culture if you want to identify what is blocking change in your organization. That process starts with an organizational diagnosis.[1]

It is most effective to bring in someone from outside the organization who can see it from a fresh perspective, free of the inherent biases that come from being immersed in internal politics. If you

Transforming Newsrooms:
A Model for Change

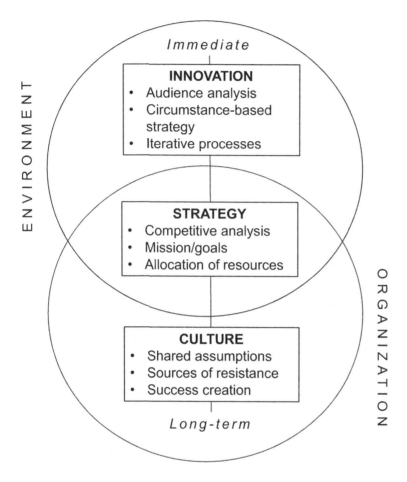

Figure C.1 Transforming newsrooms: a model for change

cannot afford to hire an experienced consultant, a journalism, communication, or management professor might be willing to help you in exchange for the ability to collect data for research projects. If outside help isn't feasible, create a diverse team with members from different departments, experience levels, and positions in the organizational hierarchy. Empower them with the time required to do this work as well as your vigorous public blessing.

Conduct an internal listening exercise through interviews, surveys, and focus groups. During this process, everyone in the organization needs to feel that his or her voice has been heard. In Box C.1 are some of the kinds of questions we have found useful.

BOX C.1 CONDUCTING CULTURAL INTERVIEWS

We prefer open-ended questions to allow participants to share their experiences in their own words. You can shape the questions to fit your organization.

- Describe how you do your job.
- What do you feel your organization is *best* at? What do you like most about working here? Are there any examples of successful transitions, past changes that made a positive difference?
- What are the biggest challenges you face in your daily work? What tends to block change in this organization? What are this organization's greatest weaknesses?
- How do people find out what's going on around here? Are there formal announcements, gossip, informal networks?
- How does newsroom leadership communicate goals and expectations around here? Do you feel you know what is expected of you? What kinds of feedback do you receive? How are decisions made, and do you have input?
- Do you think this organization is evolving in ways that are consistent or inconsistent with core journalism values? Why, or why not?
- How does the newsroom determine what "success" means in the current environment?
- Where do you think this organization is headed? What do you see happening in the next year? The next five years?

The goal: understanding how people view the organization's greatest strengths and weaknesses, and articulate its goals and values. How well do daily routines and rewards measure up to these values in their minds? Be open to their assessment of organizational communication and leadership in this time of change. When collecting information, keep questions open-ended and assumption-free to solicit honest, unexpected answers.

Surveys set up through tools such as Google Forms or SurveyMonkey may be more practical for larger organizations. Depending on the relationship between management and employees, you may get more intimate and revealing information via a survey rather than face-to-face interviews. Offer everyone the opportunity to respond to the survey to ensure a valid, generalizable sample for your fixed-choice questions, and include open-ended questions for specific details to inform your quantitative results. Appoint a group to identify themes from qualitative survey data and share the results in an easily digestible way. The qualitative and quantitative data should inform one another.

Confidentiality is a must to inspire candor and reflection. In newsrooms, remember that it can be possible to determine people's identity on the basis of job position—for example, there may be only one sports editor or anchor—but as long as you promise confidentiality and are transparent about how you are using the data, openness usually is not an issue, especially with an outside evaluator.

Members of the organization should understand that the process is exploratory; it is a way to ensure that change happens in a way that best reflects the values of the organization's members. If you find this process to be difficult, that fact alone might say something about your culture.

Besides interviews, the cultural analysts should spend time observing meetings and daily routines. Even insiders can benefit from watching silently as a newcomer might, especially in departments and divisions that are separate from their current responsibilities. Observation will help identify the gaps between what people say and what they do, a critical component of understanding culture.

When observing and studying interactions, use these questions as an analytical guide:

- Who speaks the most in meetings? Who stays quiet? Do one or two people dominate, or is conversation distributed more equally?

- What kinds of topics get the most attention? What kinds of news stories lead editorial meetings/discussions, and what (if any) are the reasons given for coverage of certain topics?
- What do interactions tell you about leadership styles, communication patterns, and priorities?
- What is most celebrated or revered in the organization? What gets ignored or de-emphasized?

Also, pay attention to *artifacts* such as the physical space and what it might reveal about the organization.[2] Ask:

- What does the space reveal about hierarchy and staff relationships? For example, who gets the offices around the perimeter of the newsroom? Who is working in the open, among the cubicles?
- Does physical separation cause subgroups to form?
- What kinds of awards or other signifiers of prestige get displayed?

These observations can uncover unspoken priorities and nonverbal forms of leadership and communication. But be cautious about over-interpreting what you see, especially at first. Experienced researchers do not draw conclusions until they have compiled observations over a significant period of time, allowing them to weed out anomalies and identify patterns in the data.

Analyzing Information

After you have collected your data, review the complete set of observations to identify themes about your culture. Here, an outside perspective is particularly valuable, as it prevents your own biases and preconceived judgments from creeping into the analysis.

Next, identify *espoused values*. What did people say were the organization's mission and goals? In most groups, these answers are fairly consistent, often mirroring language from visible mission statements or mottos. When it comes to journalists, some of the espoused values will likely be those tightly held by most members of the profession, such as the importance of verification or a strict adherence to independence.[3] Others may be more specific to your organization and its current strategy.

The next step is more interesting: What are the *underlying assumptions* about the right way to do things? What are the unspoken values governing what people actually do, even if those actions appear to conflict with the stated mission? Compare observational data with what people told you, and keep in mind that people don't always behave rationally. They may be responding emotionally or defensively to circumstances and events in the workplace.[4] This reaction doesn't mean that they are bad employees—they're just human. You will be surprised at how quickly insights emerge.

Avoid fixating too quickly on a handful of visible problems.[5] Organizations are complex, interdependent systems, and issues that arise may not be as simple as they appear. How are different parts of the organization interacting? Do they fit together in ways that allow you to adapt to both internal needs and to the changing external environment?[6] For example, insufficient budgets in one area may affect the behavior in another department in a way that makes you slower to respond to competitors.

Share the Findings

Present a summary of findings in a concise format to organization members. Ideally, host small meetings of no more than 10 people to discuss the report, and solicit feedback on the results. Does the culture you've described sound familiar to everyone? If not, where did the analysis miss the mark? What else should you add?[7]

While leaders are probably the most immediately interested in the cultural findings, everyone should have the chance to give feedback. If the organization's size makes it logistically impossible, gather feedback from people at each level in the hierarchy; a quick way to breed resentment is to make someone feel left out of the process. Problems you identify must resonate at all levels as collective issues, not the failings of one person or a handful of individuals. Employees will also lack the motivation and commitment required to meet the challenge of changing if they can blame individuals instead of recognizing their own responsibility for and stake in the problems at hand. Getting unspoken but widely shared concerns into the open develops a shared mindset critical for change. Culture is a shared phenomenon,[8] and conversations that allow people to air frustrations without feeling as if they are going to take sole blame for problems can be cathartic and build morale.

This cultural analysis will inform the rest of the road map, but the report is helpful on its own. Often, simply having a widely shared understanding of how people perceive the organization's identity and values helps identify what may inhibit change.

Before you begin venturing into the strategy and innovation levels, ask: Are there any changes that may be necessary based on what you have learned so far? What can you do to address the issues that may be making the organization function less effectively? Do you need better systems for sharing information and communicating internally?[9] How can you improve the flow of communication?

There is no universal prescription stemming from your cultural assessment because organizations, like people, are unique, and any changes you make should dovetail with the distinctive picture of your organization. Look carefully for the ways in which you could better align your daily routines, the actions your staff *actually* performs, with the values embedded in the organization as you develop your revamped processes. This reflection needs to happen continually—not just as a one-off exercise—to maintain a consistently improving organization.

Leadership and Culture

As we discussed earlier in the book, leaders play a critical role in shaping and reinforcing culture.[10] After the cultural diagnosis, leaders should reflect upon their own management style and its impact upon the wider organization. How do they model behavior for their employees? Does an authoritarian, hands-on style lead to less risk-taking among employees? Does a laissez-faire approach cause chaos or disengagement? How can leaders design policies and allocate resources in a way that reinforces and instills the values they want to be part of the culture moving forward?

After sharing the cultural findings, leaders need to think about how they can adjust incentives—even subtle cues such as what's praised publicly—in the direction of the organization's goals. Leaders can't just make new demands; they need to think carefully about how they can inspire people to take individual responsibility to achieve collective goals. Box C.2 details a common pitfall you should avoid.

BOX C.2 AVOID THE "IF ONLY!"

It is tempting to assume that all of an organization's problems could be easily solved "if only!" the right/best/perfect person could be discovered to run it. But underlying factors, such as attitudes and expectations, the organization's culture, and communication processes are often the real culprits when it comes to failing to adapt.[11] When beginning to understand your culture, you must be open to a wide and complex array of factors will impact your ability to deal with change.

STRATEGY: IDENTIFY YOUR MISSION

Some organizations devote much effort to their visioning process. We agree that it's important to root yourself in a well-articulated strategy—strategy is a central part of our model—but it is easy to fall into lengthy discussions over a single word in a mission statement and lose sight of the primary goal of the endeavor: to create guiding principles to achieve collective goals. A compelling strategy establishes the organization's place in the competitive landscape. It should explain how the organization's assets and strengths provide a unique value in the marketplace. Box C.3 explains how change is a never-ending process.

BOX C.3 NEVER STOP CHANGING

We all want a problem-free, stress-free organization, but this will, never happen. One of the first guidelines we learned from Michael Diamond, the founder of the Center for the Study of Organizational Change at the University of Missouri, was that organizations have to be prepared for continuous change with no endpoint. Our media landscape will continue to evolve; the next Facebook, Twitter, or Instagram will create new demands we will have to adapt to. Instead, you are working to develop your capacity to recognize problems and deal with conflict constructively.

Create a Strategy Team

Nimble, reflective organizations continually dust off their missions and think deeply about the *why* of their existence. They review structures and procedures, and question policies and systems that constitute double-loop learning. To start this process in your own organization, put together a strategy team to review the mission statement in the context of the current competitive environment. Do the goals and guiding principles make sense to keep the news organization a thriving, vibrant part of the community conversation? Are resources—human and financial—distributed in a way that makes achieving the fundamental goals possible? Where is the disconnect between vision and execution? And how well does the strategy connect with the underlying assumptions identified in the cultural analysis?

The strategy team, too, should bring together key people from across the organization—departments as well as levels in the hierarchy—to analyze organizational goals. As with other teams you convene to manage and inspire change, you'll want to make sure to control the size of this group to make the work manageable and the team effective. Consider the possibility of some open-book management techniques,[12] which recommend sharing bottom-line results with all organizational participants so they understand how their individual responsibilities contribute to the operation's overall financial success.

How can you use the mission to provide an aspirational guide in a way that speaks authentically to organizational members? Be skeptical of quick strategic shifts.

Conceptually, time horizons change at each level of our model. Culture evolves over many years; innovation tactics should be acted upon quickly and decisively for testing and evaluation. Strategy provides the fulcrum between the security of culture and the experimentation of innovation. A good strategy connects disparate experiments to a larger goal; if your overall strategy shifts with each passing fad, you will never dedicate enough time or resources to establishing your experiments as new ways of accomplishing journalism, ones that your communities—whether they be geographic or topical—will view with authenticity, credibility, and respect. Box C.4 offers suggestions for what to include in your mission statement.

BOX C.4 WHAT SHOULD YOUR MISSION STATEMENT INCLUDE?

A good mission statement reflects broader, larger values that the organization aspires to attain. It should be clear, concise, and memorable. People should draw inspiration and purpose from it, and it should be easy to extract tangible, executable goals from reading it. It should provide the guiding framework for developing a unique value proposition, a statement of what your organization provides of value to the community that no one else can provide.

STRATEGY: IDENTIFY YOUR ORGANIZATIONAL POSITION

With mission statement in hand, the strategy team can dig into an evaluation of the competitive landscape and the organization's place within it using a SWOT (strengths, weaknesses, opportunities, and threats) analysis. As with the cultural evaluation, it's important that this review be conducted without covering up blemishes. As difficult as it may be, organizational units must set aside their preconceived notions and sacred procedures to embrace the possibility of a better way of accomplishing goals that align with the mission. Don't just create a vanity document that affirms your own greatness. The best SWOT analyses go deeply into weaknesses and threats.

Internal Evaluation: Strengths/Weaknesses

The first part of the process is identifying what the organization does and does not do well. Strengths and weaknesses are the tangible elements within the control of the organization's leaders and members. The review should dissect the allocation of resources, human and financial, and evaluate whether some should be redistributed to shore up identified weaknesses. How should the news organization be repositioned to take advantage of opportunities in the competitive landscape?

The cultural analysis, if done correctly, will surface how work actually gets done in the organization and will help you identify the true strengths and weaknesses inside the company, beyond the image presented by individual managers. Sometimes, mid-level leaders become skilled at presenting a version of reality skewed to benefit their own departments—and often, to the detriment of others'—in the current structure of resources and incentives. This process should help uncover those unintended consequences sparked by certain edicts or policies.

Take the practice of setting and reviewing website goals based on metrics, an important part of many newsrooms' digital strategy. Examine closely how newsroom personnel are boosting traffic and revenue. Are they adopting short-term practices that meet page-view quotas but diminish content quality and damage brand credibility? How has the push for speed and quantity affected accuracy? Consider the interlocking implications of such policies, and look closely for any potential to damage the organization and its journalistic credibility.

In the strengths/weaknesses evaluation phase, you will want to review the following areas:

- *Staffing.* What human resources do you have? What are the distinctive skills and qualities of your staff that provide a competitive advantage? Does the staff have the necessary skills for newer forms of storytelling, or does the newsroom have noticeable skill gaps (e.g. programming, cross-platform creation)?
- *Equipment/technology.* What technological investments has your organization made? How do those technologies position the organization to compete? What equipment should be upgraded and improved moving forward? How could the organization's physical resources be leveraged creatively to provide distinctive journalism for the community? Are there open-source, free alternatives to proprietary options that would still meet your needs?
- *Finances/investment.* Has the organization streamlined its budget in targeted ways, or has it adopted across-the-board cuts that have damaged its competitive advantage? Where have investments been made to move the company forward to maintain its edge?
- *Policies/procedures.* Is control centralized, or do individual units/managers have some power to manage their budgets and take studied risks? Are job descriptions flexible enough to allow employees to venture into varied tasks? Do employees have opportunities to learn new skills and experiment with new ways of accomplishing work?

- *Structure.* Are there layers of bureaucracy for decision-making? Does the structure inhibit or foster innovation? How do lessons from one unit spread throughout the organizations? Do the communication flows allow for—or even reward—interdepartmental sharing of information regarding successes and failures?

External Evaluation: Opportunities/Threats

The next step in the SWOT analysis is evaluating the environment surrounding the organization, beyond the direct control of leaders and managers. Scan the horizon not only within the industry and its current solutions, but also in similarly positioned sectors. When looking for opportunities, don't limit brainstorming to those traditional journalistic pockets and advertising sources of revenue. How can you leverage your information-gathering and verification strengths into adjacent possibilities to serve your community? This view of strategy leads to thinking at the innovation level.

A little over a decade ago, the American Press Institute (API) teamed up with Clayton Christensen to develop its "Blueprint for Transformation," which offered a framework for helping news organizations analyze and seize opportunities among their audiences and communities. One of the blueprint's key recommendations for locating opportunities: Identify those in the market who are not connected to your brand or products—or "nonconsumers"[13]—and discover the information "jobs" that those community members need done.

The Media Choice Model mentioned in Chapter 4 provides a framework for identifying what those communication "jobs to be done" might be. Researchers have found that the primary needs in the online space include information, shopping/consumption, entertainment, and connectivity.[14] How can your organization effectively fulfill those roles? How can you use your strengths to best satisfy those needs in your community?

The API report also noted the importance of understanding the competitive impact of these choices. In addition to identifying the nonconsumers, look for targets being ignored by competitors.[15] Remember that your competition may not necessarily be another news outlet; consider other sources of information, entertainment, and connection that compete for time and attention. In the age of the smartphone, media consumers have become spoiled by the plethora of content choices, which allow for extreme specialization and customization.

For identifying threats at a business level, Porter's Five Forces framework,[16] referenced in Chapter 3, helps locate your organization's place in the competitive landscape. Walk through each category to determine what outside forces may threaten the long-term existence of your organization. Such a review provides the proper foundation for your innovation efforts and prevents haphazard experiments. Leverage your existing strengths to pursue sensible opportunities.

INNOVATION: STAYING NIMBLE AND RESPONSIVE

If you aren't consistently developing new products, services, or internal processes that respond to audiences' changing problems and needs, you are standing still in ways that risk your sustainability.

Fortunately, innovation does not depend upon a sudden flash of genius.[17] Design thinking, agile development, and academic research on organizational learning and tech disruption all offer a variety of methods newsrooms can use. None of these models for innovation on its own is a formula for success, but by understanding them, leaders can ensure that their news organizations are well positioned in an era of constant change. As you apply the techniques, keep in mind your cultural and strategic reviews. Apply the lessons of disruption and innovation in a way that meshes with the organization's underlying assumptions and its identified strategy.

Paradigm Shift: Focus on the Audience

The biggest and most fundamental task at the innovation level of our model is to shift organizational goals to include the needs of the audience. As Liz Danzico, creative director of NPR, says: "The user is at the center of the diagram, not the content."[18]

This insight is critical across the many different disciplines we studied to produce this book. Entrepreneurs, social journalists, designers, and innovators of all stripes know that the key to a successful new product, business, or service is to solve a problem or meet a need.

Innovation is not about pushing your product, idea, or story into the community. It's about discerning what your audience wants and meeting those needs in a variety of different ways, and then committing to testing continually to be sure that you are consistently meeting those needs.

When we think about audience, we like to think in terms of communities—not just as physical spaces, but in terms of passions or common goals that unite groups. What are specific unfulfilled content niches, and what are the interest communities in your area? Start with what you learned from your SWOT analysis to identify certain communities you may want to focus on initially, but be open to the idea that you may need to adjust going forward. Entrepreneurs often discover that the initial market identified for their product is wrong.[19]

Create a Community Team

In this part of the process, put together a team focused on audiences and communities. If your organization is large enough, this team should ideally have members independent of the culture and strategy teams. This group will be charged with finding new ways of listening to people you serve across demographic and interest categories, and identify gaps in the community's knowledge and fulfillment of needs. Find people from both the editorial and business departments who are good at connecting with others through blogs, comments, and social media, as they are more likely to intuitively understand audiences and interactivity.

Watch for media-related hackathons organized by groups such as the Online News Association that are being held nearby or at a conference you attend regularly. These events can help you learn and practice some of the skills you need to build new products and services that match community needs.

One important caveat: Don't limit responsibility for your community-centric thinking to a handful of individuals; it has to be infused into every position, every employee. The team is but a starting point. Use what you have learned about your culture to spread these lessons throughout the organization.

Listening

Most likely, you already have some ideas about what your community's problems and needs are, but you will need to test those assumptions.

Understanding the community begins with adopting new tools and strategies for listening. Identify where people gather, both in virtual and physical spaces, and go where they are. In some cases, this exploration may involve a virtual space like a Facebook group or online discussion board, but often it will happen in a meeting hall or public event. Instead of starting with a list of questions or specific story ideas you want to pursue, just listen and observe.

This process can be difficult for journalists used to operating on a deadline-driven quest to get what they need. But stepping back—even briefly—yields new insights and often, different kinds of connections. Brown's social-journalism students often find they are approached by curious community members, allowing the groups to develop less transactional and more meaningful relationships.

In these spaces, converse with people. Don't treat them as a source of the perfect quote or a "real person" who will neatly encapsulate one particular point of view. Ask broad, open-ended questions that probe experiences and concerns. Pay special attention to gaps they see in their knowledge around a particular topic or issue or their ability to take action to achieve goals.[20]

Most journalists have developed some well-founded cynicism about people's motivations and desires. People may say they want hard news, but we know too well that they are more likely to click on the sensational or titillating, whatever their aspirations. When you start to better understand people's problems and frustrations, though, the way to help them understand the relevance of hard news becomes clearer.

These questions can help you understand your community more deeply:

- What problems do they have that could be solved or mitigated with more information or the ability to take action?
- How important is timeliness in the context of this specific community, topic, or issue? When, or under what personal circumstances, do they want to receive information?
- How do they prefer to receive and interact with information? Is it on mobile? Delivered via social media? Do they need a new app or website, or could they be best served by a bot? Do they like text, video, audio, or some combination of them all?

- What kinds of stories excite, delight, and prompt them to share with others?
- How personalized or targeted do they need information to be?
- What questions do they have for you that you could use your reporting skills to answer?

Remember what you learned earlier about newsroom culture and the gap between what people say and what they do, despite their intentions. Observe and make note of actions as well as words.

A variety of tools and techniques continue to emerge that can help you gather information about your community needs. Many of these can also fuel more traditional reporting or crowdsourcing.

A few to consider:

- GroundSource (www.groundsource.co) allows readers to easily answer questions and interact with journalists via text message. Post a phone number anywhere you like with a simple but compelling prompt; GroundSource then allows you to ask follow-up questions and collects the answers in an easy-to-use database.[21]
- Hearken (https://wearehearken.com) is a platform and consulting service that helps journalists collect questions from the public that reporters will answer. You can ask people to vote on which questions are chosen for reporting if you want to, and even allow the questioner to participate in the reporting process. Stories created with the Hearken model typically garner higher traffic and audience engagement.[22]
- Set up a "listening post." You can solicit answers to a specific question online, but you can also put up a sign and a table in a place where your community gathers and ask for thoughts that way, as public radio/producer Jesse Hardman has done in New Orleans.[23]

Design-thinking practitioners remind us that empathy is the most critical part of any good listening effort. Heather Chaplin, who runs the Journalism + Design program at the New School, also reminds us to think in systems, looking for interrelationships: "Good designers from any discipline will tell you that nothing is created or consumed in isolation—and that it is important to respect the relationship between the new creation and the environment in which it arrives."[24]

Assess what you learned from these listening efforts. If multiple people or tools were involved, be sure you've captured, shared, and discussed everything that you have collected.

After this process, begin by identifying specific problems to solve. Unless you have a large team, you may want to focus on one problem at a time. In design thinking, this part is called the "define" phase, and its proponents say you should try to state the problem as clearly and succinctly as possible.[25] The statement will guide your efforts going forward, allowing you to operate with clear insight from the people you will be serving, rather than your own gut-level assumptions.

Developing Solutions

Brainstorming exercises often can help generate fresh ideas. Some recommend group brainstorming sessions with whiteboards and Post-It notes; others advocate asking individuals to think of ideas on their own before discussing them as a group. No matter what method you choose, give everyone permission to suggest anything, no matter how small or silly or unrealistic it may seem at the time. Suspending judgment is key.[26]

Think of it this way: Forward-thinking journalists could have created Google or Craigslist. Google surfaces relevant information, and Craigslist connects local buyers and sellers—two services once dominated by newspapers. You never know what kind of valuable solutions you might come up with if you are willing to consider ideas that seem farfetched in the moment. You could develop an app or vertical, or perhaps a multimedia story or new way to cover a particular issue.

With the brainstorming list in hand, it is time to select the top prospects. This sifting process should involve group discussion, debate, and synthesis of common ideas.[27] During some brainstorming sessions, participants place stickers next to the most promising ideas.

Next, sketch out your idea and build a basic prototype. Though the prototype can take many forms, keep it as simple as possible at first. If your idea involves creating an app or website, for example, you might start by just sketching what it would look like. Use this outline to note key features, such as landing-page functions and navigation, and then create a more detailed visual guide using wire-framing tools such as Balsamiq, which is recommended at Arizona State University's entrepreneurial journalism bootcamp for educators led by Dan Gillmor. Tap into developers to help build basic but functional versions of an app or site that contain a few of the most important features.

Entrepreneurs call this version the "minimum viable product." The goal is to reduce perfectionism, get started quickly, and create something that you can test.[28] This concept of releasing something with known flaws can be particularly hard for journalists, given that errors and imperfections are scorned by the profession. But testing will save money in the long run.

A prototype or sketch will help audience members understand your idea, and they can experiment with the initial features. Often, if you ask people if they might like, say, a new local breaking-news app, they might answer enthusiastically, "Sure!" But when your carefully designed app becomes available months later, community members may not find the idea compelling enough to actually take the time to download the product. Or they might find features such as your notifications annoying and delete the app. That same thinking can be applied to any approach, including a new coverage plan. But before you revamp job responsibilities for your staff, listen to the community to help shape your priorities. All too often, great ideas are met with minimal engagement because untested plans developed in isolation do not match people's needs.

The next, crucial step is testing your ideas, a key step in the design-thinking process. Are you solving the problem you identified? Eric Ries calls it "validated learning."[29] He warns of the importance of ensuring that the metrics being used to judge the product/service are rigorous—not just cherry-picked numbers designed to make yourself look and feel good. Your cultural analysis should inform this process. Organizational theorist Chris Argyris pushes organizations to build an ethic of embracing truthful, accurate information to correct errors, even if it is difficult to hear and absorb.[30]

Entrepreneurs use a similar process called "customer discovery." Memphis's Start Co. accelerator tells startups to talk to at least 10 potential customers a week. The goal is fourfold:

1 To better understand if your idea is solving a real problem people have.
2 To determine if your product or service is solving that problem, and what features are most important.
3 To see how much, if any, people are willing to pay for your product/service (this can include "paying" with their time and attention).
4 To understand how people will find out about the product/service.[31]

Your early rounds of customer discovery and testing can be fairly basic, with the knowledge that fine tuning will happen later. Your next task is to adjust based on what you learn. Maybe you need a completely different approach; maybe you just need some tweaks. You can go back and repeat the whole process described above as needed. The most important lesson: keep learning.

Although learning is ongoing, some organizations use "sprints" as a way to focus their efforts on a specific challenge in a concentrated time frame.[32] A team is given a fairly short and defined time period, such as a week, to run through the design steps described above to prototype and test a new idea.

CONNECTING THE LEVELS: ALIGNING CULTURE, STRATEGY, AND INNOVATION

Now is the time to connect all levels of our model as you seek to bring about meaningful change to your organization. Make sure your innovation efforts fit with your long-term strategic goals and do not end up getting blocked by defensive reactions resulting from misalignments with cultural values.

Cultural Alignment
- For each new product/service/change you propose, identify explicitly how it aligns with core journalism values, and communicate this connection broadly. We recommend using The Elements of Journalism

by Bill Kovach and Tom Rosenstiel as a useful guide to commonly held journalistic principles. For example, how will this proposed change make your journalism more accurate, engaging, relevant? How will it hold the powerful accountable or give voice to diverse perspectives? Or as a minimum, how will it contribute financially to your organization in a way that ultimately allows you to do more work that supports these values? You are unlikely to get buy-in from the majority of journalists if this link isn't clear.

- *Open communication is key.* Identify how you will communicate about any new initiatives, beyond the rollout. How will you report the progress as you tweak the idea throughout the execution process? Will you send weekly or monthly email updates, use Slack, hold meetings, or talk with people informally?

- *Do the changes jibe with the identity of key opinion leaders in the organization?* You don't necessarily have to appeal to every single person in the organization, but you do want to make sure that primary stakeholders are along for the change ride. Even if they don't have leadership titles, these cultural ambassadors are ones other organization members look to for guidance and approval. If those leaders aren't on board, you'll have a hard time selling your idea across the organization.

- *Identify any potential conflicts with your organization's underlying assumptions.* These will not be easily swept aside, but now that you know what the underlying assumptions are, you can discuss how they may impede progress or trigger defensive mechanisms. For example, does your organization tend to avoid conflict in ways that keep people from sharing honest information needed to make a new initiative a success?[33] If so, can you find ways to bring people or internal groups together for conversations that recognize potential conflict as an opportunity for learning or problem solving rather than something that needs to be shunned?[34]

- *Invest in training.* People who are asked to learn new skills often get anxious and therefore revert quickly to old, comfortable routines. If new skills are required, be sure people have the time and resources to develop them. You can bring trainers to your newsroom for maximum convenience, or reasonably priced courses for new skills are often available online from places such as Poynter or Lynda.com.

- *Leaders must determine how they will incentivize and support the specific changes,* both formally and informally. It's not just about obtaining the proper approvals and funding; without regular accolades and acknowledgements from above, those on the front lines likely won't feel that new projects are valued. Even something as simple as whom leaders talk with and what they discuss in more casual conversations sends signals about what is deemed important.
- *Individual relationships and structure are the two primary sources of conflict within organizations over change.* Individuals relate to others at work based on their past experiences, their own self-image, and the circumstances of a given interaction. Structures like organizational norms, hierarchies, and competitive pressures also influence how people respond to new things. The key is to help people feel empowered enough to act to solve any problems that come up in the course of the change.[35]
- *Beware of the "we already do that" trap.* In an interview for this book, futurist Amy Webb told us this statement is often a way people dismiss an innovative proposal.[36] Sometimes it's true, of course, but more often the organization is not, in fact, already "doing it," at least in a significant or effective way. Box C.5 lists some defense mechanisms to be aware of.

BOX C.5 COMMON DEFENSE MECHANISMS THAT SIGNAL RESISTANCE TO CHANGE

Michael Diamond, founder of the Center for the Study of Organizational Change at the University of Missouri, highlights several defense mechanisms that arise during times of change:

Conversion: Emotional issues turn into physical symptoms.
Denial: Pretending something didn't happen or isn't happening.
Displacement: Redirecting your negative response to something at someone less "dangerous"; e.g. being mad at your spouse or colleague when you have a problem with your boss.

Humor: Allows for psychological distancing; is often a good tool for conflict resolution.

Isolation: Paranoia, divorced from reality.

Projection: Pushing your responsibility off onto others.

Rationalization: A more conscious process than the others in which you attempt to convince yourself of something you don't believe is true.

Reaction formation: Setting out to replace "unacceptable" emotions with emotions that are directly opposite to what they really feel; e.g. saying how much they really like a boss that they despise.

Regression: Going back to your days on the playground and behaving in an immature way.

Repression: Shutting down your awareness of a situation, forgetting.

Splitting: Things are either all good or all bad, no room for gray.

Suppression: Avoiding thinking about emotions.

Strategic Alignment

- *Revisit your SWOT analysis.* How do your new products and services fit into this assessment? Top managers have to review resources—human, financial, and technological—and determine how best to balance them to make change happen. How can you best leverage your distinctive strengths?
- If your new product or service requires a substantial investment of scarce time and resources and you can't add staff or increase budgets, *you need to determine what you will no longer do.* At some point, doing more with less becomes a zero-sum game. People will burn out or make haphazard, in-the-moment choices about what to focus their time on.
- *What physical changes to your spaces do you need to make?* Are people sitting in the right places in proximity to the right people? Even without an expensive renovation, can you move some furniture around in a way that better facilitates communication and makes diverse teamwork possible?
- *Examine your daily routines, and think about how they may need to change to accommodate new responsibilities or tasks.* For example, many newsrooms

are still adjusting the workday away from a singular focus on print or broadcast rhythms, and recognize that they need to focus resources for different times of the day, when people are likely to be consuming news and looking for particular kinds of content. How are your meetings timed and structured? How well do your routines align not only with new products and services, but with your core values?

Innovation Alignment
- As you approach the end of this process, there is one important element to remember: *You need to ensure that this isn't a one-time endeavor.* How can innovation happen consistently? Develop a system for checking in regularly to review what is working and what isn't, and in many cases, repeat some of the above steps.
- *Measure and evaluate.* The key to creating a culture of continuous change is measuring your progress toward your goals so that you can adjust course as needed. Using baseline metrics that align with your culture and strategy, be transparent about how you measure success.

Unfortunately, there is no singular approach to success. Instead, you have to identify particular metrics that are easily understood and used by everyone in your organization, and communicate those benchmarks openly and accurately. Newsrooms have become increasingly comfortable with the idea of reviewing quantitative metrics, but have made less progress in integrating them into editorial processes to drive better decision-making and longer-term change.

Some organizations have started tracking areas such as number and quality of comments, social media "likes," and other metrics of interaction, even though they often reflect low levels of engagement. Chartbeat founder Tony Haile has argued that the most important metrics are those that measure time and attention, not clicks or shares.[37] And many are looking even deeper to measure more active forms of participation and impact, which are the best indicators of how much your content is valued by your audience.

Go beyond vanity metrics to tracking online interactions that reflect community building, such as a willingness to sign up for memberships or contribute user-generated content. Use a broad range of measures, but focus on those that track participation and impact, using tools such as the Reveal's Impact Tracker,[38] which was made using scientifically validated measurements.

- *Chronicle and celebrate successes.* Make sure the chosen metrics are broadly accepted as appropriate measures of success in your newsroom. Spend time acknowledging and praising what is working while keeping a critical eye on those successes. Culture moves through shared successes; it's important that the entire newsroom hear about them and learn how to incorporate those lessons into their own work.
- *Create feedback loops.* Everyone in the organization should have the opportunity to provide feedback on an ongoing basis. Many leaders who say they have an "open-door policy" often find that many employees don't perceive it as such, so you should be sure to actively solicit feedback and remind people that it is welcomed. You also need to determine how you will acknowledge and act on feedback.
- *Chronicle and celebrate failures.* Our fragile psyches are afraid of failure, as we tend to cover up mistakes and relive our successes. But an organization dedicated to learning embraces failure as a pathway to true learning. As important as successes are to building the organizational story, so, too, are the failures that the newsroom has collectively overcome.

The difficulty is knowing when to end an experiment. Leaders must give new ideas enough time to succeed but recognize when the time is right to move on.

- *Remain flexible.* In the language of startups, innovators often talk about "the pivot,"[39] where the original idea needs to be adapted to community responses. Pay attention to where your audience is heading.
- *Continually ask why.* As you tweak and refine your innovative ideas, raise the question of why. Are you changing for change's sake? Is each change in the best interest of your community? Does it remain aligned with the strategy and culture of the newsroom

and your organization? Ultimately, do these changes position you for long-term viability?

The Role of Leadership

Throughout this entire process, leaders must keep in mind their own key role in driving change. Without clear guidance and support from above, the best-laid innovation plans will go awry. Leaders have to articulate goals in a way that inspires and then set up the structures and budgets to make those goals a reality.[40] They must establish a cohesive group identity, create meaning, and serve as a kind of "container" for other people's feelings and hopes that allows them to move past obstacles and anxieties and focus on the task at hand.

It will not be easy. Expect pain and frustration. Be prepared to make tough decisions, some of which will not work out as you intended or expected. Facing the future with honesty and empathy, however, will bring together a cohesive team who shares in one another's failures and successes. Only when viewed as a collective endeavor will the successes embed themselves in the culture to give rise to a truly resilient, innovative organization.

NOTES

1 Michael Harrison, *Diagnosing Organizations: Methods, Models, and Processes (Applied Social Research Methods)*, 3rd ed. (Thousand Oaks, CA: Sage, 2004), 1.

2 Edgar Schein, *Organizational Culture and Leadership*, 4th ed. (San Francisco, CA: John Wiley & Sons, 2010), 23–25.

3 Bill Kovach and Tom Rosenstiel, *The Elements of Journalism: What Newspeople Should Know and the Public Should Expect*, 3rd ed. (New York, NY: Crown/Archetype, 2014).

4 Michael Diamond, *The Unconscious Life of Organizations: Interpreting Organizational Identity* (Westport, CT: Quorum Books, 1993), 56.

5 Harrison, 64.

6 Schein, 19.

7 Schein, 326.

8 Diamond, 58–59.

9 Harrison.

10 Schein, 326.

11 Harrison, 39–42.

12 See Jack Stack and Bo Burlingham, *Stake in the Outcome: Building a Culture of Ownership for the Long-Term Success of Your Business* (New York, NY: Doubleday Publishing, 2003).

13 American Press Institute, "Newspaper Next: A Blueprint for Transformation," September 2006, www.americanpressinstitute.org/wp-content/uploads/2013/09/N2_Blueprint-for-Transformation.pdf, 22.

14 Esther Thorson and Margaret Duffy, "A Needs-Based Theory of the Revolution in News Use and Its Implications for the Newspaper Business," August 2006, Working paper presented at the University of Missouri Columbia, Reynolds Journalism Institute at the Missouri School of Journalism, Columbia, MO.

15 American Press Institute, 27.

16 Michael Porter, Competitive Advantage (New York, NY: Free Press, 1988).

17 LUMA Institute, Innovating for People: Handbook of Human-Centered Design Methods (Pittsburgh, PA: LUMA Institute, 2012).

18 Heather Chaplin, "A Guide to Journalism and Design," Tow Center for Digital Journalism: Columbia Journalism School, 2016, https://towcenter.org/a-guide-to-journalism-and-design/.

19 Start Co., "The Four Steps to Customer Discovery," n.d., http://neverstop.co/start-launching/the-four-steps-to-customer-discovery/.

20 Clayton M. Christensen and Michael E. Raynor, The Innovator's Solution: Creating and Sustaining Successful Growth (Boston, MA: Harvard Business School Press, 2003), 74.

21 Joseph Lichterman, "GroundSource Is Trying to Help News Sites Build Community through Text-Message Conversations," Nieman Lab, March 23, 2016, www.niemanlab.org/2016/03/groundsource-is-trying-to-help-news-sites-build-community-through-text-message-conversations/.

22 Jihii Jolly, "Platform Aimed at Audience Interaction Generates Story Ideas, Goodwill," Columbia Journalism Review, August 22, 2016, www.cjr.org/the_profile/hearken_hey_area_homeless_san_francisco_audience.php.

23 Jesse Hardman, "Listening Is a Revolutionary Act: Part 2," Medium, October 29, 2015, https://medium.com/local-voices-global-change/listening-is-a-revolutionary-act-part-2-bead20954108#.ze4vrj6gl.

24 Heather Chaplin, A Guide to Journalism and Design, July 13, 2016, www.cjr.org/tow_center_reports/guide_to_journalism_and_design.php.

25 Chaplin, A Guide to Journalism and Design.

26 Chaplin, A Guide to Journalism and Design.

27 Chaplin, A Guide to Journalism and Design.

28 Start Co. Founders' Toolkit, n.d., http://neverstop.co/startco-toolkit/.

29 Eric Ries, The Lean Startup: How Today's Entrepreneurs Use Continuous Innovation to Create Radically Successful Businesses (New York, NY: Crown Business, 2011), 38.

30 Chris Argyris, Reasons and Rationalizations: The Limits to Organizational Knowledge (New York, NY: Oxford University Press, 2004).

31 Start Co., "The Four Steps."

32 GV, "The Design Sprint—GV," Google Ventures, n.d., www.gv.com/sprint.

33 Diamond, The Unconscious Life of Organizations (New York, NY: Taylor & Francis, 1994).

34 Diamond, 1994.

35 Diamond, 1994.

36 Personal interview, March 5, 2015.

37 Tony Haile, "What You Think You Know about the Web Is Wrong," *Time*, March 9, 2014, https://time.com/12933/what-you-think-you-know-about-the-web-is-wrong/.

38 Lindsay Green-Barber, "CIR's Open-Source Impact Tracker Is Live," *Reveal*, July 18, 2016, www.revealnews.org/press/cirs-open-source-impact-tracker-is-live/.

39 The Lean Startup, "The Lean Startup—Methodology," n.d., http://theleanstartup.com/principles.

40 Kets de Vries, *The Leadership Mystique: Leading Behavior in the Human Enterprise*, 2nd ed. (Upper Saddle River, NJ: FT Press, 2009), 69.

Index

24/7 news cycle 22, 38, 84,
    98, 102
2008 financial crash 28, 84

Abernathy, Penelope Muse 86, 139
accountability 84, 99, 114,
    122, 225
accuracy-immediacy tension 22–26,
    54–55, 183
ad blockers 138
Adblade 187
adjacent possible, the 98
advertising: audience segmentation 139,
    140; banner advertising 86;
    campaigns 44–45; *Christian Science
    Monitor* 52, 63, 67, 114, 173, 181,
    187, 190; engaged journalism 138;
    ethical concerns 187; online 1, 78,
    86; and page views 112; third-party
    advertising 86, 187; verticals 120
advisory boards 147
aggregated content 61
agile development techniques
    102, 218
algorithms 64, 114, 126, 178, 184
American Press Institute (API) 5, 25,
    46, 217
American Public Media 9, 137
analytics 7, 62, 64, 103–104, 113–114,
    117, 127, 198; *see also* metrics
Anderson, Chris 145
aperture of content 100
apps 66, 94, 102, 222–223
Arab Spring 24

Argyris, Chris 14, 92–93, 104,
    199, 223
Arizona Daily Star 140
artifacts of organizational culture 38,
    53, 68
Atavist 180
Atlantic, The 88
audience: audience connection models
    99–100, 115–117; audience focus
    218–219; audience-first framing 5,
    31, 57, 100, 126–127, 131–132;
    Christian Science Monitor 57, 62,
    126–127; incorporating feedback
    from 103–104, 115–117, 118, 229;
    and innovation 5; journalists'
    resistance to audience participation
    134–135; as news creators 23;
    participatory environments
    133; segmentation 139, 140,
    145, 173
audio products 81; *see also* podcasts
authenticity 144, 145, 160
awards 27, 67
Axios 80

Balsamiq 223
banner advertising 86
Baquet, Dean 38
Barlett, Don 163
Baron, Marty 160, 164
Bascobert, Paul 83
belonging, sense of 166
Benton, Joshua 91
Bernstein, Carl 30

Bezos, Jeff 85, 164

bias 21, 135

BizTech newsletter (CSM) 119–120

#BlackLivesMatter 18, 23, 131

Blair, Jayson 156

blogs: audience engagement 138, 144; breaking stories 30; changing routines 161; *Christian Science Monitor* 57, 58, 61–62, 116, 119; Gannett 84

board of trustees 178, 181, 185, 202

boards of directors 178, 181, 186, 193, 195, 202

Boczkowski, Pablo J. 68, 92

Boston Globe 5

bounce rates 66, 125, 173

Boyer, Brian 102, 103

Brady, Jim 167

brainstorming 222

brand distinction 115, 127, 139

breaking stories 7, 18, 30, 95, 132, 188–189

broadcasting 53–54, 83

Brown, Andrew 94

Brown, Lane 117, 118

Brown, Matt 85–86

budget cuts 80, 83–84, 164–165, 181, 202, 216; *see also* staff layoffs

Bui, P. Kim 18, 22, 24, 25

bundling 179

bureaucracy 12, 217

Burke, Tarana 131, 132

Bush, George W. 30

business-editorial separation 82

business-to-business (B2B) products 121, 122–123, 179

buy-in 24, 26, 41, 103, 111, 159, 166

buyouts 55–56

BuzzFeed 66, 94–95, 138

cable TV 53–54

Canham, Erwin D. 67

capabilities, assessing 79–82

Capital Times 21–22

Carroll, Jill 124

Carvin, Andy 18, 22, 24, 25

celebrity journalism 28

Center for the Study of Organizational Change at the University of Missouri 9, 41, 213, 226–227

change: change agents 56–57, 105, 154; continuous change 92, 112, 141–142, 213, 228; evolutionary change 68; model of change 3, 12–16, 207; systemic change 40; *see also* resistance to change

Chaplin, Heather 221–222

Charlie Hebdo shooting 25

Chicago Tribune 102

Christensen, Clayton 4, 5, 96, 97, 217

Christian Science Monitor 10–11, 12, 28, 51–74, 86, 111–130, 173–205

Christian Science Publishing Society 68, 181, 185, 194, 196, 201

churn problems 199

Cillizza, Chris 165

citizen journalism 30

City Bureau 93

City University of New York (CUNY) 11

civic agenda, setting the 30, 133–134

Clark, Matt 120, 174, 186

Clark-Johnson, Sue 159

Clayton, Mark 179, 192

Cleveland Plain Dealer 1

clickbait 145

clicks, pandering for 31

click-throughs 114, 119, 140, 177

Clinton, Bill 30

CNN 98

cognitive burden, reducing 140

collaborative journalism 26, 30–32, 133, 145, 147

Collins, Clay 174, 200

Colombia Journalism Review 18, 44

comments sections 115–117, 135

Commission on Freedom of the Press (Hutchins Commission) 29

Committee of Concerned Journalists. 8, 9, 19, 21, 23, 26, 29, 137

communication 43, 137, 225; *see also* internal communications

community building: audience engagement 18, 32, 135, 136, 139, 143, 146–148, 220; *Christian Science Monitor* 65; cross-platform community building 139; "jobs to be done," identifying 99; metrics 228–229; mission 84, 86–87

community journalism 86–87

community outreach 133

community teams 219

competition: analyzing 3–4; for attention 143, 217–218; *Christian Science Monitor* 183; competitive advantage 4, 77–78; identifying nonconsumers 217–218; and the Internet 75, 78; leadership 162, 166; and problem-solving 101; reflexive responses to 6; strategy development 77–78; with substitutes 77–78

conference rooms 197

conflict avoidance 39, 43, 53, 226

connectivity, as motivation for media use 99, 146

consensus builders 154

consensus-led management 122

content-management systems 55, 56, 63

continuity 124

continuous change 92, 112, 141–142, 213, 228

"convergence" 21

core tasks of journalism 174–175

core values of journalism 20–21, 133, 136–137, 175, 182, 224–225

cost accounting 78

cost leadership 79–80

COVID-19 1, 86, 88

Craigslist 86, 97

credibility 145

crises of identity, journalism's 28

cross-platform community building 139

crowdsourcing 31–32, 141

culture: building a learning culture 100; cultural alignment 224–227; cultural analysis methods 9; cultural interviews 208; cultural resistance to engagement 134–137; culture wars 61; deciphering your 37–49; diagnosing your 203–213; as the foundation of change 6; resistance to change 153

Currie, Phil 159

customer discovery 224

cybersecurity 178–179, 180, 192

cynicism 220

Daily News Briefing 184, 195, 199

Dallas Morning News 5, 146

Danzico, Liz 218

dashboards 103–104, 127

data journalism 24

DC Decoder 120, 122

deadlines 102, 220

deep-dive reporting 188

defensive reactions 44–45, 53, 68, 104, 135, 199–200, 226–227

demo days/open houses 103

democracy 2, 21, 29, 133

derivative journalism 61

Deseret News 162

design sprints 103, 190, 200, 224

detachment, norms of 135

Detroit Free Press 146

Dewey, John 133

Diamond, Michael 9, 41, 213, 226–227

Dickey, Bob 84, 159

differentiation 79, 80

Digg 117

"digital first" 7, 37–39, 51–74

directors 178, 181, 186, 193, 195, 202

disconfirming data 7

discoverability 143, 183

Disqus 115

disruption 12, 57, 96, 97

distinction 174–175, 188, 199

diversification 81, 121–123

Doctor, Ken 76, 167

Dodge Foundation 145

Donald W. Reynolds Journalism
  Institute 26

donations 195

double-loop learning 92–93, 103

Drucker, Peter 6

Druge, Matt 30

Drury University, Missouri 11

Dubow, Craig 84, 158

Duffy, Margaret 9, 99

EBSCOhost 121

economic versus journalistic impetus for
  change 21

Economist Intelligence Unit 121

Eddy, Mary Baker 52, 54, 70, 123, 174,
  181, 193

"edge of chaos" 166

editors' picks 125

Edwards, Aaron 94

Edwins, Laura 176–177

efficiency 63

egos, journalists' 135

Elements of Journalism (Kovach and
  Rosenstiel) 9, 19–21, 26, 136,
  224–225

Elizabeth, Jane 25

email subscription products 184,
  187, 191

emotions: connection with audience 146,
  178; defensive reactions 44–45, 53,
  68, 104, 135, 199–200, 226–227;
  motivations for media usage 99; and
  organizational change 13, 93

empathy 221–222

Energy Voices 120

engagement 131–152, 218–229; *see also*
  audience

entertainment, information as 86,
  99, 146

entrepreneurial mindset 91–109, 133,
  218–219, 223–224

environment scanning 4

ephemerality 22

errors 22–23, 26, 117, 223

espoused values 38–39, 210

event sponsorships 78

events 135, 180

evolutionary change 68

experimentation: *Christian Science Monitor*
  57, 59, 62, 71–72, 122, 124, 179,
  187; design sprints 103, 190, 200,
  224; and leadership 166–167; and
  objectivity 160; organizational
  culture 8; strategy development 82;
  value of 5

explainer products 120, 182

Facebook: advertising 1; algorithms 178;
  Christian Science Monitor 66, 86,
  117–118, 177, 178, 189, 190, 191;
  Dallas Morning News 146; innovation 92,
  95; listening to audience via 220;
  resistance to using 26

fact-checking 23–24, 189

failures, chronicling 53–54, 70, 229

failures, company 96

Farrell, Mike 180, 194

Federal Communications
  Commission 94

feedback, incorporating 103–104,
  115–117, 118, 229

First Draft 26

First Look Media 24–25

Fisher, Sara 80

Five Forces framework 3–4, 77, 218

Five Whys 104

FiveThirtyEight 80

Forbes 86

free press 21

freelancers 122, 179

French, John R.P. 162–163

fundraising galas 81
furloughing staff 1

Gannett 1, 5, 8, 10, 76, 83–84, 158
GateHouse Media 83, 84
gatekeeper role 5, 23, 24, 30, 119, 132, 134, 202
Gilbert, Clark 162
Gillmor, Dan 223
"good enough" journalism 139
Google: advertising 1; *Christian Science Monitor* 60, 61, 64, 71, 72, 126; major media player 86, 92, 95
Google Docs 94
Google Doodles 61, 72
Google Forms 209
Google News 60, 61, 66, 71, 72, 189
Google Ventures 190
Google+ 118
Grant, David 192, 194, 199
Green-Barber, Lindsay 133, 142
GroundSource 221
group dynamics 157
Guardian, The 132, 138

habits 142, 145
hackathons 219
Hackney, Sue 176, 196
Haile, Tony 228
Hanes, Stephanie 119
Hardman, Jesse 221
Harris, John F. 159
Harrison, Michael I. 45
headlines 58–59, 64, 182
Hearken 221
hierarchies 46, 56, 158, 185–186, 217
home-page traffic 65, 113–114, 125, 173
Hopkins, Jim 84
Huffington Post 138
Hutchins Commission 29

idealism 19, 30
identity, threats to 158–161
immediacy-accuracy tension 22–26, 54–55, 183
impact, measuring 93, 142, 174, 177, 229
Impact Architects 133
Impact Tracker 142, 229
incentives 4, 104, 138, 212
independence, compromising 135
individualism 40
"information centers" 158–159
information consumers, public as 24
information disorder 26
information needs, assessing 141, 146, 217
Ingwerson, Marshall 123–124, 174, 175, 176, 178, 182, 186, 193, 196
innovation: building into routines 102–104; *Christian Science Monitor* 71, 190–192; diffusion of 104–106; disruptive agents 57; entrepreneurial mindset 91–109; finding pockets of 136; innovation alignment 228; innovation fatigue 122; messy path of 167–168; more than just a buzzword 4–5; opinion leaders 141–142; organizational culture 8; pockets of innovation 136; "shiny diamond" syndrome 76; staying nimble and responsive 218–224; and strategic vision 13; strategy development 82, 87
Innovation Report 46, 91
interactivity 27, 144
interdisciplinary teams 196, 197
internal communications 41, 43, 57–58, 95, 103, 137, 168, 189
International Center for Journalists 7
International Symposium on Online Journalism 24
Internet: 24/7 news cycle 22; audience-first framing 5; early days of 92; *see also* Facebook; Google; social media

interns 176, 187
investigative journalism 27–28, 30
Investigative Reporters and Editors
    conference 27
iteration, rapid 4

Jarvis, Jeff 138–139
Jobs, Steve 182
"jobs to be done," identifying 97,
    98–100, 217
Johnson, Steven 98
Journal Media Group 83
Journal Register Co. 167
journalism-first strategies 81

Kauffman, Stuart 98
keywords 64, 184
Kiesow, Damon 95
Knapp, Jake 190
Kovach, Bill 9, 19–20, 23,
    24, 28–29, 31, 136–137, 224–225
Kramer, Melody 103–104

Lamar Smith, Anthony 18
Lawrence Journal-World 147–148
leadership: approachability 58; as
    balancing act 166–167; buy-in 41;
    characteristics of leaders 12–13, 155,
    157; Christian Science Monitor 57–59, 70,
    123–125, 193–194, 196; and culture
    42, 212–213, 226; engaged
    journalism 137–138; motivations and
    leadership 162–164; opinion leaders
    105, 124, 141–142, 225; power and
    motivation 162–164; strategic
    thinking skills 12; supporting
    investigative work 28; through change
    and resistance 57–59, 153–171, 230;
    transformational leadership 164, 168
Lean Startup model 94–96, 100
learning culture, developing a 8
Lewinsky, Monica 30
linear processes of news 46
LinkedIn 117

Lippmann, Walter 28
listening 141, 144, 208, 219–221
Listening Post Collective 141
listening posts 221
London riots 132
Long Tail 145
longitudinal study methods 10–11
Los Angeles Times 64
'Lost Mothers' (ProPublica) 148
Lowery, Wesley 160
lowest common denominator 135
low-income news consumers 98–99
loyal visitors 113, 115–117, 126,
    132, 173

management-by-team 122
manifestos 103
marginalized communities, connecting
    with 131
market research 87
marketing personas 173
Mayer, Joy 133
McCarthy, Joseph 29
McConnell, Mitch 176
McKisson, Irene 140
McLaughlin, Abe 120, 186, 194, 198
meaningful work 28
Media Choice Model 99–100, 217
MediaNews Group 167
meetings, effective 197
memberships 76, 78, 81, 132, 138,
    191; see also subscriptions
Memphis Start Co. 224
mental load of news consumption 140
mergers 39–40, 161–162
Mersey, Rachel Davis 139
#MeToo 131
metrics: Christian Science Monitor 65–66,
    111; community engagement 143;
    depth of visit metrics 65–66, 228;
    impact measurement 229; and
    innovation 223; learning from the
    lean startup model 94–96; measuring
    time and attention 228; and mission

216; qualitative 142, 184; *see also* page view counts
Meyer, Eugene 85
Mic 126
micro-payments 190
Milano, Alyssa 131
Milwaukee Journal Sentinel 7, 9, 10, 26, 27–28, 39, 43, 47
minimum viable product (MVP) 94, 95, 223
Minnesota Public Radio 147
mission: affirming through action 85–86; *Christian Science Monitor* 53, 128, 174, 188, 195; communication breakdowns 137; defining 82–85; identifying 213–215; mission statements 215; strategy development 76
mobile phones 30, 37, 91, 125
model of change: applying 13–16; diagram 3, 207; thinking across levels 12–13
moderation 115, 118, 134
Modern Parenthood blog 119
Monitor Global Outlook (MGO) 178, 179–180, 181
motivations and leadership 162–164
motivations for media usage 99, 138, 146
Muck-Rock 99
multimedia 27, 37, 86, 101, 144, 180, 198
multipliers 65–66
Murphy, Pat 117
Murrow, Edward R. 29–30
mutual sharing 135

N2 Innovation Method 5
name recognition 143, 144
Napoli, Philip 142, 148
narcissism 155
narrative unfolding 23
National Public Radio 103–104

navigation, ease of 144
net neutrality 94
networks of news organizations 145
New Jersey News Commons 145
New Media, Enduring Values project 9, 26
New Media Investment Group 83, 84
New York Times 7, 28, 37–38, 44, 46, 91, 131, 140, 156, 165
New Yorker 131
Newcomb, Amelia 174
Newmark Graduate School of Journalism, CUNY 11
newsletters 80, 119–120, 179, 184, 192–193, 199
Newspaper Next project 5
NewsWhip 177
Nexis 121
niches 78–79, 80, 113, 120, 145, 178, 181, 219
Nielsen, Jakob 144
Nieman Lab 91, 167
nonconsumers, identifying 217
nonprofessional voices 131–132
nonprofits 28, 80–81, 87–88, 93, 98–99, 147
NowThis 18, 24–25

objectives, setting 161–162
objectivity 29, 160
office spaces 196–197, 227
Online News Association 219
open-book management techniques 214
open-door policies 57–58, 229
operating subsidies 51
opinion leaders 105, 124, 141–142, 225
opinion-free journalists 161
opportunities, assessing 79–82
organizational culture: connecting to change 6–8, 43–45, 155; deciphering your 37–49; origin stories 52–54, 68; strategy

development 82; thinking across
    levels 12–13
organizational identity 94, 112, 155
organizational learning 8, 92–94, 218
organizational life cycles 157–158
organizational structure/processes 45
origin stories 52–54
Orr, Jimmy 12, 56–57, 63–64, 65, 70,
    71, 117, 124
Outlier Media 98–99
Overholser, Geneva 9
overworked journalists 135–136, 186

page view counts: and advertising
    revenues 86; *Christian Science Monitor* 52,
    54–55, 59, 60, 61, 62–63, 64–65,
    70–71, 111, 120, 125, 126, 178,
    187, 196; engaged journalism 143;
    gaming 65
pandemic 2020 1, 86, 88, 140
participatory environments 31–32,
    115–117, 131–152, 133, 228
Passcode 179–181, 187, 190, 192–193,
    194–198, 199
passive receipt of information 99, 133,
    139, 147
paywalls 88, 91, 190, 195, 200
Pentagon Papers 30
Perception Gaps 200
Perfas, Samantha Laine 200
perfection, releasing before 95, 223
Pew Research Center 78, 131, 153
Philadelphia Inquirer 163
Picard, Robert 80
pitching 189
pivot, the 229
podcasts 80, 179, 180–181, 199, 200
pods 197
Politico 80, 159–160
polychronic time 46, 115
Pope, Kyle 44
Porter, Michael 3–4, 77, 78, 79, 218
post-publication changes 47
power and motivation 162–164

Poynter 1
PR officials 31
premises 196–197
premium content 121
presentation of information 144
press releases 23
primary sources, becoming a user's 145
Principia, The 193
problem-solving approaches 12, 93,
    101, 222–224, 225
process, journalism as a 144
product-first mentalities 5
professional identity, threats to 158–161
professionalism, challenges to 60–61
profiling 140
profit margins: *Christian Science Monitor* 67;
    and competition 77; and innovation
    96–97; protection of 12, 21; strategy
    development
    83, 88
Project Thunderdome 167
ProPublica 31, 136, 148
prototyping 122, 222–223
proving-ground mindsets 58–59
psychodynamic theory 13, 44, 94
psychology 13, 153, 155, 158,
    162–163
public editor positions 44
Public Insight Network Project 147
Pulitzer Prizes 27, 67, 136

Quantcast 64, 173
quizzes 66, 177–178

racism 136, 148
radio talk shows 146
Radio Television Digital News
    Association (RTDNA) 29–30
Raines, Howell 156
Rapid Response Team 187–188, 189,
    193, 195, 196
Rather, Dan 30
Raven, Bertram H. 162–163
Raynor, Michael 4, 97

readership levels 52
real-time traffic 111
Redirect 190–191
redundancies 55–56; *see also*
    staff layoffs
referent power 163–164
referral mechanisms 113
reflective-style journalism 69, 183
regression 44
relationship building 1, 22, 24–25,
    31, 135–136, 139–142,
    220–221, 226
relevant, making stories 137
repeat visitors 113–114
Reported.ly 24–25
research methods 9–11
resistance to change: *Christian Science
    Monitor* 53, 59–63, 200–201; core
    values of journalism 19, 21;
    engagement 134–135, 136;
    leadership 153–171, 226–227;
    mission 83; model of change 12;
    organizational culture 6–7, 40
restructurings 55
Reveal's Impact Tracker 142, 229
revenue streams, new 52, 71, 75, 78,
    87, 138, 140, 178–179
rewards 112, 161, 162–163, 168
Ries, Eric 4, 94, 95, 100, 104, 223
risk 12, 87, 97, 154–155
Roberts, Gene 163
Robinson, Sue 21–22
Rogers, Everett 57, 104–105,
    142, 168
rolling series of stories 144
Rose, Charlie 165
Rosen, Jay 44
Rosenstiel, Tom 9, 19–20, 23, 24,
    28–29, 31, 105, 136–137, 224–225
routines: building innovation into
    102–104; *Christian Science Monitor* 56,
    72, 183, 199; engaged journalism
    138; new faces 176; questioning 96;
    resistance to change 38, 44, 45, 46,

47; strategic alignment 227–228; and
    threats to professional identity 159

Sappenfield, Mark 62, 174, 194,
    198, 199
Schein, Edgar 6–7, 38, 46, 115
Schön, Donald 92–93, 104
scientific methods of journalism 28–29
scoops 188–189
Scott, Dave 64, 66, 124, 174,
    176, 195
Scripps-Howard 83
scrum meetings 102, 196, 197, 198
search engine optimization (SEO):
    Christian Science Monitor 56, 57, 60, 66,
    70, 72, 86, 112, 126, 173,
    181–182, 184; competing for
    attention 143–144
self-evaluation 14
self-reflection 14
sensationalism 28, 29
sense of self 94, 158–161
sensemaker/referee roles 23
service, news as a 139
shadow networks 166
"shiny diamond" syndrome 76
shorter stories, moving towards
    60–61, 64
skills, new 7, 100–101, 158, 216
skunkworks 166–167
Slack 94
slogans 75
smart speakers 92
smartphones 37, 91, 125
"social first" 176–178, 187
social media: #BlackLivesMatter 18, 23,
    131; building community 86–87;
    building trust 133; *Christian Science
    Monitor* 66, 117–118, 176–178, 189,
    190, 191; citizen journalism 30;
    connection with audience 146;
    digital natives 143; engaged
    journalism 141; and the gatekeeping
    model of journalism 24; immediacy-

accuracy tension 22–26; #MeToo
131; Politico 160; promotional uses
25; resistance to 18–19; rumors
23–24; slowing down the news
cycle 24; tracking users from 115,
117; two-way nature of 31;
verification skills 7; *see also* Facebook;
Twitter
Social Sandbox 104
solidarity 44
solution-based journalism 53, 60, 102,
199, 222
Solutions Journalism Network 182
Sonderman, Jeff 105
Sorcher, Sara 180, 192, 194
Spanish language 81
special interests 86–87
specialization 80, 218
speed, pressure for 156, 183; *see also*
immediacy-accuracy tension
speed versus depth 60–61
Spike 176–177
Spirited Media 102
sponsored content 120–121, 180, 190,
192–193
sprints 103, 190, 200, 224
St. Louis protests 18, 22
Stacey, Ralph D. 166
staff layoffs: *Christian Science Monitor*
55–56, 122–123, 185–187; due to
pandemic 1; leadership 161–162;
and organizational change 28,
44, 84
stakeholder meetings 103, 137
stand-up meetings 197
Starkey, Ken 94
startups 7, 81, 157
statements of purpose 76
Stevens, Jane 148
storytelling skill 87
strategic positioning 4, 66, 71
strategy development 75–90, 213–218;
audience engagement 138–139;
Christian Science Monitor 194–198,

202–203; importance of strategy
2–4; leadership 161–162; strategic
alignment 227–228
strategy teams 214
streamlining 80
stylebooks 53
subscriptions: audience engagement
132; *Christian Science Monitor* 52,
59, 67, 113, 178, 184, 187,
191, 195, 196, 197, 199, 200;
engaged journalism 138;
entrepreneurial mindset 91, 95;
organizational culture 44; renewals
199; and social media 146;
strategy development 78; *see also*
memberships
subsidies 185, 195
substitutes, competing with 77–78
success measures 65, 70, 79; *see also*
metrics
Sullivan, Cheryl 124–125, 128
suppliers 77
surveys 121, 208–209
survival, anxiety over 70–71
sustainability 55, 75, 98, 188, 190
Sutherland, Jeff 197
SWOT analyses 79, 215–217, 227
systemic change 40

talk shows 146
targeted news 99
targets 60, 63, 195
technology: *Christian Science Monitor*
53–54; "shiny diamond" syndrome
76; SWOT analyses 79, 215–217;
as tool versus concept 22; *see also*
analytics; Internet; social
media
test-learn-adopt 62, 114
Texas Tribune 80–81, 98, 179
text messages 99
The 19th 147
The Post (film) 30
third-party advertising 86, 187

third-party resellers 121, 125
This is Tuscon 140, 145
Thorson, Esther 9, 99
top billing stories, deciding on 39
tracking stories 62
training 42, 101, 145, 197, 225–226
transformational leadership 164, 168
transparency 18, 23–24, 25, 76, 102, 160
Trello 197
trend-driven story selection 57, 58–59, 64
tribes 46
Tribune Co. 83
trolls 44
Trump, Donald 44, 91
trust 21, 41, 115, 118, 133, 138, 139, 146
trustees 178, 181, 185, 202
Trusting News project 133
Tuchman, Gaye 161
Tuckman, Bruce 157
Turner, Ted 98
24/7 news cycle 22, 38, 84, 98, 102
Twitter: #BlackLivesMatter 18, 23, 131; *Charlie Hebdo* shooting 25; *Christian Science Monitor* 66, 117, 118, 177, 189, 191, 194; community influencers 132; *Detroit Free Press* 146; journalists' own 160, 191; #MeToo 131; resistance to using 26; rumors 24
two-way information flow 135

UMP (understanding, models of thought, and progress) 175–176, 177, 182–184, 187, 189, 195, 198, 199, 202
uncertainty, collective 70
unconscious assumptions 7, 14, 39–41
underlying assumptions 7, 14, 38–41, 43, 211, 225

underpaid journalists 135–136
unique visitor metrics 176, 187, 196
uniqueness 80
University of Missouri 9, 26
usability 144, 180
user review systems 144
user testing 200
user-generated content 133, 229; *see also* participatory environments
uses-and-gratifications theory 99
Usher, Nikki 37

validated learning 94–96, 223
value chains 78–79, 80
value creation 86–88
value-added content 61, 188
values: alignment with culture 42; *Christian Science Monitor* 53, 55, 175, 189, 199, 202; core values of journalism 20–21, 133, 136–137, 175, 182, 224–225; diagnosing your culture 203–213; strategy development 82; uncovering 18–36
VendeHei, Jim 159
verification 18, 22–26, 27, 28–29, 134
verticals 113, 119–120, 125, 178–181, 199
video products 81, 190–191, 198
vision 12, 42, 115, 166, 174–176, 213
visitor return rates 65
Visual Revenue 114
voice of content 100
Voice of San Diego 76
volunteer contributors 147
Vox Media 80, 126

Washington Post 30, 85, 160, 164
watchdog reporting 27, 30, 31
Watergate 30
Webb, Amy 226

Weinstein, Harvey 131
WellCommons 147–148
Wells, Jonathan 55, 57–58, 196
WHO-TV 9
Wii 97
Wikipedia 144
Wilk, Doug 162
Williams, Joe 160
wire reports 61
WMC-TV 11
Woodward, Bob 30

workflow reconfigurations 55, 138
WTXL 85

yellow journalism 28, 52
Yemma, John 51, 52, 54, 57–59, 63,
    66, 70, 71–72, 117, 123, 174,
    181–182, 196
YouTube 117

Zamora, Amanda 147

Made in United States
Orlando, FL
23 January 2024

42832584R00143